In the words of Western Buddhists in this book:

'There are so many things I like about Buddhism.
The magnanimity for one thing. I also like the fact that you
are encouraged to question, to work it out for yourself.
You can challenge anyone, including the Dalai Lama...
the more doubts you have the better.'

'It's not some peace, love, dove, groovy, freak, crashpad,
incense-burning thing. Buddhism is real, otherwise
I wouldn't do it.'

'The essential message of Buddhism is one of hope
because the Buddha starts with the statement that we are
all potentially perfect.'

'In Buddhism....each spiritual seeker can find the
most appropriate method for his or her own personality
and circumstances.'

'There is a kind of rigor in a tradition which asks us to be
the chemist or the goldsmith of our own experience.'

'The most advanced spiritual psychology imaginable.'

'I now see beauty where I did not see it before.'

'The more you look into it, the more it reveals...
a never-ending source.'

VICKI MACKENZIE was born in England and spent most of her early years traveling with her father, a British Naval officer. She gained her BA from Queensland University, where she had the privilege to count Judith Wright among her poetry tutors. A career in journalism followed, starting as a cadet news reporter on the Sydney *Sun* before moving to London where she worked as a feature writer for several national newspapers including *The Times* and magazines. For many years she also worked in the London bureau of Australian Consolidated Press. In 1976, on impulse, she attended her first Buddhist meditation course in Nepal which triggered a continuing personal and professional interest in Buddhism. She has written many articles on the subject including several interviews with the Dalai Lama. Her books have all been published internationally: *Reincarnation: The Boy Lama* (Wisdom Publications, 1996), *Reborn in the West: The Reincarnation Masters* (Thorsons, 1995) and *Cave in the Snow: A Western Woman's Quest for Enlightenment* (Bloomsbury, 1998).

Why Buddhism?

WESTERNERS IN SEARCH
OF WISDOM

Vicki Mackenzie

Element
An Imprint of HarperCollins*Publishers*
77–85 Fulham Palace Road,
Hammersmith, London W6 8JB

The website address is: www.thorsonselement.com

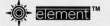

and *Element* are trademarks of
HarperCollins*Publishers* Ltd

First published by Thorsons, an Imprint of HarperCollins*Publishers* 2002
This edition 2003

1 3 5 7 9 10 8 6 4 2

A catalogue record for this book
is available from the British Library

ISBN 0 00 714228 5

Printed and bound in Great Britain by
Creative Print & Design (Wales), Ebbw Vale

For Lama Thubten Yeshe and Lama Zopa Rinpoche,
my inexpressibly kind teachers,
with gratitude, respect and love

Contents

vii

Acknowledgements

$\mathcal{M}$y heartfelt thanks and appreciation goes to all the contributors to this book, who not only let me into their homes and centers but into their intimate relationship with Buddhism as well. I am aware that this often took courage, and I am immensely grateful for their willingness to share their thoughts and feelings with the world at large. I hope and pray that their generosity will benefit many who read this book. The inspiration for *Why Buddhism?* came from my Australian publisher Jackie Yowell, whose personal curiosity, openness of mind, penetrating questions and subtle suggestions have been invaluable. My gratitude too goes to Christa Munns and Sarah Brenan for their excellent editing skills—the text is infinitely neater and shinier for their efforts. Many people provided me with assistance in the form of contact addresses, suggestions, and hospitality while I was traveling—and to them I would like to say a big thank you: the entire Dale and Eisa household, Jenny Gucci, Lois Graessle, Jeffrey and Helen Baden, Lama Palden, everyone at Langri Tangpa Center, Bob Milliken, Monica Joyce, Leila Hadley Luce, John Swindells, Rebecca Dale, Margi Haas, Jean Simpson. And my very special thanks to Andrew for his continual understanding, support and love.

Introduction

*I*n December 1976 I attended my first Buddhist meditation course in Nepal. Back then the climate was such that I did not dare reveal to my colleagues on the British national newspaper that employed me where I had gone or what I had been doing. I knew without a shadow of doubt that to do so would jeopardize my credibility as a rational and responsible journalist. The fact is that 25 years ago Buddhism and activities such as meditation were regarded as being so 'fringe' as to border practically on the subversive. So as not to lose face, I even went as far as to wrap the Buddhist books I was avidly reading on my way to work in the classic brown paper to avoid suspicious looks from fellow commuters on the train. Five years on, in 1981, Buddhism was still obscure enough for the features editor of the *Sunday Times*, no less, to ask me who precisely the Dalai Lama was when I presented him with an interview I had done with the exiled Tibetan leader during his first tour to Europe. Interestingly, on that tour the Dalai Lama did not quite fill the moderate-sized Caxton Hall, in Westminster.

How times have changed. Where once you might stumble across an obscure Buddhist center catering to a handful of intellectuals, there are now literally hundreds mushrooming in cities, suburbs and country towns across Australasia and Europe, as well as North, Central and South America. They draw people of all ages and from diverse walks of life. In Australia Buddhism is the fastest-growing religion, a fact perhaps best exemplified by the news that a giant stupa (traditional Buddhist monument) is being built in the small country town of Bendigo, Victoria. Rising 35 metres high, measuring 50 meters at its base and containing a 400-seat temple, it is being designed to last 1000 years and will be the biggest in the Western world. Books on Buddhism regularly top the best-seller list, a phenomenon that *Publishers Weekly* recently hailed as the Fifth Noble Truth. The Dalai Lama, once a remote, exotic figure, regularly fills venues like London's Wembley Stadium, New York's Central Park, and Melbourne's Tennis Center to overflowing. In fact, the smiling face with the shaved head and spectacles is now so universally recognizable that Apple thought fit to use it to sell their computers using only two words of text: 'Think different'. And I knew that Buddhism, with its once-alien message, had truly become mainstream when I was driving through

Sydney's Taylor Square, in the heart of the city, and spotted a giant billboard blazoning the caption: 'When you come back as a whale you'll be bloody glad you put Greenpeace in your will'. As badges worn on T-shirts declaim, reincarnation is making a comeback.

Why? This is what this book seeks to understand. What has this 2500-year-old religion got to offer the new millennium? Why has it crossed from East to West at this particular point? And why has it taken root in our soil with such speed and fecundity?

My own story is fairly typical. I went on that first meditation course back in 1976 as a complete ingenue, never having read a Buddhist book nor sat cross-legged on the floor since primary school, but drawn nevertheless by a need for meaning, or a wisdom that I sensed would come from the East. At one level I had acquired all the components that the West deems essential for happiness—good education, successful career, smart address, glamorous travel itinerary, full social diary and yet…in the quiet still moments when the frantic pace stopped, it all seemed rather vacuous. What was the point? My spiritual inclinations, nourished at home on broad-minded Christianity, found in the Church no more than a replica of the social service agencies bent on 'going out there and doing good'. Where was the mystery, the spirituality, a vehicle that could explain the reality that lay behind the outer show of things? The priests had no answers to my deepest questions and strongest yearnings. When my friend told me she was going to Nepal to meditate with the lamas, I leapt at the chance to go with her.

The conditions were abysmal (pit lavatories, no shower, sleeping on the floor, rising at 4 a.m.), but the content was rich beyond measure. On offer was an explanation of the human condition—why we are here, why we suffer, what makes us what we are, what constitutes true lasting peace and happiness. In short, here were people prepared to proffer answers to the Big Questions. The source of it all, we were told, was the mind, which shaped every aspect of our reality both internal and external. To study Buddhism therefore meant, in effect, studying ourselves—learning about the nature of our own minds, seeing its vast potential and the way we could develop it further. I was informed that the very word 'Buddhist' means 'interior being' and to be a Buddha—the final destiny for each and every one of us, apparently—is a matter of becoming 'fully awake'. It was fascinating and challenging stuff. The vision was vast and comprehensive, encompassing notions like 'beginningless time' and 'countless universes', forcing our mental horizons beyond nine-to-five jobs and lifespans of three score years and ten. After the theory we were presented with the tools for bringing about the great awakening, in the form of a vast array of meditations specially designed for 'looking within' and examining the contents of our own mind. For me, this was not always a pretty sight, and more often than not excruciatingly hard work. The knees hurt, the back ached and the mind careered all over the place refusing to be reined in. Patience, we were told. If we gained enlightenment in three lifetimes we would be doing exceptionally well.

What that Buddhist course in Nepal in 1976 gave me was a living spirituality—a spirituality backed up by scholarship, philosophy, ethics and compassion. Furthermore it was a spirituality that was embodied, not just spoken, by the lamas who were teaching it. It was what the West lacked, for all its technical, mechanical and materialistic knowhow. And it was what I and many others sought. Matthew Fox, the Dominican priest expelled by his order after 34 years for his mystical and too-liberal views, put it succinctly in *Natural Grace* (pp. 2 and 5):

> In twelve years of training as a Dominican I never heard Meister Eckhart mentioned once. The greatest mystic of the West and he was a Dominican, no less. We didn't have a single course on the mystics or spirituality as such. You were supposed to get it by osmosis. We practiced such things as vegetarianism, fasting, celibacy and charity but there was no reflection on why we should or what it meant. I urged my Dominican superiors that somebody should go and study spirituality... Now more than ever we have to strip down religion to its essence, which is not religion but spirituality. Spiritual experience must include worship that awakens people rather than

bores them, that empowers them, that brings out the gifts of community, that heals and brings the healers such as artists and justice makers back to the center of the community. This is the agenda for the third millennium.

Over the years my interest in Buddhism has grown. I have been a lazy though absorbed student, trying to keep up with the ever-increasing literature on the subject, meditating haphazardly and going to courses in various parts of the world (without committing myself to the really dedicated path of doing long retreats, in which the real transformation is said to occur). Still, I have discovered that the more I look, the more treasures Buddhism reveals. In this most complex of religions there is layer upon layer of meaning which gradually open up to you the more you delve into them. It is exciting and exceedingly rich. For all my intellectual and philosophical interest, however, Buddhism has had most impact where it has touched my daily life. Where would I have been when my mother literally dropped dead beside me in the kitchen if I had not been instructed repeatedly on the fundamental Buddhist tenet, 'Death is definite but the time of death indefinite'? 'You can die lifting the fork to your mouth,' said my teacher, Lama Zopa Rinpoche. My training was such that, although shocked beyond measure, I still managed to perform some of the prayers and rituals done at death to guide my mother's consciousness as it left the body hopefully to a happy realm of existence. I don't know whether it helped her, but it certainly helped me. Similarly, when I see birds swallowing berries and dispersing seeds, when I acknowledge the multitude of people who have been involved in getting my bowl of cereal to me in the morning, when the rise or fall of the US dollar affects my spending power overseas, when arms manufacturers sell weapons to countries engaged in war with their own countrymen, then I know the Buddhist truth that says that everything is interconnected and nothing is independent. There have been times of anguish when 30 minutes on the meditation cushion have provided me with a calm center from which to move. The knowledge of karma has sometimes provided an explanation for the seeming injustices of life and therefore made them more palatable. I know too that attachment is painful, as the Buddha said—that my holding on to a person (or an idea) creates much tightness around my heart which would instantly dissolve if only I would 'let go'. And after 25 years of examining the Buddha's claim that anger is a major impediment to peace, and therefore spiritual progress, I have finally to concede that life is indeed less turbulent in the supermarket queue and the traffic jam if I apply the given antidote of patience. For all this, and much more, I am immensely grateful.

Why Buddhism should be welcomed by the West at this particular time is a matter of speculation. Maybe it is due to the increase in world travel which allows Buddhist masters to jet in and teach us with relative ease. Maybe it is due to an opening up of our collective psyche to Eastern thought through the advent of mass media. And maybe it is due to the appearance on the world stage of the very special form of Buddhism from Tibet, so long locked up in its icy fortress on the rooftop of the world forbidden to outsiders. In this respect the coming together of East and West was a conjunction of extraordinary circumstances. If the Chinese had not invaded Tibet in 1950, if the Dalai Lama and thousands of his lamas had not fled into exile to India in 1959 and had the hippies of the late 1960s not gone East to seek 'love, peace and gurus', very few of us would ever have been exposed to the extraordinary numbers of supreme meditators and spiritual scholars that that small country produced. The hippies eventually returned to their homes, bringing some of the more intrepid lamas with them. The first classes were formed, the first students gathered and a movement begun. With uncanny prescience, the great eighth-century saint Padmasambhava, who introduced Buddhism to Tibet from India, had prophesied: 'When iron birds fly, and horses run on wheels, Tibetan people will be scattered like ants across the face of the earth and the Dharma [the Path] will come to the land of the redskins [white people]'.

As Buddhism takes root in the West, a fascinating process has begun. Slowly but inexorably we Westerners are taking this essentially Eastern religion and moulding it to suit our needs and psyches. This is how it should be, and how it has always been. The Buddha said that his truth was not dogmatic but as malleable as a piece of gold, which should be tested and hammered and then made into a unique ornament worn by every seeker. Over the centuries, when the flame of Buddhism has jumped from its birthplace in India to Sri Lanka, Thailand, Laos, Cambodia, Vietnam, Burma, Korea, China, Mongolia, Tibet and the Himalayan kingdoms, it has naturally taken on the culture of the country it has landed in. Thus the stark, chaste lines of Zen contrast radically with the colorful baroque hues of Tibetan Buddhism, which in turn is quite distinct from the morally strict, ascetic Buddhism of Thailand and the southern schools. Now it is the West's turn. The more broadminded teachers are encouraging their students to use French perfume instead of incense sticks and to provide Western food during the offering services rather than traditional fare. Certain American teachers are incorporating psychotherapeutic techniques into their Buddhism; Australia is leading the world with an ever-growing chain of Buddhist hospices; England is opening some of its Buddhist doors to asylum-seekers; Western Buddhist organizations everywhere are going out into the street to help the homeless and needy; one lady lama in the USA has adapted the famous twelve-step AA program into her teachings on the grounds that within the Buddhist context we are all junkies hooked on craving and desire; Western women are bringing about the feminization of Buddhism by putting female teachers on the thrones and becoming scholars and authors in their own right; and it is predicted that soon Buddha statues will take on Western features.

Interestingly, the traffic has not been one-way. As quickly as Buddhism is coming to the West, Christianity is being exported to the East. The spiritual void left by communism has resulted in some 30 million Chinese now attending church services both in officially recognized churches and in illegal 'house churches' in rural areas. Christian missionaries, particularly American Mormons, have also moved into Mongolia, the latest country to shake off the communist yoke and are converting the locals at a rate that is alarming certain Buddhists. Coming from the technologically and materialistically successful West, Christianity has more 'street cred', it seems, than their home-spun religion. The Dalai Lama, however, is having none of this proselytising. Time and time again he tells his audiences not to change their own religion but to learn from Buddhism how to become better members of their own community, their own family and their own churches. Following his own advice, he gave a moving series of lectures on his interpretation of the Gospels to a group of Christian monks and nuns in London, who received his offering with tears in their eyes.

It's not all rosy, of course. Buddhism has become horribly fashionable. Seizing the opportunity, marketing men are now producing everything from Hollywood movies to Buddha mouse pads to 'power beads', replicas of wrist rosaries worn by Buddhists for centuries. Showing how wrong they can get it, one CNN reporter recently announced that the Dalai Lama had become so chic he was spotted wearing 'power beads'. Actors and pop stars have jumped on the bandwagon. Thousands are chanting for fatter salaries and bigger cars— ironically the very antithesis of Buddhism, which states that desire and craving only produce dissatisfaction, not happiness. With this increasingly high profile, detractors have inevitably appeared. Scandals have been revealed involving eminent gurus who drank too much or had illicit sexual relations with students. Law suits have been filed, kiss-and-tell books written. Distressing schisms have appeared in newly established Tibetan centers throughout England, Europe and America with loyalties divided among different lamas and their disparate views. As Westerners are discovering to their cost, power bases aligned to interpretations of spiritual truth are particularly nasty. Discerning researchers like Brian Victoria from Adelaide are also questioning the part Buddhism played in Japan's attitudes during World War II, unleashing a wave of unease and controversy among Western Zen followers. Victoria asks disconcerting questions such as, 'How many sentient beings have been drawn to their deaths by the Zen insistence that "Neither good nor evil has any significance"?' And news flashes from Korea of monks brawling in the main temple over who should handle the annual budget have seriously dented Buddhism's once all-peaceful image! The maturation process has begun.

The froth and brickbats are peripheral, however. There

are now enough sincere and committed people investigating and practicing Buddhism to ensure that Buddhism is here to stay. Western men and women, ordained and lay alike, are dedicated and determined enough to enter retreats sometimes lasting three years and more to meditate without distraction. Others are assiduously learning the language of the host country so that they can read the scriptures in the original and become translators to transmit the Buddhist teachings more accurately. Some are embarking on twelve-year Buddhist degree courses. An increasing number of men and women in all Western countries are taking robes, in spite of predictions that the priesthood would rapidly become outmoded in the third millennium. And thousands of ordinary men and women are attending their local Buddhist center, genuinely interested to learn the teachings of the Buddha and attempt to put them into practice.

So, Buddhism has arrived. When I was approached to write a book on why it had become popular I was both delighted and somewhat nonplussed, Buddhism being a vast subject and I no scholar. In the end I decided to go for the microcosmic rather than macrocosmic view in the hope that, like a mosaic, a collection of beautifully colored pieces would make up a bigger picture. I opted to interview people from different countries and varying walks of life, asking them what had attracted them to Buddhism, what had been the joys and difficulties and where Buddhism had affected their lives. This then is a sample, but one which I hope will give insights. I have tried to choose contributors whose stories would throw light on varying aspects of Buddhism and areas that the reader would be interested in. For example, Alison Murdoch tells how she has reconciled her strong Christian leanings with her Buddhist faith; Yvonne Rand gives insights into Zen; Sharon Salzberg describes Vipassana meditation, from Burma; Robina Courtin explains how Buddhism is benefiting maximum-security prisoners; Inta McKimm shares how she is using Buddhism to help her die; Stephen Batchelor reveals how he can be a Buddhist without believing in reincarnation. All of the people I interviewed were open, discerning and incisive. Many of them also smiled and laughed a lot. Whether this is due to their association with Buddhism, I do not know, but I found it highly attractive. Interestingly, certain themes run through several interviews: difficulties with the cultural trappings and Eastern psyche; fascination with the philosophy of Emptiness; the importance of going on retreat; the recognition of death as a major motivating force; the inspiration given by the personal example of the teachers. For several interviewees, a personal tragedy or crisis was the starting point of their search. And many talk of 'coming home' when they met the Buddha's teachings.

I traveled from country to country, interviewing most of the contributors in their own homes or centers, which provided valuable background information which I have included in the introductions to each chapter. The exceptions were those I managed to catch as they were passing through Melbourne, where I was living at the time. For me, it has been a rewarding personal odyssey, feeding my fascination with Buddhism. A large proportion of the subjects are followers of Tibetan Buddhism—partly because this is the territory I am most familiar with, and partly because I believe that the Tibetan Buddhism has had the greatest impact on the man and woman in the Western street. No matter the country of origin or the school, however, at core all Buddhist teachings are the same. The Buddha was interested in one thing, the alleviation of suffering, not just for now but for all time, through the method of self-discovery and self-release. This is what the West is examining now. We are at the start of our journey into Buddhism. What we will find there and what we will make of it is the next stage in the story.

Teaching Buddhism in prison

ROBINA COURTIN
Nun among gangsters

Robina Courtin was the first Western Buddhist nun to befriend me. I'd go into her office in Manjushri Institute, in Cumbria, England (when it was still under the spiritual guidance of Lama Yeshe) where she was editing Buddhist books, and ply her with the myriad questions that came up for me during my years of attending introductory meditation courses. She'd sit me down, make me endless cups of tea sweetened with honey, and hurl a volley of questions back with the velocity and impact of a machine gun. 'What do *you* think, Vicki?' It was the Socratic method of learning. She'd brook no sloppiness of thinking on my part. Robina, short, powerfully built and armed with a rapier intellect and a razor-sharp tongue, could have been frankly terrifying if she were not always so warm-hearted and generous with her time and learning. She was (and still is) also funny, dynamic, affectionate, kind, outrageous, her speech frequently dotted with expletives. All this plus her ability to move across the ground at a million miles a minute proved conclusively to me that you do not necessarily have to be quiet, serene and passive to be Buddhist.

Born in Melbourne, Australia, she trained as a classical singer before going to London where her career took a decidedly less conventional turn. She joined a group called Friends of Soledad, which organized support for imprisoned black activists in the USA, known as the Soledad Brothers. She next took up the feminist cause, eventually becoming a radical lesbian feminist. Next was kung fu and karate. 'I was always looking, always politically active, wanting to change the world,' she told me.

At this point she felt a resurgence of the spiritual longing she had had as a child. 'It was as though I'd exhausted all other possibilities. I'd been a hippy, a communist. I'd been into black politics. I'd blamed straight people, white people, rich people. Then I'd blamed male people. There was no one left. There was only Robina.' She'd been a devout Catholic with a natural devotion to God and a strong attraction to the mystical lives of the saints, but had turned away from Christianity when she was told not to question but seek faith; this was anathema to her quick, analytical intelligence. In June 1976 she saw a poster advertizing a meditation course given by two Tibetan lamas and went along. Finally she found what she had been looking for. 'It was as clear as a bell. Of course this was what I was going to do,' she said. Eighteen months later, aged 33, she became a nun.

I kept in touch with Robina over the years as she moved from country to country at the bidding of her lama. Finally she settled in California, where she became editor of *Mandala*, a Buddhist magazine with an international readership, and a powerful, persuasive teacher in her own right. Then she wrote and told me she had started entering some of the toughest prisons in California to teach Buddhism to the inmates, and how much she was enjoying it.

I remembered a story she once told me about how she had been mugged at gunpoint while visiting New York with her sister. The gunman had pointed the cold gray barrel into her chest and demanded she give him money. There had been a nanosecond of fear before Robina had registered that she was as poor as her attacker. 'When I am confronted I get very clear and very angry,' she recalled. She pulled herself up to her 4 feet 11 inches, stared straight at her mugger and said, 'Who do you think you are, man? How dare you demand money from me. I'm just as poor as you are. Give me *your* money'. He repeated his demand, she repeated hers and the situation descended into farce. 'I remember I liked this man very much but I just didn't want to give in to him. In the end he was completely bemused. He ran his finger gently between my breasts, and walked off into the night.'

I couldn't have thought of anyone more suited to the job of taking Buddhism to criminals, and I was not surprised when the film *Chasing Buddha* was made of her work, capturing her inimitable style.

On her next teaching tour to Australia she visited a maximum-security prison in Victoria, and I accompanied her to see her in action. As the series of gates clanged behind us, Robina marched purposefully forward into the heart of the prison where the most dangerous criminals were held. Unafraid, she sat among six sullen men, some with hair down to their shoulders, others covered in tattoos, and quietly explained the fundamentals of Buddhism. Some asked for books to be sent to them. Later we moved on to a remand center filled with younger men awaiting trial, mainly for drug-related offences. She moved among them, slapping them on the back, taking their hands, telling them they were handsome young men who didn't have to be in that situation if only they would take control of their lives. They loved her. Outside on the street she burst into tears. 'It breaks my heart to see the men like this. No one really cares for them,' she said.

Ensconced in the infinitely more aesthetic surroundings of a leafy Melbourne garden, talking against the gentle sound of wind chimes, Robina explained precisely what prisoners are finding in Buddhism and what they, in turn, are teaching her.

"*I*t all started two years ago with a young Mexican gangster, Arturo, who wrote to *Mandala*, the magazine I edit. He had found the address in the back of a Buddhist book that our organization distributes free in prisons. Normally the letters go to someone else, but this one came to me. He wanted instruction on how to meditate and he wanted someone to visit him.

What was immediately obvious was his sincerity. It was clear that he really wanted to practice. Arturo was just twenty—he'd been in prison and juvenile detention centers since he was twelve, with only a few months out. His first major sentence was when he was thirteen; he got three years for armed robbery. He came out at sixteen, went back on the streets, got into gang fights, was arrested again and charged with attempted murder in three cases. He was given three life sentences. Arturo has explained to me that the violence from the gangs in prison is huge. Prison is another universe— a sub-culture. While he was in prison he got involved in a fight and cut someone's throat. They removed him to SHU (Security Housing Unit) in the Pelican Bay prison in the northern tip of California. It was built ten years ago to take the major troublemakers out of the other Californian jails. They're mostly Mexican and black, their crimes mainly gang-related. There are thousands of them in there.

Arturo discovered Buddhism first through a Zen book written by a Samurai master. He told me there was one

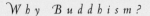

sentence which leapt out at him: 'Man yearns for what is true on earth, for only by finding truth will he put an end to his restlessness and find within himself the foundation he seeks'. The idea of looking within made logical sense to him. But it was a second book written by a Tibetan lama, with its emphasis on compassion for all—friend, stranger and enemy—again so logically argued, that really shook him. He said, 'It completely penetrated my heart and slapped me in the face simultaneously. I was forced to see that much of what I had done with my life was senseless, that my gangster way of life only brought more problems to my people, it didn't help them at all, although that was always my intention'.

It was then that he contacted *Mandala*. At first I wrote to him, then I visited. Actually I was the first visitor he had had in three years. After that it grew. I now write in a very personal way to 50 or 60 men (I lose count) and visit about five prisons in the USA. I help them with their practice, send books and generally take care of their needs. I've also given Refuge and Bodhisattva vows [the ceremony which commemorates the formal acceptance of the Buddhist path, and the vow to work tirelessly throughout all lifetimes to bring all beings to Enlightenment] on the authority of my lama. About twenty prisoners are now studying full-time on a seven-year master's program in Buddhism by correspondence.

Some men just want a bit of guidance, some a book to

read, but I could see that Arturo had a huge appetite and a very intelligent mind, and he was stuck in a cell all day. It was clear he needed detail. So I gave him explicit instructions: I told him how you start from the moment you wake up; how you rejoice that you are alive (because you could have died overnight) and how you set your motivation, 'May I use this day for my own benefit and the good of others'; how, when you get out of bed, you do three prostrations to the Holy Beings. I explained how you set up your altar, make offerings, sit down and begin to meditate. I told him how to do breathing meditation, watching the breath as it enters and leaves the nostrils in order to stabilize the mind; how to visualize the Buddha; how to meditate on the basic topics of Buddhism. I recommended various books for him to study during the day including one huge tome, *Liberation in the Palm of Your Hand*, a classic work setting out the minutiae of practice by an eminent Tibetan scholar and meditator, Pabonka Rinpoche. He said it was the greatest book he'd ever read. From the very beginning he began memorizing all his prayers and great chunks of the book, studying it, getting very clear on its meaning, writing books of notes. He had a highly disciplined daily structure starting at 5 a.m. and finishing at midnight.

The fact that he was a prisoner made no difference to what or how I taught him. I gave him nothing special. I've noticed that with all the men I write to and meet. I give them the Dharma [the Buddha's teachings] and *because* they're in prison they understand it all the more. That's what is so interesting. They are like blotting paper.

For a start, you don't have to persuade them of the Buddha's First Noble Truth—that life is suffering. People outside prison generally don't think life is fundamentally unhappy because it doesn't look like it, but prisoners know. Arturo and the men in SHU are locked up 22½ hours a day. Their cells, which measure 8 feet by 10 feet, have a naked toilet and no window. Their exercise yard, which is the size of two cells, is covered with a plastic roof so they never see any sky, tree or bird. The food is appalling. All they're allowed are eight books, photographs, the inside of a ballpoint pen and a TV. The noise from those pent-up men is dreadful—they all talk about the 'monstrous noise'. And then there is the violence. The intensity of the gang culture in the prison is beyond your imagination. Arturo says it is a war zone, a killing field—people die daily at the hands of each other. They all have knives. I once asked how they made their knives. They replied out of anything they could get, including plastic bottles. I was told, 'They're not much good because you can only use them once'. Arturo also said that because it's a culture that has grown over 30–40 years, it is so sophisticated and strong that the prisoners run the yard. They have so much power, which was why the authorities built Pelican Bay to house the most dangerous ones. They can't walk out the doors but they have enormous psychological power.

Because Arturo has been given an 'indeterminate' sentence, which means he's there for the rest of his life, he knows there is nothing for him on the outside, so he can't be conned like the rest of us. He knows he only has the choice of going crazy or going inside and finding his own mind, which is what Buddhism is all about. Buddhism maintains that one's reality is part of one's own mind-set, and that through discovering your own mind, even in the direst situations you can make your world a pure realm.

On his 21st birthday, a lama sent Arturo a birthday card:

I know you are in prison but actually it's just a concept: what you label and how you use the place. For another mind it's the same as a hermitage. In Tibet people lived in very small mud hermitages with only a small hole for passing in food. They didn't come out for many years. We think people who are outside prison are not prisoners, but actually we are. Even people who are traveling the whole world and are regarded as successful, who think they have everything—all the desire objects—actually are in prison, the prison of their inner life because their inner life is crying, so miserable and unhappy, not finding satisfaction. They are even more unhappy than people who have very little. Ordinary people who are not practicing Dharma, who do not have realizations, including kings and presidents, are living in a prison of family obligations, and a prison of self-centeredness, jealousy, desire and anger.

Interestingly, Arturo genuinely knows this to be true. That's what I'm finding with all of these men to different degrees. They are like huge receptacles, the Dharma just falls into them.

Francisco, a 30-year-old who'd been a gangster since he was eleven, shared cell 108 with Arturo at one stage. (Interestingly, 108 is an auspicious number in Buddhism.) He was also fed up with violence and thinking deeply on how to change his life, but in SHU you wouldn't dare to speak about such things. Arturo had been practicing on the top bunk completely privately for six months (with his head bent because there was not enough space for him to sit upright) when he and Francisco started to talk about their feelings for the first time. As Francisco expressed it:

> Arturo reached for one of his *Mandala* magazines to share a quotation with me and I happened to get a glimpse of a photo of the great Kirti Tsenshab Rinpoche [a highly revered meditator]. An ineffable feeling went through my body but I didn't say anything to Arturo because I wasn't sure that any sound would come out. So I asked to borrow the *Mandala* and I lay on my bunk for a long time looking at this photo and when I came out of my trance the joy that I had experienced which was so pure and so clean and which I had never experienced in my whole life was what I knew I wanted all living beings to experience. From that moment I vowed never to harm any living being.

Although the Mexicans have all been brought up Catholics and have very devotional hearts, like me they had many questions which weren't being answered. They had no problems with concepts such as rebirth and other realms of existence before birth and after death. For them it was the easiest thing. And when they heard about cause and effect it affected them deeply. Rather than making them feel guilty or ashamed, it made a lot of sense. It accounted for the situation they were in and their propensities.

I explained how the mind is continuity of consciousness —that it doesn't come from God or Buddha but is our own and whatever is in it is our own experience. I said how the situations we are born into are due to our past actions. In that way we can learn to take responsibility for what has happened to us rather than feeling like a victim. I said we have to recognize that the imprints in our mind for actions (such as violence) are from having done those actions in the past to others—that we get it done back to us and we keep wanting to do it. I told them that the actions we are doing now are the source of our future suffering and happiness. All these men have strong regret for the harm they've done to others. Francisco would say, 'I've always known there are other realms, Robina'. Another prisoner who's called Silent Death says, 'I'm not afraid of death—I've nearly died so many times and it isn't painful—but I'm terrified for my future lives'. For them reincarnation is not a problem.

When you learn about karma, if you're hearing it in the

right way, it's the most empowering thing because it's saying you are not a victim, you are responsible and you can change; you are not a hopeless case. That's important. The prisoners are treated like scum, so they identify with that. The essential message of Buddhism is one of hope because the Buddha starts with the statement that we are all potentially perfect. Our nature is perfect and clear. I am constantly reaffirming, rejoicing in their marvelous efforts, stating that they are not as people see them, that they are not innately negative, that this is just the result of past karma and also a wonderful opportunity to change. It's not me patting them on the back. It's the truth. They are innately pure—they do have Buddha nature. We all have.

We also talk about anger, which in Buddhism has to be eliminated if one wants to achieve peace for oneself and others. The level of anger and violence which these men lived at was enormous because the whole philosophy of the Mexican gangs is that anger is justified on the grounds that you're trying to help others and maintain a 'moral code' as they call it. If someone disrespects that code, the way to eliminate the problem is to eliminate the person!

No one ever teaches us how to change from an angry to a non-angry person. No one ever tells us that anger causes 'you' suffering and is not helpful. That it stops 'your' peace of mind and everybody else's. It's never talked about in a practical way, only a moralistic way. What I am noticing about these guys is that they have intelligent minds so their hearts are wide open to explanations. It is now so evident to them that anger is not beneficial, that it was making them insane and harming others. It was so clear. No one needs to convince them that anger is suffering. They know it.

In the West this Buddhist view is quite controversial because anger is often seen as justifiable—the necessary fuel for many political, social, or even religious causes. Anger is a cover-up for pain, or as one lama put it, it's the response when attachment does not get what it wants. Attachment is the huge neediness within us to get something because we have a fractured, separated, alienated, lonely, bereft sense of a 'me' in here and all the delicious world 'out there'. And so attachment is this constant neediness to get full, to fill up. When this huge neediness doesn't get what it wants, anger is the response. If you analyze it, anger is this painful response of smashing the obstacle to get to what 'I' think is right.

I know this from my own experience. I wanted answers and I had a great desire to make things better. I had my own unhappiness in childhood, but my first experience of suffering in the world was when I started reading black American literature and listening to black music. It moved me profoundly. My heart reached out (that was the good part) but there was anger in my mind. That was the political stance also, of course. The compassion I had for black people was equalled by the anger I had towards white people. And then when I became a feminist my compassion for female people was equalled by the anger I had for male people. That's why, after ten years of being very political and hating first of all the straight people then all the white people, then all the rich people, then all the male people, there was no one left to blame. I'd exhausted all the possibilities. My heart meant well but the methodology was a disaster. It just created more violence, more problems. It was so clear. It was also obvious that my own mind was becoming crazy. I couldn't hate half the human race—it wasn't on. It was logical that it was destroying Robina. At that point I began to listen to the Buddha's teaching—looking at Robina for the first time in my life.

I knew that only by looking at Robina's mind, getting rid of the pollution, would I be qualified to help or be of any benefit—to the world. We have to ask what is a Bodhisattva? It's a political activist, if you think about it. The Bodhisattva checks his or her own mind, gives up habitual deluded responses, recognizes his/her own marvelous potential, develops his/her huge compassion for others and then acts to benefit others. These actions do not come out of anger and frustration but out of wisdom that sees what is necessary to do and has the patience to wait for the right time to do it. The Bodhisattva never gives up.

With anger I wasn't constant. I changed my politics. One minute I hated these people, the next I hated those people, then I couldn't care less about the first group. I changed. My mind and my motivation were unstable.

The gangsters who've taken up Buddhism are given a

hard time, no question. Some have actually put their lives on the line. The courage that's needed is unbelievable. Francisco has vowed never to harm any living being. That means no longer shooting or stabbing, which in turn means giving up the gang. Then there is no protection. You're an outcast. Even the guards don't respect you. Francisco is almost waiting to die. Silent Death is on a hit list. Two guys I write to love the Dharma but they can only go so far with it because they're too afraid to take the huge step of promising not to harm another living being.

Arturo's behaviour is also shocking and threatening. His fellow prisoners watch him sitting in his cell reading, meditating, doing prostrations every day. They notice he talks in a different way and that he doesn't push it on anyone. They started grilling him: 'Would he let one of their enemies into his cell?', which is what you definitely would not do. He said, 'I don't have any enemies now'. He tried to explain it without being fanatical. Eventually they all rejected him and stopped talking to him. It was very brave. He knows if he were not in his cell he would be killed.

He's totally steeped in it—memorizing, meditating for hours, studying the master's program. I asked him recently, 'Does your day go quickly?' He clicked his fingers and said, 'Like that'. He hasn't got enough time to do everything. For most people who have nothing to do with their minds, having so much time is boring. Another prisoner who is just beginning in Buddhism wrote to me recently, 'I am so excited to find this; I've wanted all my life to learn about the mind and how to control it. Your letters make my week worthwhile'. He's 25, in for life and done seven years. He knows what it is like to be bored. That's why he and the others are so full of energy for Buddhism—suddenly it stops the boredom.

It's a fascinating fact that you can read, study and meditate on the same subjects repeatedly in the Buddha Dharma and never get tired of them. The reason is that when you meditate on specific Buddhist themes they become experiential. When something remains at the merely intellectual level, you get bored. The point of Buddhism is to go into your mind, discover what is there and work with it. Consequently every single moment of your life becomes a rich experience because you are growing something inside and you get the happiness you want.

As the prisoners are discovering, if you start to face reality, to look at your own mind and make an effort, you get results. In Buddhism it's only effort that makes the difference. Most of us get lulled because we're in a comfort zone—because these men live at such a grotesque level they make a tremendous effort to raise themselves above it and so they are getting results. Many are finding peace of mind, clarity, they're learning humility and patience. These guys get more results than most people I know. They see and feel Buddhism tangibly, that's why they're so blissful.

I visit Arturo and I see a happy man. Paul Dewy is 'on

the mainline' (part of the general prison population), in with 800 other men serving a life sentence for killing someone while drunk-driving. He woke up in a hospital paralyzed from the neck down amd went through a huge cathartic experience of thinking about his whole life, realizing how absolutely selfish he had been. He vowed from then on only to benefit others. The next day he woke up and wasn't paralyzed at all. (My speculation is that this is the ripening of Bodhisattva vows from past lives.) He gets up early before the rest of them so that he can do his meditation. He says it's another story in the evening—800 men wide-awake and wound up. He still does his meditation—by concentrating. If we get the slightest distraction we get irritated, but he knows he has no choice, so he actually develops concentration amid this 'monstrous noise'. He says that when he manages it, all the noise goes away. He constructed this marvelous meditation, has taken Refuge and Bodhisattvas vows, and studies Buddhist courses by correspondence. He had a vision of the female Buddha, Tara, along with her entire entourage and experienced bliss in every atom of his body. He said, 'Robina, I needed a wake-up call'. Every one of the prisoners I have contact with speaks like this. The Tibetans say that if we're really practicing the Dharma we give ourselves our own wake-up call. Many of the contemplations are to help you realize that you are impermanent, that you don't have to wait till you have cancer to realize you are going to die. Most of us have to wait till we're punched in the nose.

There's Timothy, a 40-year-old Puerto Rican ex-gangster in a prison in Michigan. He started doing yoga because he wanted to get power over his enemies, but he got bliss instead. Daily in his cell he would have this presence of green light, which he sensed had a female quality about it. Then he started reading Buddhist books and discovered the green light belonged to Tara—now he's devoted, studying hard and wants to become a monk.

Of course many of the prisoners do not have visions and bliss. Many of the men I write to are ordinary guys, young and old, who struggle and have low self-esteem like the rest of us, but they want to find something. There's one guy, Milo, a former roadie for a rock group who's in for seven years, who is a lovely human being. He's discovered Buddhism and it's still a bit of a struggle but he's getting something from it. You can tell from his letters that he's learning so much. He's looking at his mind and his life, is full of regret and trying to get a better relationship with his wife. He's appreciating his family more, he's learning patience and humility—things he would never have bothered thinking about before. You can feel how his little heart is growing and he counts his blessings every day, he says.

In Massachusetts I give talks in the chapel to a group of men. Some are Christian, although obviously not fundamentalists or they wouldn't be coming. On Death Row the men are involved in endless appeals which go on for years, so they're in a sort of limbo. They have so little communication with anybody and are hungry for intellectual and spiritual stimulation and for anyone to talk of spiritual experience. They're very sincere and use what I give them as grist for their mill. We have a marvelous communication.

We talk about karma, rebirth, reincarnation, whether there is God, why this, why that. They ask questions, trying to get clear about their truth. I'm not trying to make them Buddhists. I teach them meditation, sometimes using visualizations of Jesus with light coming from him, purifying and blessing. There is no contradiction—the technique is Buddhist but the content can be Christian or whatever is helpful, so long as the bottom line is developing clarity, kindness and morality. Buddhism knows that everyone has the right and responsibility to find their own way to truth. You cannot force. I think any religion has to be universal because if it's anything less it is merely political.

It's been my own personal meditation, trying to think through and speak the things that I am attempting to live. I have to constantly distil what I know when I talk, especially when I am addressing non-Buddhists. To me the process has always been to listen, think about it, and work with it in my own mind. Then if I have to speak it I can speak it clearly. This has been my wish and my karma too. I've always worked with words—editing, teaching wanting to comprehend and make things clear. Interestingly, the name

that was given to me on my ordination is Thubten Kunsel—
Thubten means the teaching of the Buddha, Kun is all and
Sel is clear [hence, making the Buddha's teaching clear]. I was
very happy to have that name.

There is no doubt that I am helping these men, but they
are helping me beyond imagination.

In trying to practice and integrate this stuff into your life
you learn, as they say, to see everything that comes to you
as your own karmic appearance. These letters—these jewels—
keep coming onto my desk. I haven't invited them, they just
come. To me it's the karmic appearance of these hugely
violent people in an appalling situation which is a reflection
of my own nature, which is very volatile and angry. I have
never been afraid of violence. I'm almost attracted to it.
Somehow it's as though it calms me. So working with these
men is perfect at this time. It's making me practice discipline,
to control my mind, to control my speech. Even to walk into
those prisons I have to be so careful. If I walk too fast, the
guards slam down on me. If I speak too loudly, I'm too
confronting. I have to be very calm, very clear, very quiet.
This is a huge challenge for my own mind and it's something
I'm wanting to taste. It's like nectar.

Recently I had to make a choice between teaching a
group of 50 at a center just outside San Francisco and driving
eight hours to spend two hours with Arturo with a glass
partition between us. There was no doubt what I was going
to decide. The group liked what I said but I could sense they

did nothing with the material I gave them. For them it was basically entertainment. Everything I tell Arturo he uses, and turns it into something. His appetite and his wish to practice are enormous. I said to the group, 'I'm sorry, I can't come here any more but you are all welcome at classes I give in San Francisco any time you want. It's 40 minutes away'. Not one ever came.

I want to bring Buddhism to those in the bleakest situations, where it wouldn't normally be found. I am not trying to make these men more than they are (they're just human beings), but I am inspired by their effort, energy, humility, the recognition of their suffering and their wish to turn it around. I admire their sense of responsibility and I really want to help them. **99**

From Sotheby's to Dharamsala

ALISON MURDOCH
Buddhist and Christian

I asked Alison Murdoch to contribute to *Why Buddhism?* because she exemplifies, *par excellence,* how someone steeped in Western culture, particularly Christianity, can be drawn to Eastern thought in its most potent expression, Buddhism. Alison is quintessentially English. She was born to middle-class professional parents, went to the university of Oxford in England where she read history and history of art, and then went on to work at Sotheby's. From childhood she had strong spiritual inclinations and was actually contemplating being ordained as an Anglican priest when she heard the call of the East. I first met her in 1988, shortly after she had done her first Buddhist retreat in Nepal, this tall, brown-eyed, vital, highly articulate woman who wore exquisite shawls. I remember being both impressed and horrified when she told me she would lie in her small, rudimentary room at night while rats chewed at her hair— she didn't like to shoo them away, she said, in case she woke up the other occupants. Alison has always had an intrepid, rather romantic streak. When her lama told her to go to Tibet she went in alone through the 'back door', via China, dressed as a man. Similarly, when she was in her twenties and working flat out in London she decided the way to relax was to take off her shoes. Hence she walked the pavements barefoot carrying a gray woollen blanket over her shoulder which she threw out on the Underground platform inviting strangers to join her as they waited for the train.

Alison's spirituality, true to her Christian roots, has always had a large element of 'doing'. This contrasts radically with Buddhism's emphasis on 'being'. While the good Christian will seek to feed the poor, house the homeless and relieve the sick, the good Buddhist will endeavor to find some solitary place in order to go within to develop the awakened state—the argument being that only then is one qualified to help appropriately. In those days in Nepal, Alison would regularly leave the peace of the monastery to go down to the sordid, grim prison in Kathmandu and visit a young Englishman convicted of some drug-related offence. She felt his plight keenly and pressed British officials both there and at home to do something to help him. Before then, when she was a regular attender at the famous St James's Church in Piccadilly, she made national news by persuading the vicar to open its doors to the homeless. She stayed with those homeless people for a further three or four months and later ran a day and night shelter for them, going on to create a network for all the day centers for homeless people across the United Kingdom. Next she did a research project into people who were begging in London, a job she describes as 'an absolute gift for a Buddhist'.

Today Alison is working full-time as the director of a Buddhist center called Jamyang set up in a former court house in Kennington, central London, in the midst of tower blocks, traffic and grime. With typical verve and inspiration she fought off the developers greedily eyeing this prime piece of real estate, by buying it on behalf of a Buddhist organization, the FPMT (Foundation for the Preservation of the Mahayana Tradition). With the help of a dedicated team, she has converted the courtroom into a beautiful meditation hall (the judge's bench now holds a Buddha) and the cells (which once held notorious criminals) into accommodation rooms. Not surprisingly, Alison has introduced some innovative schemes in the running of this essentially Tibetan Buddhist establishment. In this interview I was interested to explore how her Christian inclination 'to help' has been grafted onto the Buddhist philosophy and practice which she now embraces. This melding of East and West is echoed in her marriage to a devout Christian. I wanted to know the pleasures and pitfalls of such a match.

The interviews took place at Alison and Simon's home. Out of the window we could see the church which they both attend every Sunday. Downstairs some esoteric piece of European music was playing. Upstairs was Alison's meditation room. And in the hall were two bicycles, their means of transport across London and beyond. All were apt symbols of Alison's diverse life.

I was brought up in the Church of England, and was always very much at ease in churches. When I was about eighteen I was a committed atheist and rebel. Then in my mid-twenties I reconnected with Christianity through St James's Church in Piccadilly, London. It was a very natural, comfortable reawakening. That church introduced me to a wonderful eclectic Christianity. We were focusing on spirituality rather than the Church of England service, with the idea that your spirituality permeated every aspect of your life. It was an incredibly rich and stimulating time. I was living quite close by, and so I got increasingly involved.

I remember someone once saying, 'You are either a God person or a Jesus person'. I was always a God person. I had difficulty with Jesus, I don't know why. I think I was very put off by the way he was depicted in children's books, as a person with long hair, in white robe in a different culture. I had some very powerful moments in prayer from quite an early age, about limitlessness. One particularly strong experience happened when I was about ten or eleven, out of which came the phrase 'Alpha, Omega and me'. I was shocked by the audacity and arrogance of that phrase, but it was my souvenir of an experience of limitlessness and was what I associated with God. I always knew there was a power and an energy within me that the external world distracted me from.

I used to walk into St James's and feel that I could be myself in a different way. I had the most wonderful, alive, imaginative connections with people, a sense of being stripped of things I didn't need, and of being able to play like a child in that environment. I remember organizing a Christmas pageant that involved masks and clowning. We also made some ten-metre high batik banners to hang at the back of the altar at Christmas, and when the rector asked how we were going to get them up I turned to him and said 'with prayer'. In the event I went to the local fire station and they brought their ladders and hung them up. I have no idea if that's prayer or not. My spirituality was strong but undisciplined—all heart but not a lot of head.

During this time I did my first meditations with a Julian of Norwich group. [Mother Julian of Norwich, 1342–1416, one of England's most significant mystics, described her visions of Jesus in the evocative *Revelations of Divine Love*.] At that point I hadn't found actual meditation techniques within Christianity, although now I know they exist. This meditation was a going into silence, starting from the revolutionary (for the Church of England) principle that God was inside you and all you needed to do was to be quiet and listen. 'Let nothing disturb you, let nothing dismay you, all things pass, God never changes', as Teresa of Avila said.

I was also greatly inspired by Anthony de Mello, an Indian Jesuit based near Poona who was disowned by the Vatican. He collected stories from all different faiths and used to lead extraordinary retreats where he would look at what Buddhists call 'the emptiness of the self'. I will never forget reading about Tony's revolutionary discovery: 'You do not exist at all as you think you exist'. This was when I'd hardly heard of Buddhism, but I was so inspired. He always appealed to me a lot more than Thomas Merton, who I found came more from the head. I was also crazy about the Bible. I used to read the Psalms a lot. I loved the Psalms. They had the poetry, the literature and also the heartfelt cries.

At the time I was working at Sotheby's, as an expert on British nineteenth-century paintings, but was finding it increasingly unsatisfying. I felt it wasn't what I wanted to do with my life. From the age of about 25 I had someone who became my spiritual mentor who I saw on a regular basis. She really helped me explore what was happening in the realigning of my priorities. She advised me to go on Christian retreats. I loved doing retreats on my own. They were rudimentary and unmanaged, but I did them in the most wholehearted way. One time I went to Patmos, where St John wrote Revelations. I also spent a few days in an Eastern Orthodox nunnery and had the most fantastic experiences.

I made a strong connection with the abbess. I remember telling her I was thinking of going to Asia and she said, 'Don't, you will lose your Christianity', which was quite prophetic as it happened. I was there for about four or five days before going off to another island where I was frightfully intense and solitary during the day and then ate in the same restaurant every night and drank half a bottle of retsina. It was a fine combination. Although I have always been called to some kind of inner life, I am also very good at getting distracted by the world. I enjoy things. I'm a hedonist. I'm passionate and enthusiastic. Enthusiasm I find the easiest so-called virtue of all. I once had 'lively and enthusiastic' for every subject on my school report. I have to live with that personality! Back then in the 1980s I was getting the best of both worlds: the wonderful exciting London life coupled with discovering silent prayer, retreat and meditation.

After those rather powerful few weeks in Greece and with the support of my Christian spiritual teacher I decided to throw in my job at Sotheby's and to take some space. The sort of phrases I was using (which make me shudder now) were, 'I want to make my life a blank sheet of paper for God to write on'. At a more grounded level, perhaps, I was saying, 'I want to see what happens when nobody is telling me what to do'. I thought that by taking a year off I could sort my head out and be that blank sheet of paper. Now I have a much more long-term approach. I always had a yearning to go to India and Kathmandu. When I handed in my notice

I was offered a one-year sabbatical which I turned down, as I wanted to go with no ties whatsoever.

I bought a single ticket to Delhi, which gave me the sense of freedom I wanted, and flew out in May 1987, aged 27. I'd collected all kinds of addresses and contacts from people in an organized way (rather the opposite of going as a blank sheet of paper!) and someone had mentioned Dharamsala and the Dalai Lama. I knew nothing about either, but I remember thinking, 'Don't go there straightaway, you'll get stuck'. So I decided to start in Simla, where my great-grandparents had lived (there was a strong Indian connection that no one in the family had explored). I ended up a week or two later in the Manali Valley with a couple of New Zealanders who were good walking companions, and one morning I remember saying, 'I need some space today, I'm going off on my own'. I walked past a road and felt an incredible pull to go down it. At the end was a Tibetan Buddhist temple. I had never had any interest in Buddhism at all because I hated the airbrush paintings in primary colors of Buddhas done by the hippies. You see, I was a Sotheby's snob. I was into ancient stonework and medieval Gothic. There had never been any attraction whatsoever to Buddha images or Buddhas. But I was quite impressed by this temple, because within its own cultural context I could connect more easily to it. I noticed a Western woman doing prostrations and in great St James's style said, 'I'm interested in being respectful so can you please show me what to do'. Afterwards we went off to have a cup of coffee, over which she told me there was a meditation course run by Westerners starting in two weeks time in Dharamsala and that I ought to do it. I thought 'OK', and made my way there.

I registered and was given a room and then I said, 'I'd also like to meet the Dalai Lama'. My mother had been wild about Tibet in the 1950s. Heinrich Harrer's book *Seven Years in Tibet* had just come out and what she most wanted to do was to go there. She told me about a daughter of a friend of hers who had gone to Dharamsala and seen the Dalai Lama. So in a sense I'd carried this lineage from my mother. All these professional Buddhists fell about laughing and said, 'You'd be so lucky'. I said, 'What would I have to do if I wanted to see him?' And they told me I'd have to go down to the Dalai Lama's private office (ha ha ha). I walked in, said I wanted to see the Dalai Lama and they said, 'Fine, he's giving an audience tomorrow, we'll add you to the list'. So the first Tibetan lama I ever met was His Holiness the Dalai Lama.

I had some seeds from the garden in St James's to give to him because I knew he loved gardening, and I stayed up all night painting a little seed packet for him.

Meeting him was wonderful, overwhelmingly so. He had a complete impact. I realized something very special had happened. I did a ten-day meditation course run by a Canadian monk and was immensely impressed by it. I think I was the most awful student. It was extremely stimulating and intellectual and I remember arguing about everything and asking far too many questions—getting totally stuck in. I had some wonderful conversations. There were some Buddhist feminists there and we had great discussions. I wrote letters back to my Christian community saying I had had a fascinating time, that they would have loved it and how I couldn't wait to share it with them as Buddhism could really inform our Christian beliefs.

What I had found of value there were the methods. A very simple example was the meditation where you beam out love from your heart to all the world—starting with your own body, then to the people in the room, then going out to the whole world. The meditation on death made a strong impression, too. Here you imagined your whole body peeling back to the skeleton and the skeleton dissolving and going into the universe. This resonated not only with my whole sense of being part of a 'timeless universe' but also my fascination with death in literature and art. When I was a child my mom used to say, 'You're far too interested in death, it's really macabre'. But I was looking for something that I knew was definite, and then I realized it was death. To be with people who were comfortable discussing it, who could talk you through the death process without fumbling, saying, 'This is what is going to happen to you', was a tremendous relief.

The meditation whereby you learn to generate equanimity towards 'friend, enemy and stranger' alike also had a profound effect on me. It is the basis of generating true compassion towards all. Having just worked with homeless people in a very full-on way through the previous winter, I knew I had experienced a kind of transcendence of my own needs, but it was always temporary. What I noticed was that after 36 hours, 48 hours, or maybe a week, the ego would wing its way back with a vindictive possessiveness and I would then behave appallingly. I could be childish and demanding. It was a rebound of a sort. I was wanting to stretch the period of time I could work and give without the rebound, when I could be selfless without wanting a payback for it. The friend, enemy, stranger meditation gave me insights into the way I operated, which I think I had been glossing over in the Christian way. Nobody was criticizing 'judgementalism' within my Christian community. This Buddhist meditation gave me a way to bring my head and heart together. It provided a method of analyzing the way I was reacting to people and also to be brutally honest about it. I thought I was being loving but when I actually examined my behavior, I wasn't. I was saying things I didn't really mean. I hadn't taken time and space to examine my preconceptions, my prejudices. That meditation gave me a chance to examine, unpick and bring any intelligence I had to bear on this heart issue. It's an extraordinary method and has remained a very powerful meditation for me.

On that course for the first time I was introduced to the real power of watching your mind and the principle that you can control your mind, that you don't have to be controlled

by it. I had had some quite addictive periods in my life—
alcohol, art, late-night friendships, sex, passion, those sorts
of things—and I could see no reason to restrain myself. In
my teens I'd been told to be mature, which to me seemed
like a mediocre shade of gray; to me there was no justification
for not being either white or black. There was a sort of manic
mind there. Now I was being told that you could work with
your mind, and if any bits were wobbly you could patch
them up like you patch up a wobbly table. Buddhism was
saying you pick it apart and use reason. It wasn't a matter
of 'God is revealing his grace to you or he isn't'. With
Buddhism there were always things you could be doing in
times of difficulty and in times of joy. And we were reassured
that slowly, slowly there would be a difference. Every drop
will join the ocean. It was such a contrast to the powerful,
instinctive approach that I'd had. I remember someone saying
to me, 'The thing about charismatics is that they're great
when things are going fine, but they don't always have
the tools when they are not'. In Buddhism I encountered a
stunning philosophical system where you felt everything had
been thought through, everybody's experience had been
brought together and it was bigger than you. All my life I
had been searching for something that was bigger than me—
something that could take everything I could throw at it.

I've studied very little Buddhism, but I'm staggered at
what I have found. Compared to anything I experienced at the
university of Oxford, this is massive. It's the most complex,

subtle, sophisticated philosophical system in the world. It's like some gigantic flow chart, where one thing leads to another. I'm a person who loves lists. I enjoy summing things up and defining them and then seeing what goes off. And the Tibetan flow chart is just extraordinary. Whatever direction you decide to take it in, there's an answer. You don't have to accept the answer—it can become a basis for your questioning. They'll debate with you and then you'll go off somewhere else. It's the most extraordinary, detailed map. I felt I'd been wandering around without a map. If I was going to be really serious this was offering me everything I'd always wanted.

I did the course in Dharamsala as a Christian and when it was over I headed on up to Kashmir and Ladakh and then went down to a Christian–Hindu ashram in Pune. I spent over two months there and was introduced to a wide variety of texts in the library, including a biography of Krishnamurti. That was the first time I felt my Christianity was beginning to disintegrate. Krishnamurti was talking about everything being subjective—that we are hardly, if ever at all, objective and so we're projecting the whole time. That was very powerful for me because for a long time I'd been interested in this subjective–objective question. When I read Krishnamurti it was like an explosion inside. I thought, 'This God who I have been praying to, and thinking about, and having such powerful experiences with, is simply a reflection of my own mind. I've been projecting the whole time'. My idea of God was fairly abstract (he was not a white-haired figure, although he was personal to the extent that I did chat away to him a bit). What I was doing was projecting onto an experience and saying, 'This is God speaking to me'. Krishnamurti was stating, 'Maybe not. Maybe this is your deepest soul, your deepest mind talking'. I didn't discuss this with anybody—I took it away privately. But really that nuked many of the Christian beliefs I had until then. Looking back, if I had known some of the profound Christian teachers I've met since, I think they could have talked me through this time and I could have remained a Christian.

There wasn't despair. I was in exploring mood and felt the whole world was mine at that point. This was my opportunity to do anything I wanted. There was nobody on my back. I'd got away from a disciplined childhood. I'd been an obedient eldest daughter, I'd had a wild but nevertheless conventional upper middle-class time at Sotheby's, I'd been a good girl in the Church, and this was my moment of freedom.

My Indian visa was running out and I'd heard that there was a month-long Tibetan Buddhist course in Nepal run by the same organization that had run the course in Dharamsala, and I thought, 'I learnt a lot last time, why don't I go and do some more?' I arrived and was taken to my room, which had mattresses on the floor, and beside every mattress there was a little shrine with a picture and some flowers, which was just what I used to do instinctively when I was traveling. That evening I had an incredible feeling of being in the right place at the right moment—more powerful than any other time in my life. It was a transparent feeling, the whole thing was so positive. About twelve days into the course the main lama arrived to teach, and I had such a powerful feeling when I saw him. My entire stomach flopped over and afterwards I had to run away and cry. Still, I went into his teachings with a critical mind. I was a solid type, not a soft, easily influenced hippy! I asked him a question and he laughed and laughed. Someone said afterwards they could see something going on. Then he started to teach on Emptiness and it was in some way a development from what had affected me so strongly from Krishnamurti.

An intrinsic part of the Emptiness teachings was that there is no inherently existing 'I'. As someone who has been very egotistical, I just adored the idea that the 'self' that I had been living with didn't have validity. It felt like coming out of prison. I was being instructed that I wasn't entrapped by this person that I always thought I'd been, or others thought I was. That goes back to very tangible moments in childhood when my mother would say, 'Oh that's typical of you!' and I'd think, 'No, it's not, there's somebody else in here as well and I could change'. We get so trapped by an identity, then we build it up more and more until our armor is covered in concrete. And then we cling to it. Often it's our negative opinions about ourselves that we cling to most strongly. We define ourselves by our own sense of guilt and inadequacy. That wonderful childlike joy I felt in church was actually quite close to our true state. What Tibetan Buddhism was offering was an ordered, logical way into that same experience which I could use in moments when it wasn't happening naturally.

I was there with about 80 other people mostly my own age. It was intoxicating—socially and intellectually—being with people from all around the globe immersing themselves for a month in Buddhist meditation. A very interesting aspect about Tibetan Buddhism at the moment is that we are an international family who are bound together by the fact that we are in a minority and so we have these passionate international friendships. I know that in almost any country I go to in the world I will find kindred spirits and that we will share a language. It's probably temporary, but it's very nice.

During this time I recognized I was with extraordinarily qualified teachers—people who taught from first-hand experience. I felt I'd spent so much of my life listening to people with second-hand experience. The Tibetan teachers I was meeting were the closest people I had found to a living Jesus. I thought here I was being faced with everything I'd always wanted to develop myself so I could be useful to other people and was I going to say, 'Sorry, it's not quite the right package, I'm going back to Europe to start looking again there'? That didn't feel appropriate. Then, an incredible sadness came up, which when I examined it seemed to be about attachment to the members of my Christian community in London who had all given me a massed blessing when I had left St James's, to the churches, the music, the art. I felt that if that was what was keeping me Christian, then I wanted nothing to do with it. Looking at those attachments spurred me on.

I went to see the lama and said, 'I've been really involved in Christianity, but I really would like to give Buddhism a try'. Cheekily I added, 'I'll give it one year. I've got enough money for another year in Asia, so you tell me what to do and I'll test you out'. That's where I was at. He said 'OK'. He laid out the most fabulous year for me—a month contemplating Emptiness, a course on Lo Rig [Science of the Mind], a trip to Tibet to see the famous Jowo statue in the central temple in Lhasa and a retreat meditating on Vajrasattva, the Buddha of Purification. It was a brilliant response to my personality and it confirmed that here was somebody who could take the challenge. When I told my vicar in England that I'd been listening to his sermons all those years about changing your life and was giving up my job to live the Bible, he looked horrified. He didn't have a way to deal with that kind of statement because it was the exception and not the rule.

(I can recall a lovely story from that time. There was an Israeli guy who'd been quite a senior officer in the army and something had happened that totally traumatized him. He was carrying an enormous burden of guilt. He said he'd made confessions to many people and they'd all basically said, 'It's all right, it doesn't matter'. His superiors had told him never to speak of it to anybody. He went to see a Tibetan teacher who said, 'You poor thing, to be carrying all that' and who then proceeded to set out a program of retreat for him. This man was so happy because he felt that for the first time somebody had understood his anguish and was able to offer a course of action which would ameliorate his feelings.)

There wasn't a moment of conversion. It took me years to say, 'I'm a Buddhist', and it felt like coming out when I did. It was totally unpremeditated. I wasn't expecting to be anything other than Christian for the rest of my life. What I felt was that I had found the methods that would enable me to follow Jesus's path, understand what he was saying and put it into practice, rather than simply meeting once a week to praise and worship him. The obvious example is the great command of Jesus that inspires me above all others, which is to love thy neighbor. I have been gripped by the Buddhist teachings on Emptiness because I see those as the key way to be able to love thy neighbor—ever more deeply, ever more thoroughly. The teachings on Emptiness help you get your own sense of self out of the way so that you can really respond to the needs of others. My old selfish habits would get in the way of my being able to do that. It happens on all levels. I am also Buddhist because it offers the culture of fearlessly being able to use my own mind.

At the moment I'm doing meditation practice in the mornings because I know it will change the whole of my day. It enables me to center myself, to face any naggings, worries or regrets and leaves me flexible to deal with whatever the day brings. I can introduce it into my day in all kinds of ways. If I'm speaking publicly or running a training course I specifically pause for inspiration, to make myself a channel for something that is beyond the ego. Or in tiny ways I pause before going into conversation. One teacher, Lama Yeshe, said, 'What I teach you will never leave you. You won't even be able to get away from it in the supermarket'. That's what I wanted. And that's what I got.

I used to have an annual evaluation of whether Buddhism was still suiting me, because I feel free inside. I am bound to no one. I know that is very shocking to some, but I am comfortable about the sincerity of what I'm doing. But I don't do that any more. I do get the odd panicky superstitious moment when I think maybe I've made a massive mistake and the 'otherness' that I experience is actually a personal god, but if it were, you could hardly see him being annoyed with me.

There have been areas of difficulty. In the first few years, I had enormous trouble with the liturgy, which to me represents the sacred art and music as well as the sacred space. I think I'd gone into it far more quickly than someone like the Dalai Lama would advise. I had problems getting to grips with what I considered alien chanting and alien imagery. By doing a daily practice and using some of these images in meditation, I have discovered a technicolor layer in my psyche. It's almost like a prism. The technicolor comes before the pure white. I believe there are enormous benefits in dealing with that technicolor layer. Tibetan Buddhism in particular has developed very skilful, profound methods of working with it.

I don't have nearly so much trouble with Jesus now, because I have been introduced to his story in the most powerful way possible. My husband is a Christian and about three years ago he introduced me to his church choir. It may sound strange because I am a full-time Buddhist in a Buddhist job, but I sing in this choir most Sundays. It's an Anglo-Catholic church, a beautiful Grade 1-listed building in a mixed-race neighborhood which my husband has been attending for eighteen years. To begin with, I did quite a lot of complicated intellectual interchange; I'd change words around and things like that. Now I operate at much more of a heart level. The vicar is interested in Eastern Orthodox and the highlight of the year is Easter week. Today was Good Friday and we've been singing a mixture of plainsong, medieval John of Portugal and Bach's St Matthew Passion. There was light filtering in on faded stone (there wasn't incense because it was Good Friday, but usually there's plenty of that). It brings up all my cultural resonance. I've found a connection with Jesus through the symbolism of absolute, limitless compassion. There are things in the Christian service I don't participate in, specifically the creed, and I have problems with ideas like Jesus buying us with his blood. I remember Gandhi feeling the same way. He thought it was an outrageous concept.

I love the Church's liturgical year—the moving with the

seasons. If you do that with one Church repeatedly you get an incredible sense of a wheel of the year. I love the intercessions. Apart from one lama, I've never known a Buddhist who can deal with people's prayers as effectively as the Christian intercession. And I really appreciate the idea of a community coming together at a set time once a week. Although Sunday trading is eroding it, our English and European culture was built around giving people the opportunity to do that. And my parents and my husband's parents are comfortable with me having an interaction with the Church.

In some ways my husband is a more natural Buddhist than I am. He's incredibly peaceful, generous to a fault, and has the most extraordinary patience. He's very clear-thinking and balanced, and often teases me when he sees that I'm not acting in accordance with my professed beliefs. But culturally he is a total Christian and an Anglo-Catholic one at that. He does not come to my Buddhist center. He comes from an intensely Christian background—his father, his grandparents and many of his cousins have all been priests. He broke the mould by not going into the Church. I think he's still working with the fact that there is something very powerful going on in his wife's life that he doesn't have access to. That's something we're working with. We've been married four years and the trust deepens. It's a path for both of us. When people ask us if there is a problem with a Buddhist being married to a Christian I always fall about laughing, because to me the real problem is not putting your beliefs in the center of your life. You can see it when you have stupid arguments about what film to go to. You don't have arguments about church. I feel that there is so much in common between the religions that it is completely ludicrous for them not to unite against the common danger which is materialism, the breakdown of relationships and family, and things like that.

The way we've found the most common ground has been through going on pilgrimages together (to holy sites in Tibet, India and Europe) and through the World Community for Christian Meditation, an international organization established by the late John Maine to rediscover the ancient methods of Christian meditation practiced by people like the Copts and the Desert Fathers. It is now headed by Father Laurence Freeman, a Benedictine monk whom Simon and I find most inspiring. Laurence Freeman has developed a close bond with the Dalai Lama and is carrying out a three-year program called 'The Way for Peace with His Holiness'. They've done a series of events together which we have had the enormous privilege of being invited to.

For all that, we should take on board the Dalai Lama's advice that it is ridiculous to try to combine the two religions and 'put a sheep's head on a yak's body'. I am fundamentally Buddhist in philosophy and practice. It feels as though I'm on a Buddhist bus where Christians have put in some of the glazing. A qualifier on all of this is that I am working it out as I go along. This has proved to be my path. I'm married to the only man I've ever loved to this extent, and I believe this is what I am meant to be doing. Maybe in two years or six months' time or even tomorrow I'll decide church is just distracting me, I'm not going to go any more. But this is where I am at the moment and it feels like a very exploratory, rich and growing period.

I'm quite ashamed of the fact that although I was meant to have quite a good intellectual brain I haven't done any solid philosophical study and I wonder if I'm not in a position of intellectual woolliness. My Buddhism has been very much Buddhism in action.

For the past five years I've been involved with Jamyang Buddhist Center in the heart of London. I think it is probably my work for this lifetime. The core community is practicing Buddhists and we have an extraordinary Tibetan teacher, Geshe Tashi, who is a direct student of His Holiness the Dalai Lama. He constantly stresses not the esoteric but everyday practice in the Western world. Jamyang is like the opposite of a chocolate—soft around the edges and hard in the middle. We are hard in the middle in terms of knowing where we come from and offering people a gateway into that incredible Tibetan Buddhist teaching if they want to take it (and if they can deal with all the cultural challenges). But it's soft around the edges.

We were encouraged by Lama Zopa Rinpoche, the director of the FPMT, to buy a building which was manifestly too big for us. We knew the only way we were going to survive financially was to share the building with other appropriate people, and so we created a room that we could let out to groups for meetings and seminars. To date we've opened our doors to mainstream organizations dedicated to helping people: the London Cycling Campaign, the National Homeless Alliance, a mental health team, and an agency that works for mentally disordered offenders. When we're asked to do something I ask, 'Why are we doing it as Buddhists?' I want to strike a balance between compassion and wisdom. We've built up a reputation as a welcoming peaceful place offering healthy food served with warmth and care. Just in the last few weeks we've been asked to run a meditation class in Brixton Prison—some of the inmates begged us to do it. We've also been asked to teach meditation to a local organization that works with people with mental health problems. We're not going out asking. This is us establishing ourselves as a resource and people are coming to us. We also hire out a therapy room. The therapists are not necessarily Buddhist, but we interview them to be sure of the quality of their work. We hold meditation and relaxation classes and also run a Buddhist bed-and-breakfast—so people can pass through London and stay with us for a few days at affordable prices. Sometimes people who aren't specifically Buddhist arrive, and it's interesting what can happen next.

I believe in the incredible potential of Buddhism to help those who have become separated from Christianity or Judaism. It offers a way back into the spirit. One tangible example is that we now advertize our classes on a weekly basis in *Time Out* and 'Hot Ticket'—which is the *Evening Standard*'s free listing. We've got some serious Tibetan Buddhist practitioners that way—one is working full-time as a volunteer. Christianity couldn't do that. If you advertized that in *Time Out* it would be taken as the most unappealing evangelism.

Our latest scheme is to open a café. Our center is in one of the most deprived boroughs in the whole of the United Kingdom. There's overcrowding, lack of facilities, lack of meeting places. We plan to create an adjoining garden where people can sit safely outdoors. The local authorities are extremely enthusiastic—they see it as supporting their own goals in creating a healthy and regenerated neighborhood. We're toying with the idea of having philosophy evenings in the café where you can have coffee, cake and philosophy (not necessarily Buddhist). Still, there has been some anxiety over the idea from the members—we are leasing off part of our building and we don't know what impact the general public will have on the center and the garden. I've organized meetings, private and public, where we've talked through the issues. I've had no flak from the Tibetan community. I feel tremendous support from our teacher—who has just suggested I continue in my role for the foreseeable future. It might sound pompous, but I do take things back in prayer and meditation. I find when you become more sensitive you can feel when something is niggling you.

I believe the way we do things matters as much as what we actually do. In some way the center is a vehicle for people to offer service and develop their minds. For me working in this way is an absolute joy after being in a target-led, funding-driven homelessness charity. Sometimes we stop and make alarming U-turns and that feels fine.

I am constantly redefining what 'Buddhist' activity is. It's fascinating both personally and at a work level. About a year ago I stopped using the word 'religion' because I felt it was such a barrier and began describing Jamyang as an educational charity. In the last six months I've been saying we're about health as well. The government has just introduced a new funding scheme for organizations that promote the mental and physical well-being of the local community. What else are we doing? What else is Buddhism?

Although I no longer judge myself a year at a time, I can see this weird recipe is definitely bringing a change. I have to be careful telling people how happy I am. 99

A tremendous
ripening effect

THUBTEN GELEK
Itinerant monk and pupil

*B*y a stroke of good fortune I
happened to bump into Thubten Gelek on his first visit back
to Australia in seventeen years and grabbed the opportunity
to talk to him. Australian-born Thubten Gelek is a well-
known, much-liked figure within Western Tibetan Buddhist
circles. He had the distinction of coming from one of
Melbourne's wealthiest Jewish families. On a wave of youthful idealism he had enlisted in the Israeli Army to fight in
the Six-Day War—an experience which left him partially
deaf from standing too close to exploding artillery. More
significantly, Thubten Gelek was among the first wave of
Westerners to be ordained as a Tibetan monk in 1978. Unlike
many of his contemporaries, however, he did not disrobe
after the initial wave of enthusiasm wore off and to this day
remains totally committed to his life of renunciation and

celibacy. In fact he is so committed to the monkhood that he insisted that I not use his Western name in his interview. Lastly, Thubten Gelek is also notable for his ecumenicalism— finding in other faiths and philosophies elements which he happily incorporates into his Buddhist practice. When I met him he was excitedly poring over Socrates's discourse in the last hours before his death, in which he expounds on his philosophy of reincarnation and how one is reborn according to the causes one creates right now.

For the past twenty years Thubten Gelek has led an itinerant life: sometimes living in small hermit huts in the high mountains above Dharamsala, north India (home of the Dalai Lama); sometimes making pilgrimages to Buddhist holy places in India, Nepal and Tibet carrying very little besides a small cooking stove and a pot; sometimes being on the road in search of teachings and initiations from eminent Buddhist masters; sometimes being involved in the organization of important ceremonies and conferences. Wherever he goes, whatever he does, it is always at the bidding of one of his many teachers. He has literally placed his life in their hands.

The interviews took place in the sitting room of his mother's flat in the Melbourne seaside suburb of Elwood. On the mantelpiece was a photograph of Thubten Gelek before he became a monk. It showed a bearded man with brooding eyes and a rather heavy expression. Beside it was Thubten Gelek on his ordination day, looking ten years younger, his freshly shaved head gleaming in the sunlight, his blue eyes shining with happiness. Today his eyes still hold the same sparkle, and he smiles often. Thubten Gelek is a strong man bursting with vitality. He told his story in his characteristic squeaky voice, the words often spilling over each other.

It was 1977, and I was living in what I guess might be called the fast lane. I was making huge amounts of money, thousands of dollars a week. I had a Mercedes sports car and lots of girlfriends who other people thought were gorgeous. I traveled the world first class on business and stayed in the smartest hotels. I'd be picked up from the airport in a Rolls-Royce, taken to the most fashionable hotel in the smartest part of town, installed in a luxury suite—and I'd be filled with a deep dissatisfaction and loneliness. I'd been brought up in an environment in which rich people were respected, men with attractive wives and girlfriends were admired and successful people were applauded. These were the goals that were meant to make you happy, but it clearly wasn't the case. Underneath there was always 'you'. I was acutely aware that I was miserable. I was getting drunk on Friday as the only way to wipe out that insane money-oriented mind and to create a break from it for the weekend. I was taking pills to get to sleep, coffee to wake me up, and was fundamentally unhappy. My life had its moments, but in fact the pleasures were all the same—

another car, another first night at the opera, another glamorous holiday. After a while the high price didn't seem so much of a good deal.

In the midst of all this my dad died of stomach cancer. His illness went on for eighteen months and was a traumatic family event. He was a jolly, popular person with a strong personality and he disintegrated before our eyes. We watched him shrink from a man of 19 stone to a skeleton of around 7 stone. He died in some expensive hospital room. As I stood there looking at him, utterly helpless, I saw myself lying there. I knew it was quite inevitable and only a matter of time.

The day after the funeral I woke up and prepared to go back to the office. As I was pulling on my socks the thought struck me: 'Why? What am I going into the office for?' And I was completely unable to answer it. To this day I still can't answer that question. Earning a buck is one thing, but as a philosophy of life it is absurd! That was the turning point. I sold the business and started looking for answers. I was absolutely serious. For the first time in my life I wanted to have a life that was meaningful and significant. My big question was 'Is there anything more to life than pursuing worldly goals and striving after a happiness based on merely material values?' The question hung there in the air. I wondered if I was being arrogant even to think there might be something more.

The problem was I had no idea which way to turn.

I knew that making money and acquiring things was not

the answer. I'd tried fighting for my country and been utterly disillusioned by that experience. Shortly after arriving in Israel to enlist, I discovered that the great emblem of the American hand clasping the Israeli hand in friendship which was displayed on all the billboards was also decorating the enemy's tanks and fighter planes. It all looked like business as usual to me! In one battle alone, the Arabs reportedly lost 2000 tanks—it was the mother of all windfalls for the arms manufacturers (who would heroically replace them with more). Seeing my friends killed and having to answer the questions of their tearful parents, it occurred to me that to lose one's life for a few kilometres of countryside was nonsense. Are the sons and daughters of the weapon makers and of the politicians who decide the war is so very necessary ever on the front lines?

I had been involved in a few relationships. At one stage I had lived with a woman and her children for three years. She was a wonderful person and her children were gorgeous. I was extremely proud of them. But whenever I thought about maintaining that sort of life for the next 40 years I couldn't do it. I had no guarantee that I wouldn't change, that we would feel the same about each other, and I simply felt I couldn't make the commitment of always being there.

I had no truck with religion—to me it was a prop for people who couldn't stand on their own two feet, for those who needed a fairy tale to get through life. My attitude wasn't surprising. My education, like most Western children's, was based on science and provable facts, which made religion seem implausible. My family was Jewish but not religious. I remember my father and I sitting at the back row of the synagogue telling each other jokes and the rabbi threatening to throw us out if we didn't keep quiet. To me it was mainly meaningless ritual. Once I did hear that there was an esoteric branch of Judaism but when I asked the rabbi about it he told me to go away and study the five books of Moses for 40 years and then come back and talk to him! When I was older I read my first spiritual book—Herman Hesse's *Siddhartha*, about the life of a holy man meant to be the Buddha, which indicated there might be another world based on something other than making money, eating good food and being entertained. I was clearly a very slow developer!

By the early 1970s some of my friends had begun to get into Tibetan Buddhism, and because I couldn't think of anywhere else to look, I enrolled on a course. I had little confidence in what I would find and went along with a lot of cynicism. This was upheld when I saw the way the participants bowed and lowered their heads to the lamas who sat up on thrones. I found the whole reverence thing disgusting. I was one of the group of people who adamantly refused to prostrate. Still, I had to admit there were elements of the course which were very effective. I can remember this squat, powerful Tibetan lama sticking out his jaw and saying, 'Why you people come here? You want to see some Tibetan gorilla mountain monk? Huh! You want to learn to fly?' Yes,

I thought, wouldn't that be amazing and worthwhile. I had heard stories about lamas being able to fly. Then he said, 'Birds and insects can fly but they are not happy'. That hit home. What the lama in effect was saying was that any 'trip', including spirituality, was not going to do the trick. I certainly knew the truth of that. I'd tried every trip imaginable, being sophisticated, being a hippy, riding motorcycles and flying a plane. I knew there was no real happiness in superficial things and that no half-baked transformation would do.

But what really clinched it was when we were told this really *big* lama was coming to visit. I thought big lama, big deal! We were told we had to spruce ourselves up, wash, put on clean clothes. There was a procession of monks with musical instruments and a golden silk umbrella held aloft. I thought the whole thing ludicrous. I was expecting some high, haughty church person but in came this old man, bent completely over, his hands pressed together, his eyes wide open with excitement and awe at seeing us! Serkong Rinpoche was the total antithesis of what I thought religion was. All my projections were overturned. He had complete humility, together with what looked like a tremendous appreciation of each one of us. He refused to sit on the high throne that had been assembled for him, but they lifted him up bodily from the floor onto it anyway. He gave a talk on compassion—speaking of the necessity of taking responsibility for the welfare of all living beings oneself. He gave many clear and obviously heartfelt reasons. All around me, people had tears streaming down their faces. I made my first prostration.

Over the next twelve months I attended more Buddhist courses, and became the deputy attendant of one of the teaching lamas, traveling around Europe with him. It was a privileged position and a remarkable time in my life, the like of which I am unlikely to experience ever again. By the end of that year I was committed to the Buddhist path. Unlike everything else I had tried, Buddhism offered a way to transform your lifelong efforts into something beneficial on a wider scale. It said that by working on yourself, through developing great compassion and profound wisdom, you could escape the sufferings of ongoing cyclic existence life after life and become a Buddha—in which capacity you could bring the same ultimate good to everybody without discrimination. I couldn't think of a better contribution to the human race than that! But I knew I was easily distracted, that there were girls out there, a myriad money-making business plans to entice me, and the transient fun of a social life. The only way I knew of protecting my mind from distractions and making any progress at a spiritual level was by becoming a monk.

In December 1978, aged 34, I took robes. My abiding memory is of feeling incredibly happy and light—as if I had taken off a heavy backpack that I had been carrying for 34 years and now my feet were hardly touching the ground. This load had gone. At the same time I also realized that in my dealings with others 90 per cent of my brain had been preoccupied with how I appeared to them. With only robes to wear and no hair, it didn't matter any more. Now I had the space to be with others unselfconsciously. That feeling of lightness and happiness has remained.

My big question was to see if there was anything more to life. Is there any other type of happiness other than that which comes from looking after the body and from very limited moments of happiness? Is that all there is? Is there another purpose, another dimension? Is life just a short-lived biological flash in the pan? A flash of biological functions, physical needs, doing a few things for our transient mental states, physical feelings and then death? Buddhism maintains there is more. This mundaneness is to be transcended. The problem is that people immerse themselves in the mundane to find happiness because they don't think there is anything else. Nobody has told them otherwise. Secularists can be as dogmatic as anyone. Religion has gone into disrepute and transcendence is a fact in few people's lives. I discovered that the issue of happiness is *the* central theme in Buddhism. In Buddhism supreme, unequivocal happiness is a very valid proposition because happiness—like suffering and everything in the universe—depends on causes which we individually create.

In Buddhism you're involved in the pursuit of perfection, the eternal development of an ever more subtle, ever finer, ever purer mind whose very nature is untrammelled compassion and wisdom. With that aim in mind, you reach an astonishing level of well-being and capacity to benefit others. Simplistically, there's a big difference between being involved in your own physical needs, immediate happiness and the cultivation of friends for that purpose (which takes up so much time but in the end leaves you empty-handed) and being involved in developing a mind which is totally altruistic and which, due to cause and effect, goes from life to life in ever-increasing loving-kindness and compassion. At the same time as being totally oriented towards the transcendent, Buddhism never divorces you from the conventional world of which you are a part. This reality is augmented by one's vow always to come back to help others. So I found in Buddhism a transcendent spiritual development which is totally related to people and the world as I know it.

There are so many things I like about Buddhism. The magnanimity for one thing. It doesn't have all these strictures and dogmas, 'You can only come in if you do this and that; you are not important—our structure is'. Buddhism is based on logic and reason. Buddhism is concerned with the individual. It's part of Buddhism's openness. The person is the most important thing—the maturation of the individual to his or her highest potential.

This magnanimity stretches to embrace evil people. In Buddhism, instead of condemning them, you make them objects of your compassion and prayer, because it's reasoned that through causing such incredible and widespread pain to others they must eventually suffer the most. This aspect of Buddhism is really nice, because it opens your heart to all 'bad' people and even good people who occasionally do the odd bad thing. Buddhism maintains there is no such thing as an inherently evil person anyway. It's only because people are deluded that they make mistakes. They haven't understood the law of karma. Had they known they wouldn't have done whatever they did. They plunge others and themselves into tremendous pain in this life and the next, and it all comes right back on them, because they are ignorant of the fact that causes inevitably bring about effects.

I also like that you are encouraged to question, to work it out for yourself. My first lama during a discourse asked us, 'Is this right?' and we all nodded. 'You fools, it is not right, why don't you check up,' he reprimanded. In Buddhism blind faith is considered a bad thing, because with it you can be led anywhere like a blind person. You don't want to waste your life getting into something that is a farce! You can challenge anyone, including the Dalai Lama, and he will enjoy it. In fact, in Buddhism the more doubts you have the better, because it shows you are thinking, working hard, clarifying every moment. Every proposition and tenet has to be backed up by reason. By very definition you can't attain perfect Enlightenment unless your understanding of Truth is correct. If there were a flaw in your approach you simply couldn't get there.

Because of this openness and magnanimity, Buddhism

is always open to all religions. One lama at the end of a course said that if we returned to our homes and became better Christians, Jews, Moslems, or whatever, he would rejoice. I belong to a religion which sees the Dalai Lama being able to give discourses to Benedictine monks and nuns on the Gospels, as he did in London recently. As His Holiness says, 'You don't need temples, you need a warm heart'. Buddhism has this universal principle. One of my lamas also says, 'If you think your religion is the best, you will never get Enlightened'. It's obvious. Discrimination is the opposite of altruism, and without altruism you cannot get Enlightened.

My life has completely changed. Once I had a lot of money, now I am dependent on whatever people offer. My income is very irregular. My mother and brother help a lot. Friends chip in. The amount I have at any one time varies. It's OK. My life is much simpler now. Whereas before I had so many possessions to look after, things I thought I needed for my life and which cost money to maintain, I now need very little. There is nothing from my old life that I miss.

I spend time in the mountains, in retreat. People in the West don't understand why you leave society in order to develop compassion. I get challenged on it a lot. I reply that the analogy is wanting to be a physician and going off to medical school for six years to train. In the meantime there are all sorts of horrible accidents happening and onlookers might criticize you saying, 'What are you doing locked away in medical school when people are bleeding on the streets?'

The answer is, 'If I continue and finish my five years plus internship, I can benefit people on a much greater scale'. It's the same with being a monk or a hermit. In retreat there's a tremendous ripening effect. There's an integrating into your very being of the step-by-step spiritual methods which you learn. Eventually you transform yourself into a totally spontaneous and aware altruist. To do that you need solitude for a while.

Solitude is a hard workplace. You sleep almost not at all. You meditate intensively on the transformational steps needed to develop the mind of total benevolence. It's not that you sit there listening to the birds and looking at the flowers. It's not spacing out. Quite the opposite. It's complete concentration. You sit long hours—it's painful and difficult, but at the same time it's rewarding. It's definitely the place to be. I could think of nothing more wonderful than to spend many years in retreat working on these absurd mental fluctuations that I call me. The only thing more wonderful would be the results of the process—to find oneself the embodiment of love and compassion, the effortless servant of others.

I've learnt to do without comfort. In retreat you see that the pursuit of comfort is so fleeting—so changeable. It doesn't deeply move you. It's superficial. We forget that the nature of the body is so painful—if it's not hurting now, it certainly soon will be! Sickness, old age and death are never far away, yet we put so much of our time into seeking comfort and kind words. When we hear some brief nice thing said about us it transforms our whole day. It doesn't really matter if it was meant or not. Physical comfort is the same. 'The sky is a bit cloudy today and because of that I'm depressed.' Our whole life is at the mercy of water vapor moving by wind! And then the water vapor disperses. 'Oh, it's blue—I so love blue!' It's very strange when you think about it. All these likes and dislikes. If you could switch them all off, life would be wonderful. Good food! People, especially more affluent people, spend a huge amount of time cooking, thinking, buying and reading about food. They're completely involved. Good nourishing food is important, but why make it an obsession and spend so much money on what simply ends up down the toilet, or as a small pile of ashes under a rose bush? It would be great if life went on for thousands of years, but it's so brief. To spend your life thinking about your next meal is so short-sighted. If there were only blackness after we die we'd be 100 per cent right putting all our effort and energy into acquiring as much comfort and pleasure as we could before our last gasp. Before making such a momentous decision, however, we should first investigate if there is nothing else whatsoever. It might be more plausible to work on one's mind—the source of happiness now and hereafter.

I'm guided by my teachers. I have about 40 from different Tibetan Buddhist traditions, some of whom have already passed away. They advise me on my spiritual development. They are very kind. They suggest I study this or research that, or take these teachings or those initiations. They guide me through my meditation practice, telling me if I'm on the right track or not. If they were not there, there'd be a tremendous amount of confusion and blind alleys and a lot of wasted time. It's like being in an apprenticeship to someone with a great deal of intuition and compassion. It's all made much easier. It's as if you enter a bubble of protective care and guidance, and you work within that. Of course other religions have their spiritual guides too. Eventually you learn to trust and have faith in yourself, to know that whatever happens, your mind will be calm. You become more concerned with others' welfare and unconcerned with your own—beyond selfish hopes and fears; at ease with whatever happens.

I have been a monk, and celibate, for twenty years. Giving up women and sex has not been so difficult. I knew from experience the problems relationships could bring. All too often it was an emotional roller-coaster which involved a great deal of pain, no doubt due to my egocentric viewpoint. The Buddha said that attachment is the cause of suffering. If you look deeply into it, from babyhood until now all the troubles, needs and strife has come from this underlying egocentric view of existence. Over the years you realize that the sex drive is more mental than physical and in Buddhism you are offered a range of mind-training methods to help you deal with it. There is a whole system of non-suppressive antidotes to anger, frustration and sexual desire. The mind

training is part of the process of becoming perfect. Some
people ask, 'Don't you want to be hugged, to feel physically
close to another human being?' and I reply, 'Yes, but there
are other more important things that I would be missing out
on if I disrobed'.

Within Buddhism there is a practical point to celibacy.
In order to progress in meditation, to reach the stage where
you realize Shunyata [the profound wisdom of Emptiness,
or Absolute Truth] and Bodhicitta [the universal altruistic
attitude], you need intense concentration. That requires
uncompromising practice, not just in short bursts. Someone
like me would probably not achieve the ultimate goal if my
energies were scattered about by close physical and emotional
situations—they need to be put wholeheartedly into
meditation to get there.

I have at times stepped outside my own tradition, to
help me on my way. It's feasible so long as you retain a clear
appreciation and respect for your own religious framework
and confidence in it. As a Westerner I sometimes find
examples from my own culture are more useful because they
are easier to relate to. I read St Teresa of Avila and find in
her the epitome of what I would call perfect Buddhist
humility. I have come across a Christian monk who told me
that at his monastery in France everyone sits 6 feet down in
their own grave to meditate, every day—that's exactly the
kind of emphasis traditional Buddhist practitioners have. Page
after page of St Ignatius of Loyola is almost identical to what

Tibetan sages and saints have written. In 1994 I was doing a retreat in India trying to learn about healing myself and others. I found it extremely difficult to generate a lot of compassion using the techniques given. After some months, when I still was not getting anywhere and my frustration levels were rising, I suddenly remembered my first guru's advice, 'Touch Earth!' Pondering on what he had meant, I deduced he meant, 'Touch or feel the pain in people who are suffering'. To my mind, part of being a monk meant taking care of those in need, but in my life I hadn't had to take care of anyone. I recalled Mother Teresa and her mission. During an interview with the Dalai Lama I asked if I could go and work with her and he gave his permission and suggested I went in lay clothes. On the train to Calcutta I sat next to a Dutchman named Harry and told him what I was planning; he offered me his clothes from his suitcase on condition I donate them to the poor when I had finished with them.

During the next month my heart opened a little. I learnt how to get over my own revulsion and wash the crippled, the wounded, the mentally retarded, those with open sores and the old who were covered with excrement. The horror of finding piles of shit on the floor and in the beds dissipated when I realized I was not made of rainbows but full of shit myself. And the cheerfulness with which Mother Teresa's nuns picked up a shovel and dealt with it was such an example. One day I was shaving a man who had been blinded at birth so he could be a more effective beggar, and I discovered a feeling of wanting very much to please him and make him smile, and this feeling spread to many. After a while you feel completely at home with the destitute and just want to hug them. Your days turn into days of just wanting them to be happy. Later I learnt to sit with the dying, holding their hand. Ironically, I was helped in this by a rather devout Catholic, John, who had a marvelous way of relating to all the beggars and was loved by them in return. He handed me a book written by the well-known Tibetan teacher, Sogyal Rinpoche *The Tibetan Book of Living and Dying*. It gives the most heartfelt practical and spiritual advice. I discovered holding someone's hand as they die is one of the most marvelous things you can do—helping them through the most critical time of this life. No words are spoken but there is communication and you can feel how much they appreciate just your being there for them in their last hours. By the end of my stay I'd walk out of Mother Teresa's homes, look at all the people in the bazaar and on the streets and want to protect and care for every one of them. The things I'd learnt about compassion in Buddhism were just beginning to become part of my experience. I try to go back to Calcutta every year now.

I've also started to go to Burma to learn their Buddhist methods of concentration because this was my big difficulty. Again my teachers recommended it. The Burmese have a marvelous system, completely set up for meditators, where everything is provided, including a master who interviews you daily to assess your progress and give you personal guidance and support. It's incredibly strict. There's no talking, no reading, no writing and you have to practice awareness in everything you do—eating, lifting the spoon to your mouth, closing your teeth, every muscle used in swallowing. It's the same going to the toilet, going to bed, even blinking. You have to be mindful of every detail. That is one way to develop powerful concentration. The day is divided into one hour of sitting meditation and one hour of walking meditation—for fourteen hours a day! However, your concentration becomes very strong and you begin to get results so quickly that instead of it being a chore you long to be doing it. We found ourselves wanting to get up at 3 a.m. instead of 4 a.m. to get at it! One begins to get one's first glimpse of the nature of the mind, of what impermanence really means, of what the Buddha meant by suffering—the thing we need to leave behind forever.

In Buddhism there is a cornucopia of methods, so that each spiritual seeker can find the most appropriate method for his or her own personality and circumstances. There are literally thousands of methods presented in over 100 volumes of the Buddha's direct teachings. King Indrabhut, with the thought of responsibility for his many wives and offspring, and the welfare of his kingdom, said to the Buddha, 'How can I, who am in no position to become a wandering mendicant, become enlightened too?' The Buddha, aware of the King's sincerity, taught him a method whereby he attained enlightenment in that very life. Everything in the Buddha's teaching to the King related to this transient world. Impermanence doesn't ever mean annihilation. It's just the end of our seeing things as concrete and graspable, as we wrongly thought they were.

Of course at times I encounter problems within Buddhism. One is that there is this encrustation of Tibetan culture. When you live in the milieu, as I do, it's easy to take on the customs and the way of thinking until you find you've absorbed it without it necessarily contributing to your development as the Buddha had intended. My own kind teachers have predicted that there would be American, Australian, French, etc. Buddhism, all a little different according to people's characters. At the same time it seems to me an enormous problem that we Westerners want to change things according to our liking rather than making the effort to understand the psychological significance in the Omniscient One's purpose and to practice it. If we don't follow the methods, how will we get the results? I feel that if changes are to be made, an all-Buddhist council should be convened as has been done from time to time over the centuries, so that the changes can be properly ratified and incorporated in the Buddhist canon for the benefit of all. Otherwise the lineage of transmissions from the Buddha to his disciples and from teacher to disciple, which has remained marvelously intact for 2500 years until now, becomes irrelevant; and what develops can no longer be called Buddhism.

As for the future, my wish is that day by day everyone everywhere, including myself, should grow more in step with spiritual guides whose undiscriminating love enfolds every single being everywhere and that we should all develop energy and wisdom to transform the world into paradise. This will only happen if we as individuals root out from our minds all afflictive emotions—hatred, greed, intolerance, impatience and the rest—that torment us and those around us. A place does not become a paradise according to the amount of gold and diamonds in it, but because of the mind streams of the people in it. How to transform our everyday mundane minds into a paradise mind, a source of continuous enjoyment, is clearly set out in many step-by-step methods. All we have to do is practice them. In my case that means an awful lot more retreat. What I have been saying here is just words. I need to bring them into reality. **99**

The cultivation
of mindfulness

SHARON SALZBERG
Teacher of a way of seeing

I was looking forward to meeting Sharon Salzberg, one of the best-known teachers of Vipassana or Insight Meditation in the USA, because she sounded as friendly and warm in her emails as she did in her popular book *Loving-Kindness*. Also, this was going to be my first encounter with Theravadan Buddhism, the 'Southern School' of Buddhism which is practiced in Sri Lanka, Burma, Thailand, Laos and Cambodia. I was curious to see how it differed from Tibetan or Mahayana Buddhism that I was used to.

Sharon was to be found at the Insight Meditation Society (IMS) in Barre (pronounced Barry), Massachusetts, about a two-hour drive inland from Boston. The journey took us into the heart of the New England countryside, in March crisp with ground frost. We passed white wooden houses, white churches, and village greens cordoned off by white picket fences. Paul, my driver, told me that the area had once been filled with farmers and millers but that now only elderly retired folk lived there. Still, he added, there were plenty of moose, deer and bear in the forests nearby. He was also a long-term participator at IMS. 'It helps me keep relaxed with the stress of driving. I've learnt to live more in the now,' he said.

There is only one word to describe IMS itself: impressive. As the car turned up the driveway, a vast, red brick mansion with tall, elegant chimney stacks and imposing white-pillared entrance came into view, looking for all the world like a smart country club. It stood in 300 acres of its own land and the buildings included a small but equally beautiful study center complete with shrine room, living accommodation and a library which contained contemporary works plus the entire Buddhist canon in Pali and English. There are plans afoot to build a permanent retreat center there too.

Walking through the doors which had inscribed above them *metta* [loving-kindness], I was met by an eerie sight. Scores of people were moving along the corridors and up and down the staircase, heads bowed, in ultra-slow motion. No word was spoken, no eye lifted, no smile flickered across a mouth. I thought I had walked into a sci-fi film about the living dead. Later I found out that this was just one of several 'walking meditations' that are done throughout the day, interspersed with 'sitting meditations'. In fact, the timetable at IMS is daunting: 5.30 a.m. wake up, 6.00 sit, 6.45 breakfast, 7.30 work or do walking meditation, 8.30 sit, 9.30 walk, 10.30 sit, 11.15 walk, 12.00 lunch (early line), 12.30 p.m. lunch (later line), 1.45 walk for those in early lunch line, 2.15 sit, 3.00 walk, 3.45 sit, 4.30 walk, 5.15 tea, 6.15 sit, 7.00 listen to Dharma talk, 8.30 walk, 9.15 sit and do *metta* chant, 9.45 take late tea, rest or do additional practice. In spite of this gruelling schedule, over 2000 people a year come to IMS to take Vipassana courses with Sharon and her equally renowned colleague Joseph Goldstein. Indeed, the courses are so popular that lotteries are often held to select those who will get in.

The meditation hall revealed a very different scene from the Tibetan temples that I was familiar with. Here were 'no bells and smells', no walls festooned with richly colored cloth paintings of Buddhas, no row upon row of burning candles or water bowl offerings, no incense-laden air. Instead there was just one beautiful Buddha in the front with a few discreet potplants at its base. This was clearly the plain-song of Buddhism, at least externally.

In contrast to the sombre silence in the corridors, the staffroom was filled with much laughter and friendliness. I met Joseph Goldstein and asked why so many people these days came to learn Vipassana. 'It's stopped being freaky. Meditation has become so mainstream that doctors are recommending it for anti-stress. It's happening all over the USA, even in places like South Dakota. People come looking for answers to the big questions in their lives and we deliver them in a straightforward, commonsense way. Buddhism is deep and so it hooks them in,' he said.

Sharon herself was a short, round woman with tousled hair, a warm, smiling face and a look of extreme exhaustion. Her workload is colossal. Apart from teaching, writing books, running the organization, embarking on teaching tours and sitting in on many of the sessions, she also sees all 100 retreatants at least once for private interviews, and answers notes passed to her. Sharon Salzberg had an easy way with words. She was also honest, self-deprecating and funny. As the interview progressed it emerged that she was an integral part of a small and inspired group who were instrumental in bringing Vipassana meditation from East to West. I was grateful that she took time out to talk to me.

❋

66 *I* was eighteen, confused and unhappy and struggling to understand my life. I don't know why or how (if I did I would bottle and patent it), but I had an instinct that if I could learn to meditate I would find some relief from my pain and get some peace of mind. My university at Buffalo, where I was studying, had a program where you could spend a year in another culture and so I proposed to go to India to study Buddhism, which had intrigued me when I'd come across it in a course of Asian philosophy.

My first stop was Dharamsala, home of the Dalai Lama

and a thriving Tibetan community. I studied with an eminent Tibetan lama there, and then went to New Delhi where I heard about an intensive ten-day meditation retreat being held in Bodhgaya, the place where the Buddha attained Enlightenment. It was being run by a man called Goenka, an Indian national and businessman who had lived and practiced Buddhism in Burma. What he was offering was exactly what I was looking for, a practical application of meditation. What particularly appealed was his emphasis that it was a mind training and an art of living rather than a question of becoming a Buddhist. That was helpful because I was looking for tools, not a set of beliefs.

That first course was excruciating. Physically it was agony. This was India in 1971 and there was absolutely no comfort anywhere. In the meditation room there were no cushions so we rolled up our sleeping bags or our clothes and sat on them. And with Goenka you sit a lot! You start at 5 a.m. and go on from there. For three days we watched the breath, after that we moved on to being aware of the sensations in the body. This was interspersed with days of silence. It was very intense. I wasn't used to sitting cross-legged on the floor. Just on that level it was a strain. Sitting still for so long without my normal distractions, I began to notice the more deeply hidden tensions of the body—the aching shoulders, the stiff neck, the tense jaw. Buddhists say that on a purely philosophical level there is the pain of just existing in the body. I certainly realized that!

Mentally and emotionally it was horrible too. I was eighteen, and didn't have much psychological sophistication at all. As much as I wanted to learn how to meditate, I wasn't familiar with the contents of my own mind, so everything I found there was shocking. I sat down with the goal of being with my breath and found my mind was wandering all over the place. That was distressing because I was extremely self-judgemental. I didn't have the patience to say, 'OK, my attention just wandered—let me bring it back'. I'd get into a frenzy and think I was doing it all wrong. The content of my mind was also a big surprise to me. 'Wow—that much anger! That much fear!' In Buddhist psychology, anger and fear are the same mind state. At one point I said to Goenka, 'I never used to be angry before I did this meditation', which of course was not true: I had plenty of anger but I was simply not aware of it. Along with the anger and fear I found a lot of sleepiness and restlessness.

Goenka himself was a powerful, loving teacher; very strong. Even though it was so hard, from the very first moment I sat down and Goenka started talking, it felt right. This was what I had been looking for. There were no doubts.

What resonated about his message was the same now as then. When I left Buffalo for India I had had images of the magical, esoteric, supernatural, fantastic technique I would be given. I walked in the door and Goenka said, 'Feel your breath'. I thought, 'I could have stayed in Buffalo to do that. Where's the real thing?' Then I thought, 'Maybe this is the stuff they give to real beginners and when I get really good at this he'll take me into another room and give me the next step and the magical transmission'. It's been almost 30 years and it's still the same instruction. My whole experience of myself and my life has changed, but the instruction hasn't changed at all.

Being in Bodhgaya was very special. I loved it. As Joseph [Goldstein] so poetically put it, the temple is so beautiful it's commensurate with what happened there. In those days you could just sit under the tree where the Buddha attained Enlightenment. Nowadays it is much more difficult and touristy. Sometimes we would be there all night meditating. Because it was Bodhgaya and because of the way I was taught I have always felt the human-ness of the Buddha. To me he has always been a person rather than a superhuman, symbolic figure, and that springs from spending time where he sat in meditation and where he taught.

There was also a great circle of people there—Joseph, Ram Das and many people I am still close to were at my first retreat. We formed a community which has lasted for 30 years. How I met Joseph is a nice story. I was a couple of days into the retreat and I was so frustrated at not being able to keep my attention on the breath that I said to myself, 'The next time my attention wanders I am going to bang my head against the wall'—and I meant it. Very fortunately for me the lunch bell rang at that moment. I was standing in the line for lunch when I heard two people having a conversation behind me. One said, 'How was your morning?' and the other replied with apparent great lightness of spirit, 'I had terrible concentration, couldn't keep my mind on the breath at all but this afternoon it will probably be better'. I was really shocked. I thought, 'He doesn't understand how important this is and how hard you have to work'. I turned around and it was Joseph. The difference of course was that he had been there for four years and I had been there four days. He knew that practice has its ups and downs, ebbs and flows, that it is not always going to feel great and that it is really all right.

Goenka stayed on in Bodhgaya to conduct a series of ten-day retreats and I stayed as well, to keep practicing. During this time I met Munindra, who became another one of my early teachers. Munindra was also an Indian national who had trained in Burma in the Theravada tradition. He made one comment that affected me profoundly: 'The Buddha's Enlightenment solved the Buddha's problems, now you solve yours'. What he was drumming home was that Buddhism wasn't about admiring the Buddha for what had happened in that very same place from a perspective of 2500 years away but about one's own capacity to learn, grow and change. I needed that message from Munindra, that I could do it, that I could come to awareness. One's own effort was the whole point. Goenka gave me the technique and Munindra provided the context. It was an important combination. After that I spent six months with the Tibetan master Kalu Rinpoche, who opened up the whole world of Buddhism by introducing me to the vast expanse of the philosophy and how to apply it to daily life, which was very enriching.

In 1972 I went back to Buffalo and then quickly returned to India and Bodhgaya. Munindra had a woman student called Dipa Ma who had an enormous impact on me. She was an extraordinary person. Dipa Ma was barely 4 feet tall and always in frail health. She had gone through tremendous suffering in her life. She had lost two children shortly after birth which had caused her health to deteriorate rapidly. At the point when she was just beginning to make some peace with her loss, it was discovered that she had a serious heart condition which her doctors thought could threaten her life. As she faced the possibility of her own imminent death, her husband came home one day with a fever and much to her shock died later that day. She was living in Burma at the time and was told by her doctor that she would die of a broken heart unless she did something about her mind—that is, unless she learnt how to meditate. When she arrived at the monastery she was so weak she had to crawl up the temple stairs in order to get to the meditation room. She became an extremely accomplished teacher. Dipa Ma was a role model for me. She was a woman, a householder, mother, grand-mother and very, very loving because she had come through so much suffering. Like so many of the great ones, she was inclusively loving. You would look at her and think,

'That one too!' If you've had a comfortable life and you're nice to everybody, how deep does that go? But when someone has been through tremendous suffering and is kind to everyone, it's a much stronger role model. I cried when she died, thinking no one would love me like that again.

It was Dipa Ma who told me to teach. In 1974 Joseph had already returned to America and I was going back too for what I thought would be a brief visit to get money and sort out visas. I went to say goodbye to her in the little tenement where she was living with her daughter, Dipa, her only surviving child. The external atmosphere was quite sleazy—I walked up dank stairs with rats running around— but inside her room there was just a beautiful light. I explained I was going for a short, recuperative visit to the States. She said, 'You will start teaching with Joseph'. I said, 'No I won't'. She said, 'Yes, you will'. This went on for some time. I didn't think I was capable of anything like that. I had had extremely accomplished, wonderful teachers but never imagined I could talk as they did. I was thinking this, but not saying it out loud, when she looked at me and said, 'You can do anything you want to. It's only your belief that you can't that is going to stop you'. And then she added, 'You really understand suffering, which is why you should teach'. Her words were redemptive because they gave my own experience of suffering meaning. I realized that because I really did understand suffering I had something to give. She sent me off and of course she was right.

Actually it was a lot easier coming to terms with one's own suffering in India. The cultural norm in America is to hide one's pain and to consider it somewhat shameful because there's such a picture-perfect image that we are supposed to conform to. Our consumer society promotes the idea that supreme perfection is right around the corner if you'd only buy this or that. Living in such a climate it's not easy to admit to one's feelings of inadequacy, to being different, unhappy, sick or old. But in India nothing is hidden, the suffering is everywhere. And when I first heard the Buddha's words, 'I teach one thing and one thing only—suffering and the end of suffering', I thought, 'Isn't that great, finally admitting it. It's right out there, straightforward, truthful, real'. My mind was chaotic and my body hurt, but I was not spurned because of it. Instead it was considered workable. I was tremendously grateful for that.

Through meditation you learn to look suffering in the face and work with it. When I first started sitting I was in a lot of physical pain. In retrospect I saw two tremendous tendencies of my mind—one was to take the present moment of discomfort (even when it was very mild) and project it into the future. 'What's it going to feel like in half an hour? In 40 minutes?' I'd be sitting there stunned. I'd anticipate it in 40 minutes time and then try and bear it all at once. As a result I'd feel helpless and overcome. I saw this was a strong tendency in my mind whether it was physical, emotional or any kind of pain I was dealing with.

The other main tendency was to judge myself for it. 'I only have pain because I don't have a free flow of energy in my body.' 'If I were a really clear person, I'd have a free flow of energy.' So not only did I have to bear the physical pain, I had to bear the mental anguish of all the self-judgement. Learning to disentangle those two, seeing that they were different, was very important. The question 'Where is the suffering?' is a very good investigative tool for anyone to use. 'Is it in my knee, actually?' or 'Is it in my *relationship* to that?' I'm not saying there is no suffering in the knee, it would be pretentious to say that, but where is the deepest suffering in this experience?

Although this type of investigation may not actually stop the suffering, it certainly alleviates the add-ons—the shame, the judgement, the anger, the fear, the projection to the future, the comparing. This in turn can help the suffering because then it's held in a different context.

For example, say someone has died and you feel a tremendous sense of grief and loss. One might start with an understanding based on an awareness of how you feel about the grief and the fact you think it will never end. From that you might surmise, 'I am a person who has been abandoned and who has had to suffer this loss'. If that becomes our entire image of ourselves, then we become crushed by the grief; because it's not just the pain of the loss we're bearing but the added pain of the future. When you start to sit in meditation it's not that your emotions flatten out and you won't feel grief or sadness perhaps, but you watch for the add-ons.

By 1974 when Dipa Ma sent me off to teach, my meditation was a lot better. The physical pain was not so bad, the mind wandering sometimes not so bad (sometimes bad) but I had matured to where I had Joseph's understanding. I knew it changes and you just have to keep going, when your attention wanders you have to begin again and not make a drama out of it. Because my understanding had grown, my practice changed; because I'd learnt not to be so self-judgemental, I was gentler, I could begin again more easily. Also I had more experience with the stuff of my mind. I had more compassion with myself. I had some of the same experiences content-wise but I was relating to them very differently—which was the development of the meditation. That's where people get so confused. They think you shouldn't have the same experiences any more, but the transformation is in how you are relating to them. That's what I saw, though not every day.

I returned to America and Joseph, Ram Das and Jack Kornfield were all teaching at Naropa University. Naropa was the grand vision of Choygam Trungpa, one of the first Tibetan teachers to come to the West. In that summer of 1974 it wasn't a campus. They'd rented a warehouse and various apartments. It was an extraordinary summer. Ram Das was teaching a giant course of 1000 people, and had sub-sections in his course for chanting and meditation which Joseph led.

Joseph was so popular he was asked to stay on for the second session and I became Joseph's assistant. That's when I began teaching.

After that people started asking us to lead a retreat, so we did; and then we did another one, and another one. Jack Kornfield came and we taught together. That's where the teaching partnership with both of them started which has continued to this day.

We were teaching in a very grass-roots way. Someone would write, 'I can get a cook and fifteen people, will you come and teach a course?' and we'd go. At the end of the course we'd never know if there was going to be another one. We'd crash in people's houses and then we'd get another letter. And we'd go and teach another course. Then the letters started coming more frequently. One of our friends suggested we start our own center because it would be like a sacred site, an energetic gathering point. We said, 'Sure'. We were very young! (I was 23.) The people who were most interested in helping us were on the east coast, which I'd never been to. They formed a non-profit organization and we all looked at properties; some we came close to buying. Then while we were teaching our first three-month retreat in a Catholic seminary in Maine, some nuns who were visiting suggested we call the Catholic archdiocese because the Church was selling off a lot of property. We did and they told us they had this place in Barre, Massachusetts for sale.

We saw it in December 1975 and it was perfect. There

were just twelve monks and a few nuns living here. It was so quiet and peaceful, nothing was happening. On the other hand it was so huge and we had only been teaching a few people here and there. We went down to Barre for lunch. It was a typical New England town and there in the middle of the green was a monument with the town motto inscribed on it: 'Tranquil and Alert'. We looked at each other and said, 'It's an omen. Any town which has a motto like that has got to have a meditation center'.

The whole place cost $150,000, which of course we didn't have. It was unthinkable but we got some very generous contributions from people for down payments and a bank gave us a mortgage, thinking we were the Transcendental Meditation organization, which was wealthy and well-known and has initials similar to ours! And the Fathers of the Blessed Sacrament, who owned the building, gave us another mortgage.

Joseph and I were very inexperienced. We wanted to keep to the Indian model whereby we would not take any money for teachings (which we've kept to). The daily rate that people are charged here goes towards the facility and the staff. They don't get a lot of money but it pays for their health insurance. Joseph and I live on donations. At the end of a course there's an opportunity for people to give. At the beginning we charged $6.50 a day, now it's $30. When we opened, it was all confusing. There was a big discussion on whether we should have Buddhas in public places, because the whole tenor of the transmission was that you did not have to become a Buddhist to get benefit from the practice. You could do the practice and stay faithful to Christianity, Judaism or whatever. That was how we had been taught. In the end we said, 'Yes'. We debated over whether we should have the word *metta* inscribed over the doorway. That was yes. There were money problems, days when the staff could hardly eat. We have had a lot of rocky periods. People have commended us for our vision and courage but it wasn't that way—we just did it, making decisions based on what was in front of us, and worked.

Our first course had about 30 people. Now 100 come regularly throughout the year.

They come for what we have to offer—Vipassana, which translated is Insight Meditation. Fundamentally what it means is the cultivation of mindfulness. It's a quality of awareness that allows us to see clearly what our experience is and not be so confused by bias, judgement, or projection into the future. To see clearly is to really understand. When that happens we come into harmony. Based on mindfulness there is wisdom, based on wisdom there is compassion. We use the breath as the first object of meditation in order to learn how to concentrate the mind and collect our energy in the present moment. Then we practice mindfulness of the body and the mind.

Vipassana makes you more sensitive. I said to Goenka that before I began to meditate I was never angry, which was definitely untrue. I had a lot of angry thoughts and feelings. I wasn't aware of them but that doesn't mean that they were not affecting me nor that they weren't bearing fruit in action. They had become motivators. Through becoming more mindful, I became more aware. That was definitely a disagreeable phase! There are still often times when anger or fear arises and I act. I say or do something to someone that is hurtful or which diminishes me. Becoming aware in the moment, not three weeks later, is the first step. And part of wisdom, or insight, is seeing that everything changes. That anger has the nature to arise and pass away. That I don't have to fall into it, get carried away by it. Nor did I have to suppress it or hate it. What I have to do is develop a different relationship to it.

The same applies for all the negative emotions and feelings. The list is long. Take craving. I saw in my first meditation retreat I had a very hard time just being with one breath, because as soon as I was with that one breath I'd anticipate the next. I'd wait to be ready for it. I was sort of leaning forward into the next breath even as this breath was still happening. That is a craving, a wanting. In Buddhist terms it is what constitutes 'becoming', the very building block of Samsara, the endless round of birth, death and rebirth which is the foundation of all our suffering. It's very subtle. At the time I didn't realize it in those terms, I just recognized it was hard to be with one breath. That's how we live, always leaning forward rather than settling back. Learning how to do that is a big part of practice. In this light the Buddhist principle of Right Effort is a little confusing sometimes because it also involves settling back.

Like all forms of Buddhism, Vipassana has Enlightenment as its ultimate goal. It works because mindfulness leads to wisdom. In the classical sense, when wisdom is developed our energetic relationship to our experience comes into balance so we're not acting out of greed, hatred and delusion. In any moment, if something arises and we respond with grasping, we're leaning into it, we're trying to hold it, preserve it and keep it from ever changing. If we're responding with anger, aversion or fear, we're striking out against it. And if we're responding with delusion, we're either out of touch or consolidating a sense of self in that moment. By cultivating mindfulness, seeing clearly rather than acting in these ways, we are balanced. And from that place of balance Enlightenment can happen. There's a piercing through of a veil, an experience of Nirvana.

Our tradition talks about four 'turning points' in this journey. One would be that first glimpse, then there are three more after that. In the Buddha's time people would just sort of 'pop', they'd be fully enlightened just listening to him. They say the reason why these days we don't generally do it (though it is not impossible) is because we can't open to the nature of suffering so fully right away. If we go back to what the Buddha was saying, 'I teach one thing and one thing only, suffering and the end of suffering', there has to be a deep awakening to the general unsatisfactoriness of life in order to come through the other side. My Burmese teacher would say nowadays people can't do that all at once, they have to do it gradually.

Another vital step in my own spiritual development was in 1984 when Joseph and I brought over Sayadaw U Pandita, another Burmese meditation master. We entered a three-month retreat with this teacher, whom we had never met. He was very strict and demanding, so he brought forth a new level of effort from me. His message was particularly continuity of awareness. We saw him six days a week for interviews. You're supposed to describe one sitting and one walking period from the previous 24 hours, and I had this little bit of paper on which I'd written some comments, but he wouldn't let me read them. He would say, 'Tell me everything you noticed when you washed your face', which I hadn't paid the least bit of attention to. So I had nothing to say and that would be my interview. I'd leave and do my sitting and walking meditations very mindfully and I'd wash my face really mindfully. I'd feel my hands in the water, the water on my face, be with the moment and the next day he'd say, 'Tell me everything you noticed when you took off your shoes', which I hadn't paid the least bit of attention to. I could see where things were going. Everything is an act of meditation—sitting, walking, eating, taking a shower.

The next year in Burma he taught me loving-kindness meditation, in a structured way. It was always part of

Goenka's teaching, but I'd never done the formal, structured, classical progression. That became hugely important. Although the word *metta* is usually translated as loving-kindness, actually a more accurate translation is 'friendship'. It's developing an art of friendship first towards oneself and then to all of life. I think it has a very important role in the teachings of the Buddha and in the transmission of the teachings to the West. Certainly insight brings love, because when we see clearly, we notice that we are connected. Spontaneously there is a shift, we're automatically kinder, more inclusive. The Buddha also specifically taught loving-kindness practices which open the heart and facilitate the sense of belonging to ourselves and to life.

When I teach I often emphasize that loving-kindness is not a feeling, a sentiment, or an emotion, it's a way of seeing. If you think of it as a feeling, it's kind of disgusting. One person said to me, 'I hate that practice, it's like a continually enforced Valentine's Day'. If you think you have to go round smiling, it does seem pretentious and phony. But it's not that. We see that we're all connected and we respond to that.

There were two very important junctures in that practice for me. One was the fact that you start with yourself, which to my mind was an unusual spiritual perspective. I would have expected more self-denigration in honor of other beings. The Buddha in the Theravada tradition is quoted as saying, 'You can search the entire universe for someone more deserving of your love and affection than you are yourself and you won't find that person anywhere'. That's extraordinary. To think that that is the foundation!

The second was when I started to open up to loving-kindness towards what is known as a 'neutral person', someone you don't strongly like or dislike, a person who hasn't been either kind or unkind. Just because they exist we pay attention to them rather than ignore them. What I found was the most amazing thing. You never learn this person's story, you may not even learn their name, but there is definitely a bond created simply by paying attention. I once led a loving-kindness retreat here and months later this woman came up to me and said, 'I've fallen in love with my dry cleaner. Not romantically, but he was my neutral person on the retreat'. She'd been holding him in her heart, wishing him well, and because of that she really learnt to care for him. I don't know if she ever learnt his name. She said, 'I go into the store and I'm so happy to see him. I really wish him well'. That's the change. It's not having to manufacture feeling, or trying to convince ourselves, the bond emerges.

It's particularly appropriate in the West where most of us do not think very highly of ourselves. Easterners do not have this trouble, generally speaking.

I will always remember a conversation I had with the Dalai Lama in Dharamsala in 1991, at a conference about emotions. At one point I asked His Holiness, 'What do you think about self-hatred?' He replied, 'What's that? Is it some kind of nervous disorder?' The room was full of psychotherapists who began to describe the condition to him in great detail. He kept asking questions because it was a new concept to him. Finally, he said, 'How can you think that? You have Buddha nature, you have mind, you have cognisance, you have the ability to comprehend. That means you have the ability to be liberated, to be free. How can you think that!'

I don't know why we Westerners are like this—whether it is the Judaeo-Christian ethos, the culture or the nature of our family—but it is a problem. It is a hindrance because it does affect the way we hear the teachings and therefore the way we practice. We explained to the Dalai Lama that when the texts say, 'Cut all self-cherishing', 'Give up everything for others', it plugs right into our self-denigration. He got it. He now talks about self-esteem regularly in his teachings.

Similarly when we hear about the fundamental Buddhist principle of Right Effort, we think 'I can't'. Then we try too hard, struggle and hate it.

Buddhism has been my whole adult life. I've never married nor ever thought of having children, although I have had relationships. I've never wanted to do anything else but practice and teach. I've never thought of joining 'the real world' but then 'the real world' is coming here now. Actually it's not a cloistered existence. I teach all over the world and teaching is a very engaged activity. I've lived here half my life and learnt things I never thought possible, such as finances and septic systems. We had a nine-year struggle to fix our septic system in a way the town would approve of!

I started on this path aged eighteen, confused and suffering, and 28 years later I can say I'm pretty happy. Of course I have bad days but they are not on the same level. When I wrote *Loving-Kindness*, people would sometimes come to me and say, 'It must be so wonderful never to have any anger or fear—just to be totally loving all the time'. I'd reply, 'No, it's not like that. But what I do have and what I try to convey in my work, is a complete and utter faith that we can do it'. That's a great thing. My next book is on faith. The word for faith in Pali is *saddha*, 'to place the heart upon'. It's one of the five spiritual faculties, and in my view is more important than is usually thought. Traditionally we're told to have faith in the Buddha, Dharma and Sangha, but ultimately the faith is in ourselves—in our capacity to have awareness and compassion and to be free. ”

Something spoke
to my heart

BOB SHARPLES
Counsellor and psychologist

I met Bob Sharples in 1995 at
a dinner party in Melbourne and was drawn to sit by his
side by the sheer warmth and friendliness emanating from
him. At the time I was mourning my father's recent death
and was badly in need of comfort. I sensed that this man
with the round smiling face could give it. I was not alone.
Hundreds of others have felt the same way. For years Bob
Sharples has been dispensing a very special brand of wisdom
and reassurance to streams of cancer patients who flock
to the Gawler Foundation in Yarra Junction, about 80 kilometres outside Melbourne, a center famous for its alternative
approach to the disease. Apart from working as a psychologist, an integral part of Bob's job is to lead groups in
meditation, based on his 25 years' experience of Buddhism. It
is a measure of how much he has integrated Buddhism

into his life that he manages to do this without making any overt reference to Buddhism, instead weaving Buddhist ideas into his themes. He has gleaned the essence. This is the gift he brings.

I went to interview Bob at the Gawler Foundation, a beautiful building set among mysterious white gum trees, with delicate-faced wallabies and the evocative call of the bellbirds in the bush. It was a serene, idyllic setting. Bob walked through it with confidence and pleasure. He works incredibly long hours—running residential courses and weekly support groups, talking to medical students at universities on death and dying, leading a healing meditation program for those with life-threatening diseases at Tara Institute, a Melbourne Buddhist center, as well as working as a private psychologist at home. For years he has been regularly teaching meditation to groups of Vietnam War veterans. He is on call constantly from people in distress. He loves his work. It is the fruition of a long and often sad journey to find meaning—and then to live it.

I've always had a religious instinct. My parents were not church-going but I used to take myself to the local Baptist church in a Melbourne suburb. It was pretty fundamentalist. I think the fundamentalism gave me a method of dealing with the anxiety in my life. I had a difficult mom whom I loved extraordinarily. She was deeply troubled and would have these wild mood swings. These days we would call it manic depression or bipolar disorder. When I was eight she tried to kill herself by throwing herself off a train. She spent eight months in hospital and we were never allowed to visit her, so we never understood where she had gone or what was happening. She was patched together and came back to live with us. My mother's disappearance from my life at that age and the wild energy that was driving her produced a lot of fear.

I was a twin and knew the extraordinary intimacy of living *in utero* with another human being and pushing down the birth canal together. We were very premature. I was the second and no one was expecting me—it was a complete surprise when I popped out. My brother and I shared the same room, and the maturation process from infancy to childhood to adolescence, and we dealt with the crises of our mother together.

By eighteen I had started to question evangelical Christianity and when I got to university I decided I didn't believe in a god who designed a universe where you could go to hell for ever and ever. Instead I joined the Student Christian Movement, which was more progressive and liberal.

I came from a poor, working-class background but did well at school and won a scholarship to Melbourne University. I really wanted to study history but didn't qualify for Arts as I didn't have a second language. Instead I did Law.

It was a silly choice but seemed like an easy option at the time. I graduated, got a job and practiced for three years—hating every minute of it. At 26, on the evening when I had thrown in my law job, I had a heart attack. It wasn't surprising. I was eating badly, smoking and was still terribly anxious and confused. I was also socially inept, especially where relationships were concerned. I'd had a number of distressing break-ups. So there I was, lonely, upset, and having a heart attack in the middle of the country, on a camping trip in the Flinders Ranges. I was lying in my sleeping bag on the ground with radiating pain shooting down my left arm and incredible pain in my chest. I knew exactly what it was. I spent a week in intensive care, and two weeks in hospital in a small country town called Whyalla, 1200 kilometres from Melbourne. No one was able to visit me. That was a blessing. It gave me time to think. The universe had picked me up and shaken me by the scruff of the neck, but I still didn't get the message. I decided to do a Masters in Politics, which involved going to Indonesia to do field work with trade union leaders. I got so caught up with that I buried what had happened in Whyalla.

The following year a much bigger tragedy struck. My twin brother committed suicide in Nigeria. That was so overwhelming psychically that it put me in a state of shock for some years. I was always the robust one, he the very sensitive and vulnerable one. He'd had a breakdown previously and I had helped him come through that. My feeling is that the chaos of Nigeria pushed him over the edge. The tragedy was compounded by the fact that his wife was pregnant with their first child. I also felt I had to carry the burden of getting my parents through it. At the time I buried my anguish under a competent management style which was warm and helpful to clients. A few years ago I began to feel the deep distress I'd not felt then. The Universe was saying, 'You'd better get the message this time'. And the message was, 'You are a bloody slow learner—get a hold on your life'.

I got married on my 29th birthday—I talked Jenny into it. I wasn't a good bet. Apart from my medical record, I brought to the marriage a life that had been shaped by fear and tragedy. Of course there was a lot of joy too, especially being present at the birth of our children. These are among the most amazingly uplifting experiences of my life. Still, there was constant lingering confusion. I was also carrying certain hangovers of Calvinism—fear of sex and intimacy— together with a general existential anxiety about being a father, husband, lover. Basically, I felt I was failing in every part of my life.

I gave up my academic life, moved to the country, became a teacher and started to lead 'a wholesome life'. I also began searching. I started reading spiritual books and went to hear visiting Indian gurus like Muktananda when he came to Melbourne, but I was really put off by the exotic Hindu-ness of it. Then in 1976 a friend turned up. She had just returned from India, where she had met some Tibetan lamas. She raved to me about them. 'They're extraordinary beings—you've got to check them out,' she said. And something clicked in my head. I discovered I didn't have to go to India as there was a Tibetan Buddhist center in Melbourne, so I went along. I did a weekend course with a Tibetan lama, a Geshe [a title equivalent to Doctor of Divinity]. I didn't understand much but I detected a seamless wisdom there that I wanted to be part of. The Buddhist philosophy was clear, logical, straightforward and seemed relatively mumbo-jumbo-free. What really appealed, however, was the quality of this man who was teaching. He exuded a very masculine, upright spirituality that I was drawn to. There was no artifice about him. And he had a strength that was awesome. This feeling was borne out when I met other lamas. It was the model of these men that initially drew me. I felt really good being in their presence. Now I know that the finger that points to the moon is not the moon itself, but back then I was lost, with no sense of my personhood and no vision for my life. The lamas gave me back a sense of meaning.

I liked the people at the Buddhist center too. I liked the lack of dogma. Something spoke to my heart very directly in ways which I could not ignore. The religious instinct, which had been in abeyance so long, had found somewhere where it could be expressed again. I am someone who has always needed a religious expression, a religious component in my life. Within a month I took Refuge [the ceremony whereby you declare your faith in the Buddhist path]. I was very thirsty and I just gobbled it up. My commitment was total. I drove two and a half hours every week to the Buddhist center, for fifteen years. That's a lot of driving. I listened to hours of teaching and took copious notes. I went on group retreats and solitary retreats. I took loads of courses. I set up an altar on the window ledge of the big upstairs family room and put on it a statue of the Buddha, photographs of various lamas, texts and water bowls. I also strung rows of Tibetan prayer flags across the garden.

After about two years I did a ten-day retreat with a lama called Lama Zopa Rinpoche at Noojee, in the mountains about 120 kilometres east of Melbourne. It was life-transforming. At the first talk I didn't understand a word he said. His English was poor and he mumbled. But I was incredibly drawn to him. He was interior, his head was down, he shuffled—but ten days with him and my whole world shifted. Hour after hour he went on and on and on about incredibly deep things—death, suffering and the preciousness of the tiniest living creature. And all the time he was urging us to change, searching his mind for the right words, the right expression to get his meaning across. Here was this small, bowed man doing his absolute best to convince 40 motley Westerners to change their lives. It was cold and uncomfortable; there was thunder and snow and I was living in a tent. But those ten days were like living in a pure realm. I think I fell in love with him. It sounds puerile but it was like being with a radiant being. He absolutely affected me in ways I still don't understand. Even now I find it hard to think about Lama Zopa without being emotional. It's the closest I've come to being in the presence of a fully awakened human being. I still do courses with this lama every time he comes to Australia.

Looking back I can see the key features of Buddhism which attracted me so strongly. I liked the overriding emphasis on altruism, Bodhicitta, that integral commitment to developing the good heart. Mahayana Buddhism [the form of Buddhism practiced in Tibet, China and Japan, for example] states that the only reason to be a spiritual person is to bring benefit to others. That resonated with my basic Christian leanings. When I was a church-goer I always believed more in original blessing than original sin and that people were intrinsically good and kind. I was always touched by the kindness of Christ. I liked the parables and the Sermon on the Mount—not the hell and damnation bit, but those parts of the Gospels that show a warm, loving, selfless person in Christ. So I connected with that in Tibetan Buddhism. At a personal level I was trying to be a good parent, a good husband, a good teacher, and Buddhism offered me a place where I could get another handle on those issues. Learning about Bodhicitta helped me to get in touch with a softer, more loving, giving part of myself. It made a big difference to my life.

I liked the teachings on the Precious Human Rebirth, the

absolute blessing of being alive. We were told that this life
is extremely valuable because of what we can achieve with
it in terms of personal development. The lamas said that
the levels of wisdom and compassion that can be attained
are limitless.

Then there were the Four Noble Truths, the Buddha's
core teachings in which he diagnosed the predicament of the
human condition and mapped out the cure. When I heard
the First Truth about universal suffering I believed it, because
that was how I had experienced it. My brother had leapt
out of a window. I knew life was suffering. My mother had
jumped from a train. She had disappeared from my life when
I was eight. The Four Noble Truths put that misery into
context. The Buddha said quite baldly, 'That's the way it is'.
Before then I thought I was different. Now I knew I was not.
The Buddha said that if you were prepared to see and
acknowledge this, then there is a way through it. This wasn't
spacing out on a bliss trip, but a deep understanding of the
human condition. And Buddhism gave me a method, which
was to sit on your bum and meditate.

There was an intellectual vigor to it all. The whole thing
was presented in such a logical way. It was so muscular. It
gave you something to chew on! We were all constantly
invited to check up, to see for ourselves if what was being
said tallied with our experience or our reasoning. If it didn't
we were at liberty to discard it.

I appreciated enormously the teachings on death and

impermanence. I have had so much death in my life—
Buddhism gave me a language and a technique to use to deal
with it. Buddhism says that death is a gateway to whatever
follows, and that in this light death is an awesome power
and a precious moment. To find teachers and a tradition
which talked about death and impermanence with such
regularity was an enormous relief. In one way, facing death
legitimised a deep part of me which was shaken by death.
I was frightened of facing death and thinking about it.
They said categorically, 'Death is a given, nothing lasts;
acknowledge it; live in the truth of this'. To me this was
deeply transforming.

The ethical tone of Buddhism was deeply influential. I
took on board the basic Buddhist precepts not to kill, lie,
steal or become intoxicated, and to be sexually faithful. (At
the start I think I was a little bit puffed up about all this,
proud of being a Buddhist—but that gave me something to
hold onto while the years of maturation took place.) After
three years I became a vegetarian. At university I'd been a
keen duck shooter and there was a lot of rejoicing in it.
According to Buddhism, killing is bad but rejoicing in the
killing is the worst karma of all. So I took a lifelong vow not
to eat meat. It was my way of saying sorry to the animals
I'd killed. A way of expiation if you like. We have no insect
sprays in the house—I even try to catch flies that come into
the house and release them. Thank goodness I've never had
a mouse plague to deal with!

The practice of meditation has been amazingly helpful. On that first retreat I found a deep state of stillness in myself. After that I did daily meditation practice—watching the breath, saying prayers and mantras and doing visualizations. At the beginning I meditated for an hour a day, in the morning and evening. It centered me and gave a structure, an anchor which helped me keep my life together in those tumultuous years of my early adult life. I set up an altar in my bedroom and would do prostrations in front of it.

There are certain aspects of Buddhism which I do not find easy. I struggle a lot with the ritual side of things—the pujas [prayer ceremonies] and all the spiritual paraphernalia. Even after twenty years it still feels alien to me in a way that going to a Christian service never will. In a puja I've never had that sense of sacred connection that I get in taking the sacrament. Recently I have started going back to church for the occasional service because the music and the ceremony speak to me in a way Tibetan services never do. The whole Buddhist idea of collecting merit from doing virtuous deeds and the notion that on specific 'auspicious days' your karma increases thousandfold are very difficult for me to accept.

I struggle with the ideas of reincarnation and karma. I used to accept them totally because they were presented in such a logical way. It was part of the seamless quality that I admired. Now I think that the way they are taught is simple and childlike and that these questions are far more complex. I believe there is some powerful experience of continuity after death and that there is a connection to people who are close to us, but it is not in our notion of linear time. Rebirth and karma may or may not be true. I hope they're true but I don't know if they are. Similarly I hope it's true we all have Buddha nature and will over time manifest it, as is stated. One of the hardest concepts in Buddhism is that of 'beginningless time'. I like it, but it's tremendously difficult to get your mind around it. Few people know what beginningless means. Within Buddhist circles these terms become clichés, people roll them off their tongues without rigorously thinking them through.

I struggle with the Tibetan emphasis on the suffering of the lower realms—the hell beings, hungry ghosts and so forth. I find that very difficult. It paints such a bleak picture and has terrible parallels with the fear-driven notion of original sin in Christianity which trapped me as a young boy. In my view it's more logical that human beings are more likely to go forward because of their level of development.

Buddhism has also caused huge problems between Jenny and myself and I'm still amazed the marriage has survived. Jenny, who does not share my 'religious instinct', was profoundly irritated by Buddhism. She viewed it basically as irrational and superstitious, and thought I was clutching at it as a way of avoiding married and family life. To some degree she was right. I think I was frightened of commitment and clung to Buddhism like a life-raft. I had to do it, I had no choice. I was out of the house so much at teachings and on retreat it caused enormous rows, and a lot of unhappiness in the family. It went on for a long time. It led to secretive withdrawal in me. Now it's pretty much resolved. Jenny still regrets those years but recognizes how important it is to me. I endeavor to negotiate time away. Our marriage has lasted so long, we both know each other very well and in that context we've become more forgiving and generous. And I think even Jenny would say that being a Buddhist has made me a better person.

For fifteen years I clutched at Buddhism. It was an 'ism' which made me feel OK. It took me ages to integrate it. Now I am less fundamentalist—not so much a Buddhist, more a simple practitioner. I no longer need that altar in the home and I don't want an altar to separate me from my friends and my family. I have some paintings of Buddhas in my house and two Buddha statues on top of my bookcase. In my office at work I have a little statue of the Medicine Buddha along with a picture of my guru. And above my desk I have a painting of the Madonna and Child. The people I teach meditation to often give me Buddhist things, but I give them away. I don't want the trappings any more. The inner state is what is important. I now have a strong sense of my lama in my heart.

One of the biggest problems is spiritual pride. I thought I had the perfect path and the perfect teacher and was therefore much better off than anyone else. In this vein I'd meet issues (especially difficult discussions) with Buddhist platitudes. There was a certain amount of spiritual snobbery involved! Of course that is an enormous impediment to the practice of compassion. Compassion means my similarity with others, not my separation from them.

Working at the Gawler Foundation I daily meet people who are living with death, and who are devout Christians, Jews or of other faiths, including wonderful nature-based beliefs. They have confronted me for ten years with what I truly believe. They eyeball me and ask, 'What do you think?' It's forced me to realize I have to work it out for myself and discard a lot of the dogma. I am left with a few things, particularly the preciousness of living daily life as well as you can. It's taken me years to be jargon-free, to let go of the Buddhist terminology and get down to the universal language. I strive to use the core of what the Buddha taught without belaboring the point. I try to bring in some practice of compassion. I tell my groups that if you live your life with loving-kindness to yourself and others, something extraordinary might happen. I try to set a big goal—as my lamas have shown me. Most people I work with see meditation as a tool for getting well. They limit it to the symptoms of their life. That is a narrow use of meditation. I say it can lead to a sense of universal connectedness. I bring in the mind transformation techniques of Buddhism, showing people how they can transform what is happening to them to deepen their connection with life, how paradoxically they can use their disease as an opportunity for growth. At the beginning and end of every meditation session I establish the motivation as Buddhism has taught me: 'May my efforts bring healing to myself and the world'. I say that the world is just waiting for us to do this work, and we don't want to let it down.

The great gift of my work is seeing huge inner trans-formations because the people I deal with are no longer living in the illusion that they have plenty of time left. For them every breath becomes important. I worked with a man who had three episodes of malignant mouth cancer. When the last one occurred he was written off by his doctor as a hopeless case. He was deeply depressed and despairing. During our work together I suggested he read *Start Where You Are* by American Buddhist nun Pema Chodron. It totally transformed his life. He found a doctor who would operate on him, then he decided he had to heal the deep, painful rift in his marriage. Then he dealt with his whole elaborate lifestyle. He sold his BMWs, his big house, and bought a place in the country and a small unit in town. He's fantastically well now and training to be a counselor to work with other cancer patients. There have been many people like him. So often people say, 'Cancer has given me the opportunity to live the life I wanted to lead'. It was the same with me. My heart attack and my brother's death gave me the opportunity to go on a spiritual search.

I now believe that Buddhism is not the only way. There are many paths and they are all valid. Within Buddhist circles it is very radical to say this, but many paths have the potential to take you to a higher, awakened state.

For all that, I still think of myself as Buddhist. I do my practices every day and still keep the Buddhist precepts. Retreats are core to me. I yearn for them. Usually I manage to do two- or three-week group retreats and one ten-day retreat a year. Retreat helps me deepen my meditation practice and my ability to be accepting of myself. It also connects with the possibility of a transcendent world. I know when I emerge from retreat the qualities of kindness and generosity are in me more fully and effortlessly. They come out of the meditation itself.

I still read Buddhist books, but I'm more interested now in learning how Westerners have put Buddhism into the context of their lives. I think I've got enough information and now want to integrate it. To be as awake as I can and to live in the moment is sufficient. I do that best from sitting in meditation, watching my breath. That's when I get the stillest. Mindfulness is my core practice. I like Einstein's words, 'Imagination is more important than information', and Meister Eckhart touched me with these words: 'There is nothing more like God in the universe than silence'. That is the stage I am eager to explore.

I feel that in a tentative way I've connected with the core understanding of Shakyamuni Buddha, which is to allow life to come to me as it comes. I try to greet it with as much spacious good-heartedness as I can. 99

Digitizing the Dharma

MICHAEL ROACH
Diamond merchant, meditator and scholar

$\mathcal{N}$ews of Michael Roach, American Buddhist teacher and monk, had been reaching me from around the world for some time, most of it in the form of rave reviews. 'Michael Roach puts a blowtorch to your practice.' 'He taught the Sutra [Buddha's discourses or teachings] direct from his laptop, effortlessly combining the best of old and new.' 'He delivers traditional teachings with references to cultural films, literature, even pop songs.' 'One night he gave the most extraordinary presentation of what actually happens as one progresses through the path to the realization of Emptiness and beyond.' And on and on.

By anyone's standards, Buddhist or otherwise, Michael Roach is extraordinary. First there is his Geshe degree from Sera monastery in south India, the highest scholastic rank in Tibetan Buddhism, and to date awarded to only three Westerners. Before that was Princeton University, where he graduated with honors, and before that the Presidential Scholars medallion, presented by President Nixon himself. Other notches on his intellectual belt are his mastery of Tibetan, Sanskrit and Russian and the numerous texts he has translated and published in those languages.

Then there are his projects. Down on the lower east side of Manhattan you will find the Asian Classics Institute, a Buddhist organization which offers meditation classes, drop-in lectures, long-term formal study programs, Tibetan language classes, and teacher training facilities—all funded by donation only. Round the corner is a cafe-cum-bookshop where the lost and lonely can go to find peace over a cup of coffee while watching a Buddhist video. Not far out of town is Diamond Abbey, a monastery and nunnery Michael Roach has established for Westerners who want to take robes. Then there is his active and enthusiastic participation in the renaissance of Buddhism in Mongolia, still fragile after recently emerging from 70 years of uninspired and repressive communist rule. Last but not least, Geshe Michael Roach is working on a hugely ambitious scheme to 'digitize the Dharma'—a plan to put all of the Buddha's teachings (some 200,000 texts) on disk, which he claims is the best way of preserving them and making them accessible. It took the Tibetans some 700 years to translate the canon from Sanskrit into Tibetan, but Michael Roach is unfazed. With the help of dedicated teams in the USA and India he's produced some 2500 scriptures (which he distributes freely) and claims that his own laptop already contains more books than any single monastery. There is also talk of producing multimedia programs that will combine a text, the voice of a chant master and film to illustrate rituals.

Arguably the most fascinating of all his activities, however, is his founding and directorship of one of New York's biggest diamond and jewellery firms, Andin International. Michael Roach's success at Andin has been so phenomenal, and unlikely, that the prestigious business magazine *Forbes* has featured his meteoric rise—twice. Michael Roach's love of diamonds is total (some would say obsessive). Apart from specializing in teaching the Diamond-Cutter Sutra (the Sutras are the canon of the Buddha's teachings and discourses), he has a diamond implanted in his tooth and has gone on record as saying that he would have one placed in his forehead too if he could. He's also considered having the Heart Sutra (symbolized by the diamond) tattooed all over his body. Not content with working with the stones all day, he even bought the equipment to cut diamonds at home, for relaxation.

When I heard he was giving a lecture at Melbourne University as part of a teaching tour, I hurried along to see for myself what Michael Roach looked like. I found a tall, rather gangling man with pale skin, blue eyes and, most exceptional for a Buddhist monk, unshaven black hair. He spoke very quickly, as though the words could hardly keep up with his brain, driving his points home with tremendous conviction, and making his audience repeat key Tibetan phrases 'to imprint them on our mind stream'. Afterwards, when I approached him for this interview, he graciously agreed because, in spite of his tight schedule, 'I like the idea of talking to non-Buddhists'.

The meeting took place in a small room at a local Buddhist center filled with his traveling retinue who continued to digitize the Dharma into their laptops as we spoke. As time was short (he was off to Mongolia that afternoon), I focused principally on the most obvious question: how a renunciate Buddhist monk came to be vice-president of a lucrative diamond company and how he reconciles such blatant materialism with his spiritual calling.

" One day in July 1975 I was meditating and something very extraordinary happened. It was very special. I had a vision which was to do with diamonds. I can't go into much detail except to say that the diamond has a special meaning in Buddhism. In particular it represents absolute truth, or the philosophy of Emptiness. There are several reasons, but the most important is that the diamond is the closest thing to an absolute in the physical world. Nothing in the universe is harder than a diamond; nothing can scratch a diamond; a diamond is perfectly clear. If a diamond wall were built around us, we wouldn't see it, because it's perfect. Similarly, ultimate reality is around us all the time, we live in it. If we could see it, we would be very close to reaching Buddhahood, Enlightenment.

When I had that vision, I knew I had to be working in the diamond business. It was part of my spiritual development. I asked my lama, Khen Rinpoche, a great, high lama who before the loss of Tibet had been the administrator of the Tantric College in Lhasa, and afterwards was the abbot of Sera monastery in south India. The day after graduating from Princeton I had gone to live with him at his monastery in New Jersey, where he had been sent by the Dalai Lama. I was being trained in the traditional manner. That meant, in effect, that there were only two things you could do without asking your preceptor, clean your teeth and go the bathroom. A real lama is meant to help you with everything. Khen Rinpoche, who was always very practical, approved of my plan. 'Grow your hair a little bit and buy a suit,' he said. 'Am I allowed to deal in money?' I asked. 'Sure,' he replied, 'if it helps people'.

Until that moment I had no interest in diamonds, no background in diamonds. My family is Irish. I was like Candide trying to join this business, which is run almost exclusively by Hasidic Jews and is very tight and closed. It needs to be, because you can steal a million dollars in your pocket. For that reason, diamond traders only employ their relatives. I applied to 30 firms and was rejected by all of them before I met an Israeli man who was opening a diamond business in the States. He didn't know anyone in the USA, so he took a chance with me. I told him I would do anything: I would be a messenger or clean the windows, but I needed to work with diamonds. He said OK.

He taught me from scratch. First he let me be a messenger. Then he let me touch diamonds, then he let me sort them. For the first year we worked an eighteen-hour day. I didn't sleep much. One thing, I'm celibate and I don't have the commitment of a family, so that saved a lot of time. My commute to New Jersey was a three-and-a-half-hour round trip, which gave me time to study my Buddhism and say prayers. After that first year, when things settled down, my day was divided into waking up at 6 a.m., meditating for an hour, getting the bus and being at work by 9 a.m. At 5 p.m. I'd go home. At 7 p.m. I'd have a class with my lama till 9 p.m. Then I'd meditate till 10 p.m. or 10.30 p.m. Simultaneously I was taking my Geshe degree, which necessitated going to India to debate with thousands of monks, literally. My company gave me chunks of time off to do that, but as the monastery was close to Bombay, a major diamond center, I'd combine it with business.

Shortly after starting the company my boss invited me to head up my division, which at that time consisted of two people. I made a deal with him. 'I'll do it providing I can run it along my own principles—Bodhisattva principles [the altruistic ideal of only benefiting others]. You can't interfere so long as I make a profit.' He agreed, and it worked very well. We started with $50,000, which we borrowed, and now we do $125 million a year and have about 900 employees. Until recently I was vice-president of the company in charge of the diamond importing. We have branch offices all over the world and play the markets in Tel Aviv, Brazil, Antwerp, Russia, Australia, South Africa, Zaire, Botswana and Bombay by phone and email.

The first Buddhist principle I established was that of 'exchanging self with others'. The managers have to do this Bodhisattva thing of putting themselves in the other person's shoes. The idea is that whenever you are dealing with an employee, even the janitor, you only think of what they would like and what would benefit them from the situation. I'd instruct them, 'Even if you're having a ten-minute conversation, think, "What would help this person?"'. I trained all my people this way and I never told them it was Buddhism. For five years no one knew I was a monk. I wore a suit, I didn't shave my head. I really wanted to move in the workplace, to make moral decisions there without them being labelled Buddhist. They knew I was making millions of dollars without knowing why.

Another principle is what is called in Buddhism Lojong, or mind training. The idea is that whenever there's a problem you turn it into an advantage. You use it. The Kadampa Geshes developed this 1000 years ago in Tibet. So, say we get an order from a big jewellery company for 10,000 diamonds which we would proceed to buy, and then the order gets cancelled. The result is we're stuck with 10,000 diamonds. Instead of trying to sell them and take a loss, which is the normal practice, we would design a new piece of jewellery using exactly 10,000 diamonds, go to another customer and suggest they make whatever adjustments to the design they want. Inevitably we would actually make more money from the second deal than the first.

I have rules, too, for dealing with outsiders, such as the suppliers. The main one is total honesty. We never ever pay a payment late and never cheat someone out of a deal. If someone makes a mistake in our favor we phone them immediately and tell them the payment is, say, $2000 too little and please bill us correctly.

According to the theory of karma, if you behave like this you'll get richer and richer, which is what happened to us. By using Buddhist principles the place started to go like crazy.

My division, which now has around 200 people of eighteen different nationalities, runs like clockwork and is very harmonious. The reason why most businesses do not flourish is because of problems among the people inside. It's not the market. We work on the Buddhist principles of no anger, no jealousy. If someone was being jealous or angry I would take them out to lunch and give them Buddhist logic. There are lots of Buddhist arguments about how destructive anger and jealousy are. I spent a lot of money on lunches! On a mundane level the reason is that a mental affliction takes time. A good jealousy attack lasts twenty minutes. Anger takes two days—it ruins your concentration. Even after the object of your anger is gone and the argument is finished, you still think about it. So if you teach your employees not to get angry, their whole mind is freed for other things. It's the same with desire. If a person's mind is free from desire for any object—food, sex, money, fame, whatever—then they actually save lots of hours of their lives, and so you can do lots of projects because you're not thinking about those things.

I pass on my techniques to other business people through a series of seminars called things like 'Ancient Wisdom for Motivating Employees to Reach Business Success', 'Two-Minute Office Meditations for Learning Business Focus' and 'Doing the Right Thing: Increasing Profits Through Honesty and Ethics'.

Another condition of heading up my division was that I took a month off twice a year to go on retreat. This is unheard-of in New York corporations, where the annual leave is two weeks. I insisted my staff got a similar deal. All of my people who work in the computer office are required to break twice a year—for a five- to six-week retreat. And they're paid for it. It's for the creativity. The level of creativity is extraordinary when they come back! They see things totally differently. One good idea, one good solution in the diamond business and you're talking millions of dollars. For example we worked out a way to weigh the diamonds to 1/1000th of a carat which saved one per cent or $1 million. That's the budget for the whole office.

My boss initially complained about my methods: 'The other divisions are getting angry because they don't get two months off'. 'Hang on, we've got a deal,' I'd reply.

People often ask me what a monk is doing working in such a materialistic and lucrative field. My reply is that the reason I went into the diamond business had nothing to do with the money—it was due to the vision, and nothing else. It was a coincidence that I got paid for doing what I would have done anyway. I can say now that the purpose of that vision has and continues to be fulfilled completely and very nicely. The vision was 90 per cent of the reason. The other 10 per cent was due to the fact that so many monks needed help. Back in Tibet, Sera monastery had 8000 monks and only 108 made it to south India. They started all over by living in tents in the jungle. It was wild! People were being killed by elephants there.

If you have just the basic Buddhist vows, you can't work. Among the basic 250 vows that all monks take there is a rule that says I can't own anything except my robes. Nothing. So if someone gives me a piece of red cloth I can only hold it for ten days. If I don't make it into a robe within ten days I have to give it away. But with Bodhisattva vows that Tibetan Buddhist monks take, if someone offers you a warehouse of red cloth you keep it until such a time as you can use it to help other people. There's a big difference. If thousands of monks in India are dying you *must* work. You must try to find the most lucrative work you can.

Now I support 2000 monks. I don't keep any money for myself. I donate my salary. I take enough to live on—the rest has been given to the monasteries and to Tibetan refugees. It goes directly to the charities. We have helped establish schools, water systems, buildings, temples, a library, a diamond factory. We are teaching computers to refugees—monks, nuns and lay people—in twenty different camps. We train them to input Buddhist scriptures. We then put these onto CD-ROMs and give them away. To date we've given away about 10,000. We take handicapped people, deaf people, teenagers at risk, we teach them how to type and pay them $1 a page. Every time a handicapped boy or a bad boy earns $1, we put $4 into a village food fund we set up, and so he is helping to feed everybody in the village. It's a real incentive. Everyone starts to love them—and they start to work hard.

People often wonder if spirituality is compatible with making money, having a comfortable house, a nice car. Generally the idea that a Buddhist is not meant to desire to own nice things and have a comfortable lifestyle is false. It's true that the Buddha said that most people if they have more material things will start to experience more suffering because there's the suffering of not having enough and the suffering of having it. But the Buddha also said that if you have a good attitude and are generous, then the more you have, the happier you will be. If you are constantly getting it and giving it away, it works very well. There's absolutely no problem with being extremely wealthy and being a Buddhist because you can do wonderful things. The greatest first tantric practitioners in India were the kings and the aristocrats—the Buddha constantly went after that sort of person because they were in a position to really help people. An important principle of Buddhism is that if everyone were a perfect Buddha, everyone would be wealthy. The idea that there's not enough to go round is only created by our negative thoughts. If we were all perfectly ethical there would be more than enough. There would be limitless money for every person on this planet.

The goal of Buddhism is that physically your body transforms into a body of light, your mind becomes omniscient and materially you have all the money you ever dreamed of. All Buddhas are incredibly wealthy. They own a lot and they use it. And there's no problem with that.

I love my work. It's very useful for a spiritual person to have a whole life around normal people. You get to understand the suffering that normal people go through—the stress that's involved in earning a living to feed your family. When I travel about as a big lama, no one criticises me to my face. Everyone's always telling me what a wonderful person I am, and congratulating me on the things I do. But when I'm at work the boss screams at me. There's greed to deal with. There's the jealousy of my other vice-presidents to deal with. Your spiritual life gets challenged every few seconds. It's a laboratory for Buddhist practice which you don't get in a monastery.

There are also beautiful women to deal with. We would go to the Diamond Fair at Basel and there would be hundreds of exquisite women modeling the diamonds. Buddhist monks are given methods for dealing with that sort of situation should it arise. There's a famous work by Nagarjuna which suggests we see how the body is mortal—so, you visualize the woman getting sick or performing human functions like defecating. That doesn't work very well. The other way is to see the Emptiness of a person—to see that the woman has no inherent existence. That works better for me. I was not in robes, so if a woman seriously approached me I would have to tell her I was ordained. After that it didn't happen. I grew up in the USA where there's a lot of pressure to engage in relationships with the opposite sex. It's very much drilled into you since childhood, yet if you go to a monastery and stay celibate for decades, as I have done, you discover you don't need that sort of relationship. There are much higher things to be interested in.

Actually, as a young man I was very troubled about relationships—it was one of the main things that got me into Buddhism. My parents had a very tough divorce. I saw how impermanent relationships were. I saw the swing from deep love to deep hatred. Even my own experience with my girlfriend in high school showed me how you could go from loving someone one minute to disliking them the next. That deeply disturbed me. I wanted to know how people could do that. Buddhism says that the disintegration of relationships is caused ultimately by negative thoughts and that when you change your negative thoughts that disintegration doesn't happen any more. Most relationships, however, end in sorrow, and when they don't they are ended by death.

There are so many ways I have benefited from being in the workplace. The translation work I put out afterwards was much better. You learn, for example, how normal people speak. If you deal with business people all day, you get to know that. I also now know how to teach in normal American terms. We started the Asian Classics Institute, in the East Village, Manhattan with six people; now 300 turn up. It's because the teachings are delivered in a language ordinary people can grasp. They're coming like crazy. We keep having to rent bigger places. We started in a Christian church, now we're in a basketball gymnasium. We do no advertising, they just come in off the street. They really want to know.

Positively what they're looking for is contentment—because it's totally lacking in New York. No one is content there; no one. Of all the places in the world, New York city is the hardest one to find happiness in. I'm not sure why. Maybe because we have everything. In the negative, the people who come to us are trying to explain the pain of human existence. They want to make sense of why people suffer, why they get old and die. I wanted to know the same things. The year I joined my monastery, my father, my mother and my brother all died. If you're brought up believing that God made you and that God is compassionate, then the question has to be asked why did he kill three people like that. I found that Buddhism dealt with the issue of death more thoroughly than Christianity.

Buddhism has a lot to offer. Mentally it makes you very happy. You remove your negativities, the qualities of your emotions improve and you become content. The individual becomes responsible for the individual's world, so any misfortune you might have is not blamed on an external force, like God. Rather it is due to your own state of mind. If you learn to observe your mind throughout the day, from hour to hour, and are very careful to be compassionate to other people, very, very careful to be good to other people, then the result after months or years is that your own mind becomes extremely contented. And that's what people want. So Buddhism works.

Ironically, watching out for other people's happiness becomes the best way of reaching happiness yourself. You would think that doing things for yourself would make you happy, getting things for yourself, but actually it's the reverse. It's so unexpected that most people never try it. Yet the more you try it, the happier you are.

There are certain techniques that can be used to foster mindfulness like this, other than meditation. My students and I do an exercise where we have a little book and every two hours we examine the state of our mind and jot down what it is. Actually this was invented by the Buddha, it's a deep tantric practice. You do this all of your life. Once you get good at it you can do it anywhere—even in an office in Manhattan with thousands of transactions going on and the pace so hectic that people are actually running up and down the aisles.

These days I am drawing away from the diamond industry. I just go back when they want me. I told them five years ago that I wanted to quit and it has taken me that long to get out. For a while I worked eight months a year, then six and last year I cut back to one month. Now I am concentrating on my teaching.

I plan to do a three-year retreat in Arizona where I grew up. I will have spent seven years transmitting the Geshe degree to my students in New York, and one year reviewing it. Then I hope to build a place in Arizona to start a community there made up of serious practitioners who like to study and meditate. It will be a lifestyle which doesn't require them to be in a city. We're designing some adobes, and a meditation temple with a courtyard in the middle. It will be a large property. It looks like we might get 7000 acres. I think Western monasticism is going to consist of people living in communities like that, with monks, nuns and lay people who have made lifelong vows earning their living through computer-related skills. I'd also like to keep the center in New York open and to come back periodically to teach.

It has been suggested that Westerners are so excited by their discovery of Buddhism that they are overly gullible and naive. There might be a slight danger of that, but it's overstated. A person who's infatuated with Buddhism will come down after their honeymoon period to a true Buddhism. Westerners are actually the best Dharma students in the world. Here you have hundreds of millions of people who are well educated and who are not looking for their next meal. They have time and they're critical. They're not going to believe something unless you can prove it to them. My students are extremely cynical and skeptical; 75 per cent of them have rejected something. This makes them perfect for Buddhism. There's a huge customer base for Buddhism in the West—in the diamond market you call it an overhang. **99**

A place for the heart to rest

TRACY MANN
Actor

When I read in a magazine that well-known Australian actor Tracy Mann was cleaning toilets every week at a Sydney Buddhist center, I sat up. The slight woman with the soft eyes and wide smile known to millions through her appearances on *Heartbreak High, Gates of Janus* and countless other shows must have had a significant conversion, I thought. I was intrigued to know how and why.

Happily she agreed to see me and tell me her story. The interviews took place over two days in her doll-sized, pink terrace house with lacy ironwork in Paddington, one of Sydney's trendiest inner suburbs. Down the road in Oxford Street are arty cinemas, ethnic restaurants, rows of fashionable boutiques and the launching pad of Sydney's annual gay Mardi Gras. It's a world throbbing with worldliness and commerce, but upstairs in Tracy's house, the back bedroom is a haven of peace of tranquillity. This is the 'Buddhist Suite', holding Tracy's altar, her Buddhist pictures and statues, and the ritual implements she uses during her meditations. Although a relative newcomer to Buddhism, she comes here most days to meditate.

She curled up on her sofa, and with many interruptions for cups of tea and phone calls from her agent told me how she incorporates the inner world of Buddhism into the outer domain of show biz.

*For me Buddhism came right out of the blue. In 1994 I was in Melbourne working on the TV show *Janus*. It was a prime job but for some reason I felt incredibly flat. I'd get back from work and find I couldn't leave the house. A woman I met on the set told me about a kinesiologist and I booked three sessions thinking it would help. Just before my last session I had started to read *The Tibetan Book of Living and Dying* by the Tibetan teacher Sogyal Rinpoche, which made me feel very happy for some reason. I told the kinesiologist about it. She mentioned she had been to Nepal and had met a yogi there, and gave me the name and telephone number of a Buddhist organization in Melbourne. She hugged me as I left and said, 'You are on your journey', which struck me as being really strange.

Minutes after I had left her I was driving home when a thought hit me on the back of the head: 'Go to Nepal'. It was so strong I couldn't ignore it. I went home and rang the Buddhist center, and they told me there was a very good course in Queensland, but I heard myself say, 'No, I have to go to Nepal'. I was adamant. They told me there was a course happening at a monastery called Kopan in Kathmandu, starting in a week's time. By 'absolute accident' I had a five-week break from filming, and so I jumped on a plane and just headed off—by myself. I had never been to Nepal but I knew that was where I wanted to go. I arrived at the very end of August in the middle of the monsoon. It was extremely hot, pouring with rain and no taxi would take me to the monastery because the road to it was down from all the rain. All I could think was 'I've got to get to Kopan'. I grabbed a taxi to take me to the foot of the hill, and carrying a huge backpack given to me by a 6-foot friend, I trudged up on foot through the mud and rain. I got lost several times. Finally I arrived, drenched in sweat and filthy dirty, only to be told the showers were not working. They put me into a room which had a breathtaking view of the famous Boudhnath Stupa, a huge white shrine with Buddha eyes painted on all four sides looking out over the Kathmandu Valley and then they took me to the tea room. There I found all these little monks sitting at tables chanting their texts and I cried with joy. I felt as though I'd come home. It was an extraordinary feeling.

The course was designed as an introduction to Buddhism for Westerners who were holidaying in Nepal. No one could believe I'd come all the way from Australia to do it! There were about 30 of us from different countries and walks of life. Our teacher was a Swedish nun, Ani Karen, who had been a Buddhist for twenty years. There was something of the schoolmistress about her but she was also deeply impressive. She was calm, self-contained and was an excellent teacher with an immense knowledge.

I found it really hard to sit cross-legged. I had about ten cushions all around me propping me up. Still, for some reason it all made sense. There was no need to question, either then or later. I loved the stories of the Buddha—Ani Karen's devotion to the Buddha was so strong it was infectious. I loved hearing about the Four Noble Truths—the Buddha's description of why we suffer and the way out of it. I loved the silence, the contemplation, the walking meditations we did around the hill. It was wonderful. The explanation of ideas such as reincarnation seemed like common sense; completely natural. I had always, always thought that life was too big for us to have just one go at it. Apparently when I was born my mother turned to my father and said, 'We've been diddled. She's been here before'. I was a very calm baby, born on 21 December and so good they used me to model the Christmas party hats. As a child I always yearned for the sense of the spiritual, but it wasn't there at home. I used to want my parents to say grace at meals, but they didn't. My religious education consisted of going to Sunday School really just to give Mum and Dad a break.

I found the meditations really grounding. There were so many but I remember particularly liking the ones about the mother. We were told that because we have had endless rebirths we have all been each other's mother at some stage or another. The mathematics were a bit of a problem because of the increasing numbers of beings in this world until it was pointed out that you count the sentient beings in many different universes and all realms of existence. Down in Boudhnath among the teeming crowds I felt the truth of this. 'Yes, you've all been my mother,' I thought, which made me feel enormous compassion for everyone. Somehow, thinking of us all as mothers made us equal. I felt as though the whole human race was connected.

Specifically, we meditated over and over on the kindness of our own mother. We had to remember all she had done for us, how she had looked after us day and night when we were a baby, how she went without sleep, how she washed and clothed us, how we simply could not have survived without her love and care. By the end of it I recognized that I had been truly nurtured. I remembered my mother slipping into bed beside me when I had had a nightmare. I'd put my parents through the wringer. I'd left home at sixteen, moved in with a man much older than myself (who had a son), started taking drugs. Now I truly appreciated all they had done for me.

Nothing on that first course was strange—not the teachings, not the statues and certainly not the ritual.

Especially not the ritual. I found the pujas [the chanted services] very comforting. They evoked such well-being and centeredness in me. I continue to love the ritual of Buddhism.

However, there were some misgivings.

At one point we were joined by a Western woman who was on a purification retreat which involved her saying 100,000 mantras. I went into a deep depression, thinking I could never do that and therefore could never be a Buddhist. I also worried generally that in order to be a Buddhist too many things would have to change. I talked to Ani Karen about it and she said, 'Take it slowly'. By the end of the course four of us felt committed enough to take Refuge—the official ceremony for becoming a Buddhist. I went into Kathmandu and bought a special outfit, a plain cotton pant suit in charcoal gray. It was like getting married. I felt I was making a commitment for life. During the ceremony itself I was really excited. I knew something big was happening—even though I had no idea what I was saying because the words I was repeating were Tibetan. Whatever I was promising I knew I wanted to do it. As in baptism I was given a Buddhist name, Lobsang Choezum, which means something about amassing the Dharma. Later I looked up 'refuge' in the dictionary and it said, 'coming home'. That was it.

My diary entry for that day reads:

Today I took refuge in Buddha Dharma and Sangha
in the Gompa [temple] at Kopan monastery,

Kathmandu. I am now a Buddhist. I have taken vows to practice Dharma in my daily life until I die. This means I am now mindful of my actions. I shall not kill, lie, slander, use harsh words, steal, engage in sexual misconduct. I shall cherish all sentient beings with the kindness that my mother bestowed upon me. I shall work towards the liberation of suffering for all living beings. I shall use negative situations as lessons of patience. I am very happy about taking these vows. I will develop my inner wisdom, develop my mind. It has given purpose and meaning to this precious human rebirth. It makes sense now—all these fortunate qualities that I have. I feel the spirits are rejoicing. I have finally come home.

In Buddhism my heart had found a place where it could rest. Something it could live with and sit with. Now my life began to make sense. Before, existence had seemed so small, a constant round of running from pillar to post, hoping someone would give me a job, waiting for approval, the constant struggle to find my own worth. Buddhism presented a bigger picture.

Buddhism didn't come out of a need. I was flat but not unhappy. What it gave me was a spiritual component, a purpose and meaning to life.

For years and years I'd said that if I were to do anything spiritual I'd be a Buddhist—although I had no idea what that meant. When I was sixteen I left home to be an actress and was introduced to drugs and Eastern religion of the Rajneesh and Muktananda variety. This was the 1970s, when we were all meant to be 'free' and 'open', and I was drawn to people who were into Indian artefacts, cushions on the floor, burnt joss-sticks, gurus—that sort of thing. For a little girl from Adelaide it was quite eye-opening. I took the drugs but not the religion. Somehow it didn't click. There seemed to be too much adoration and devotion about it, and I was into being an individual, not a follower. But I really took a lot of cocaine, the designer stuff. It made me feel confident, speedy and I talked a lot of bullshit. In the end it made me feel less strong. Then when a relationship broke up and I needed help I started to go to self-transformation groups. This was the 1980s and real New Age stuff. I would do weekend courses where there would be no alcohol, healthy living, and meditation. This consisted of taking a mantra which we had to choose. They were very simple, like 'Ho hum'. You'd breathe in on the 'ho' and out on the 'hum'. We also used to beat mattresses to get rid of our anger and shout things like 'Get off my back'. I'd always lose my voice. Often this would be done to pictures of our family. We always came away hugging everybody. There was some benefit to all of this, as I did find some sense of joy which I recognized came from myself. But nothing has opened me up like Buddhism.

I stayed at the monastery for a month in all, reading, meditating, talking to others and going for day trips to the mountains. Coming back to Sydney I couldn't wait to set up my own altar in 'the Buddhist Suite' upstairs. I would do simple meditations and prayers that had appealed to me: the Four Immeasurables—wishing all beings to be free from suffering and its cause, wishing them all to abide in equanimity, wishing them all to exist in permanent peace and happiness, wishing them never to be parted from joy; the Seven Limb Prayer which consists of seven components— taking Refuge, making mental offerings to the Buddhas, confessing my negativities of body, speech and mind, rejoicing in the noble actions of Holy and ordinary beings, and requesting the Buddha to remain until all suffering ceases.

I also joined a Tibetan Buddhist center, Vajrayana Institute, in Newtown. When I'm not working I spend a lot of time there listening to teachings and helping out. I very much wanted to be of use. I started off cleaning the lama's toilet—now I've graduated to making his meals once a week and organizing the cooking roster. I love looking after the lama, as living alone my life is very selfish, but it's quite a commitment. Finding people to come in every day and cook is not easy because the members are very busy working. I've had to learn to ask for help. I'm about to take on running the bookshop too. For all the difficulties, it's extremely fulfilling.

Two years ago I went back to Kopan to do a solitary retreat on a deity called Vajrasattva, the Buddha who purifies negative karma. Just like the woman who had so overawed me on my first visit. It lasted for eleven weeks and two days.

I had prepared well, going to Dharamsala for six weeks to take teachings from His Holiness the Dalai Lama and spending a lot of my time alone. I was given a beautiful house in Kopan with all mod cons, including a double bed and hot water. I'd brought my own pillow and mosquito net. Still, I was terrified. I knew it was an extraordinary thing to put yourself through and I suspected I was going to go through hell. The idea of being by myself for that long without distraction! I knew I was not going to be able to pick up the phone or open a bottle of wine when the going got tough.

The first thing I did was to set up my altar. It was rather eccentric. My offerings were a jar of South Australian jam and some honey. My effigy of Vajrasattva was not the usual big painting but a small postcard I'd bought in Dharamsala and had laminated.

The second thing I did was to shave my head. If you're going to do something you might as well do it properly! I used the scissors of my Swiss Army knife and finished the job off with a razor. It felt wonderful—very clear. I'll always remember putting my vulnerable, rather raw bald head on the cold pillow that first night. When the stubble began to poke through, it would catch on the mosquito net. But I would get up in the morning, wash my head and clean my teeth, and it was done. People commented that I looked beautiful, but I felt a bit shy about it.

For the first few days I was visited by a woman who had just finished a group retreat. She advised me on certain aspects of the practice and generally gave encouragement. I called her 'my angel'. Other than that, the only person I saw was another retreatant who I would meet every Sunday for a chat. That event was so exciting I'd shave my legs for it. Every day I followed the same routine: Up at 4.30 a.m., cup of tea; first meditation session 5.00 a.m. till 6.30 a.m.; breakfast at 7.00 a.m.; second session 9.30–11.00 a.m.; lunch at 11.30 a.m. then a long break; third session 3.00–4.30 p.m.; tea and watching the sun set over the Himalayan foothills; 6.30–8.00 p.m. fourth session. Then bed.

I was right, it was hard. Actually it was everything. It was a lifetime. Heaven and hell. In those eleven weeks and two days what I discovered was the nature of my own mind. The first two weeks were terrible. I sat on my cushion and sobbed and sobbed. What I was experiencing was the unfilled-in gaps, the missing bits, the deep loneliness of being a human being. And it was so deep and so painful. I had put myself in the position of experiencing it. That was the most profound thing that happened and the beginning of the process of unbecoming. The rumblings of the demons about to leave. As a result the empty middle does feel filled in, although I certainly would not say I was fearless. Now I understand that no one else can help me. I have become more self-reliant. That was the great gift of doing the retreat by myself.

There were interesting physical effects too. I got this great pain in my gut and my stomach blew up as if I were six months pregnant. I was completely unattractive bald and fat! I'd been bulimic when I was younger, as well as taking drugs, and I think the body was clearing itself. Since that time I've really looked after my body—in order to live my life properly. With no distractions or 'pleasures', my mind became obsessed with food! My main meal was lunch (it was brought to me) and I would spend much of the afternoon thinking about what I would eat for supper. Eventually, to stop this craving, I stopped eating supper altogether. In that retreat I could really watch my 'monkey' mind, as the Buddhists call it, flitting here and there grasping at one thing then another, never at rest, never at peace. Wanting, wanting. If I wasn't thinking about food I was planning a holiday in Bali. I had the whole thing worked out! All my life I'd wanted to be somewhere else, thinking it would be better. I really got the importance of being in the moment, of being where you are. Since then I am now much happier being at home, or wherever I happen to be. The great need to travel, to be somewhere else, has abated.

And then there was the torment of the Hindi music coming up from the valley below. It had started just after I'd begun my retreat, the same song playing over and over again. I thought, 'It will stop soon', but it went on all morning, then all afternoon, and all evening. The next day it was still going. It lasted for seven days and seven nights, non stop! At night I had locally bought earplugs called 'Fearlessly Deeper' which went in so far they blocked out everything, but during the day it was dreadful. I got so angry and frustrated. 'I've come here to meditate. And it's meant to be peaceful, and quiet!' I'd rage.

What could I do but work with it? I did my meditations as taught, looking for the inherent existence of a thing. 'Where is the anger?' I inquired. 'Is it in my toe?' 'Is it in my stomach?' and so forth, looking for this inherently existing anger and the inherently existing Tracy that was experiencing it. I did the same with the music. 'What is music?' I'd ask; 'Is it the wind, the wood of the instrument?' I was looking in meditation. Finally, on a day when I couldn't find either my anger or the music, the noise stopped. That was such a useful thing to have gone through.

At times my longing to be free was truly enormous. From my house I could see the life of the villages below and it looked so alluring. I watched houses being built, saw the crops change from wheat to corn to rice, witnessed children running home from school, wedding parties. I wanted so much to be down there, walking on those roads. I told my friend on our Sunday meeting and she said, 'Do it; go'. So, halfway through my retreat I escaped. I put on a hat and sunglasses, climbed over my fence, walked down the hill and shimmied under the barbed wire around the perimeter of Kopan, much to the astonishment of a group of children who watched me emerge at the other side. I started to walk along the roads, through the little villages and everything seemed so much smaller. The people were poor, their belongings shabby. I saw old women threshing their wheat on the road, working so very hard. Suddenly I saw it for what it was— the daily grind of what Buddha called Samsara [the fundamental unsatisfactory nature of life]. With that I turned round and walked back to Kopan and my retreat—through the front door.

What has Buddhism done for me?

With live theatre I've found that it isn't to do with 'me' any more, it's about giving the audience the best possible time. They've spent a lot of money and made the effort to come. In this respect a great weight has been lifted. It's no longer about pandering to my ego (we actors love to be loved), but about giving the very best time and bringing the audience on the journey with me. That's what I think about now when I'm waiting in the wings ready to go on. It's one way I can try to lead a mindful life and benefit others while doing this job. If I can walk into a rehearsal room, a film set, a stage with the Dharma in my heart then I am being a Buddhist. If I can meet people with kindness then I am living up to my Refuge name—amassing the Dharma.

Buddhism has also helped keep me calm and grounded, which has been extremely useful. Being an actor is very insecure. Last week, for example, I earned only $25. Often I wake up in the morning with no job at all—then, like today, I'm suddenly offered three. I never know where I'm going to be in three weeks time, so that it's impossible to plan ahead. Buddhism has taught me that's the way it is. The whole of life is in a perpetual state of flux. Nothing is fixed, everything is constantly changing. Understanding that reduces the anxiety somewhat.

I understand now that we're all suffering, we've all got fear, so there's a bit more compassion. It helps when I have to work closely with people who push my buttons. Rather than focusing in on their faults as I used to, I attempt to generate patience as I've been taught. I try to remember 'It's all an illusion and it doesn't really matter'. I feel I'm getting better as I get older, and that the generosity has got bigger.

Still, I haven't quite conquered the praise and blame syndrome yet. They are two of eight pairs of opposite qualities which you are meant to rise above. The praise lifts you up, the blame brings you down, and it's all ego. I have to admit I still feel pleased when someone taps me on the shoulder in the bus and says, 'Miss Mann, I love your work'— although it's not quite so chest-puffing as it was. Similarly, when I've tried hard for a part that I've really wanted and been rejected, I can still cry with disappointment; but the pain does not last as long as it used to. I haven't yet reached the stage where I can walk away and not mind, but then I've only been a Buddhist for three-and-a-half years. And if I get a bad review I have to tell myself I'm not going to die from one person's opinion.

I never talk about Buddhism, but people ask. There was one show I was doing in Adelaide which required my building a house in the second act. The frame was already on stage and I had to nail in the cladding—while talking all the time. It was a very hard thing to do. Right through rehearsals I couldn't get it to work, which was terribly stressful. On the very day before the show was to open, I discovered that the frame was shifting because it hadn't been placed correctly, which was why I couldn't get the nails in. I tried to remember my Buddhism not to get angry but to stay centered, and the others were amazed. 'Whatever it is you're on, we want to have some,' they said.

Living in the middle of Sydney has presented me with many opportunities to put Buddhism into practice. I walk past so many crumpled bodies in doorways. Yesterday there was a murder outside a nightclub. Today I watched a policeman standing over a collapsed woman on a street corner—the ambulance wasn't hurrying so I presumed she was dead. Living in such an environment really brings home the teachings on the preciousness of this life and how fortunate I am to be walking around in an able body with a relatively clear mind in a country which is not torn by war, famine and religious persecution. I was told by Ani Karen and subsequent teachers that these attributes are rare and should not be wasted. Now I look at the bodies in doorways with compassion, seeing them as equals, people wanting happiness like me. They just haven't been fortunate enough this time round to meet the teachings. It's their karma. At other times, however, living here is hard—the days when the drunk vomits just when I'm passing, when the demented woman sticks her face in front of mine and pokes her tongue out, when the neighbors start playing Julio Iglesio so loud it's as though it's in my own sitting room. Then I seriously consider moving up to the mountains. In my calmer moments I know it's a lesson in learning to live with people.

Now my daily practice consists of meditating for at least 30 minutes in the morning. I'm quite strict with myself. I always do my meditations and practices before 9 a.m., which is when I consider my working day begins. So, 8 a.m. is a good time for me to sit. I think it works on a very deep level. Then there are days when it is difficult to meditate, when sitting on my bottom seems a waste of time and I wonder if I shouldn't be out there, doing something like voluntary work. Buddhism is like a marriage: there are good times and bad. But generally I can say that over the last three years there has been a build-up of 'something': an inner peace, a groundedness. At times I can actually feel my heart opening in a physical sense when I'm sitting there. And I pray to be put in the right direction where I can be of most benefit to others. **99**

Life as a question,
not fact

STEPHEN BATCHELOR
Author, teacher and skeptic

Stephen Batchelor seriously caught my attention when he wrote a critique of my first book *Reincarnation: The Boy Lama* in the prestigious American Buddhist magazine, *Tricycle*. It was not the style or the story he was questioning, but the fact of reincarnation itself. For a former monk, author, translator of several seminal Buddhist texts and well-known Buddhist lecturer, this was surprising to say the least.

He wrote:

> While all religions believe that life continues in some form after death, that does not prove that the claim is true. Until quite recently most religions believed that the world was flat, but such widespread belief had little effect on the shape of the planet. Even

though the Buddha accepted the idea of rebirth, one could argue that he simply reflected the ideologies of his time. Long before the Buddha, India had developed a cosmology which included the ideas of karma, rebirth and liberation. These ideas were taken for granted, just as we take for granted many scientific views which, if pressed, we would find hard to prove.

Stephen Batchelor could make a useful contribution to this book, I thought, precisely because he is a skeptic—an audible voice of dissent among the eager new converts of 'Western' Buddhism. He agitates, he irritates and because of that he is invaluable. His email address is 'agnostic'. One of his most popular books is called *Buddhism Without Beliefs*. And the brochure for Sharpham College, Devon, England, where he is Director of Studies, states specifically that the Buddhism he offers 'is understood as a way of life inspired by Gautama Siddhartha that is continuously undergoing redefinition in response to changing conditions'. As a result of his secularisation of Buddhism, he appeals to a large section of the seeking Western public.

He was born in Scotland, educated in England and, like so many of the early carriers of Buddhism from East to West, he traveled to India in the 1970s, ending up in Dharamsala, that thriving center of Tibetan Buddhism. Stephen plunged right in. Aged nineteen he became a novice monk in the Gelugpa (Yellow Hat) school, learnt both colloquial and classical Tibetan and then moved to Switzerland when his teacher, Geshe Rabten, became abbot of a monastery there. Following the traditional education of a Tibetan monk, he studied the major subjects of Tibetan Buddhism—debate, logic, epistemology—and went on to become Geshe Rabten's translator. His career next underwent a radical change. He decided to go to Korea to train in Zen Buddhism, still as a Tibetan monk. He was there for four years, learning, meditating and taking long retreats. During this period he met a French nun Martine. They married in 1985 in Hong Kong and returned to England together, settling at Sharpham College, a splendid Georgian mansion set among 500 acres of farming estate, which offers a year-long course in 'Buddhist Studies and Contemporary Enquiry', before moving to France. It comprises three terms of twelve weeks each, and apart from Buddhist study includes meditation, retreat, yoga and work on the land.

My train journey wound round the idyllic Devon coast and ended up in Ashprington, near Totnes, a town so picturesque and archetypically English it could have served as a film set for a Jane Austen novel. There was the ancient stone church, the winding lanes, the quaint cottages, the hedgerows gloriously dotted with spring flowers, and the river Dart snaking its way through the patchwork fields. Stephen met me outside the 'wing' where he and Martine live, a former barn with commanding views over rolling emerald hills. It bore no hint of Buddhist paraphernalia unless you count the Zen-like blank canvas hanging over the wood-burning stove. He had, I thought, a distinctly professorial air with his baggy cord trousers, gray woollen cardigan, balding head and bedroom slippers.

As could be expected from a man of his scholarly background, Stephen was an articulate and erudite inter-viewee, directing the interview towards the conceptual rather than the personal. He was also at times rather pedantic. He quibbled for a long time over my use of the word 'Buddhist' and 'Buddhism' before going on to use them liberally himself throughout the session. Because I personally disagree with some of his views (particularly his rebuttal of reincarnation which I feel he does not substantiate), I found the interview challenging until the end when he began to discourse on Buddhism raising a 'culture of awakening'. This was pure inspiration and made the long journey worthwhile.

66 *I* get a bit irritated with the word 'Buddhism'. It suggests a kind of belief system that you ascribe to and hold certain opinions about, whereby you can be identified as a Buddhist. That's a very misleading idea because it's difficult to define what beliefs would hold together Buddhists of all different persuasions. 'Buddhism' isn't a word that Asians use. They simply say they practice the Dharma or the Buddha Dharma. It's a term I prefer because that's how I would speak of it to myself. Although

Buddhism has become quite popular these days and there's a huge literature on the subject, it's incredible the extent to which people are not well informed about it. People say, 'You're a Buddhist, you must believe in reincarnation' or 'You don't believe you have a self' or 'You bow to golden idols'. These views are prevalent and are not accurate.

Yet out of necessity one talks about 'Buddhism'. Why people are attracted to it now is a complex matter. There are two things going on for most Westerners. On the one hand, there is still a very strong exotic mystique, especially around Tibetan Buddhism with figures like the Dalai Lama and Tibet. It's mysterious and foreign, presumably carrying deep wisdoms and traditions that have been lost in the West or maybe have never been here. The attraction is often a romantic longing coupled with idealism. On the other hand, there is an alienation from Western culture. It's often regarded as being overly materialistic, very superficial, only concerned with money, fame, consumerism, and it's seen as having lost touch with any deeper spiritual values. When I look back I can see that trait in myself, which was fed by the 1960s counter-culture. It was certainly a very sincere yearning, but it was caught up with a reaction against something you don't like, rather than a recognition of the values these traditions have. At the same time that romantic longing has deeper within it a genuine spiritual–religious yearning—a search for meaning. Despite the affluence of our Western culture, people often wonder what the point of it all is and where our society is going.

I have been involved in Buddhism for 27 years now and I can't say it has delivered for me, because that supposes there is some sort of Enlightenment that is going to break through and give one answers. Increasingly as I pursue Buddhism I move away from an idea that it's all about some kind of spiritual or mystical Enlightenment, some highly private internal revelation or insight that initially I saw as the be-all and end-all of practice. I think that's a very naive way of looking at it which fails to take into account the richness of the Dharma. I prefer to regard Buddhism as offering a trajectory, a perspective, which as one pursues it continues to be illuminating in all areas. Generally speaking it has given me a framework of ideas and values that I find compelling. I certainly don't claim to understand all of these ideas. That's part of the attraction. I don't find ready-made answers very attractive. This template for living was outlined by the Buddha back in the earliest discourses. He called it the Middle Way and it is formed out of the elements of the Eightfold Path: right view, right thought, right speech, right action, right livelihood, right effort, right mindfulness and right concentration. In other words, the Buddha consistently presented the path as one that engages all areas of one's life.

Buddhism engages me philosophically in terms of finding a way to approach questions like 'What is the meaning of life?', 'What is the nature of reality?', which I'm personally very interested in. It also provides (not as a separate compartment but as integral to the whole) a recognition that such insights are not just of intellectual fascination but have also ethical and moral preconditions and consequences. That reflects in one's view of the other person, of society, life as a whole, as well as in how one might choose to speak and act. Then it moves into economics—the way in which one earns one's living and how we utilize resources. These were all laid out 2500 years ago. You see that at the core there is a consistent process of reflection, meditation, awareness and sensitivity that is cultivated both through formal meditation and through encouraging a particular kind of consciousness. Buddhism also provides a framework within which one can reflect on these matters in the context of 2500 years of other people's thoughts on these matters. One feels one is very much part of a tradition, and a tradition which is continuously evolving and changing.

Another thing I really value about Buddhism is that it's not centered on a textual cant. There's no equivalent in Buddhism to, say, the four Gospels. All Buddhist traditions give equal if not more weight to the insights that the founders of the various schools have had as articulated within the context of their own times. If you train in Zen you're more likely to work with the writings of the early Zen patriarchs. If you train in the Gelugpa school of Tibetan Buddhism, you're likely to work with the writings of Tsong Khapa. Over its history Buddhism has moved through many different cultures and at each time has managed to re-imagine itself in a way that is suited to the needs of the time and place. To me that's extremely rich and vital.

I also appreciate that there is no central authority in Buddhism. There's no monotheistic sense of there being an omnipotent and omniscient creator who somehow drives the whole show. That resonates with my own intuition that the notion of God is somehow superfluous. If anything, it is simply consolatory. I see Buddhism primarily as a system of liberation.

I can tell you that my relationship to the Buddha Dharma never ceases to interest me. I never get bored with it. The overall project of trying to understand and live by it is continuously engaging. In a sense that is what holds me to it. On the other hand, I'm particularly lucky in that I manage through Buddhism to find a lifestyle that by any standards is fairly privileged—living in a beautiful place, being able to make a living from my writing (which is what I want to do anyway), being able to spend a fair amount of time on retreats. I'm able to do the things I like doing. Whether that is due to Buddhism or whether it is due to certain ways in which I've managed to appropriate Buddhism is another matter. But it has led me to travel widely, to meet people from all walks of life, often well-known and interesting people. It's been a wonderful thing.

I'm extremely grateful that I made that irrational decision at a very early age to follow this course. We had no idea in the early 1970s that 25 years down the line the Dalai Lama would be one of the best-known people on the planet and that there would be an enormous movement growing out of those very small beginnings. It is quite exciting to be part of that and also affirming that one tapped into it way before it became the 'in thing'. That confirms that there was something to it. But then people who ended up in power in Hitler's government in the late 1930s might have consoled themselves likewise!

By dint of my work, my writing, my love of words and my interest in questions that are generally considered intellectual, I suppose I could be considered a cerebral person. But I feel an almost visceral aversion to Western academic life. I've never been to university, I don't have any degrees of higher education. In fact, effectively I'm unemployable in the 'real world'. What is attractive about Buddhism is that while it certainly can enrich one's intellectual life it's always aware that intellectual life is one part of the whole. I became a monk as a way of really getting 'this Buddhism thing'. It was a means of cutting off all sorts of other possibilities and making a very public statement about my commitment. There were other Westerners who were monks and nuns by vocation. I suspect that if we move towards a Buddhism that is more adapted to the increasingly secular world we inhabit, then Buddhism will undergo a degree of secularization itself. That does not mean that communities of monks and nuns will not continue to flourish. There must always be centers of excellence where those who are 'called' are supported.

Buddhism permeates everything I do, but not in a selfconscious way. Recently I've become interested in visual art and photography. The way my photography is developing is also infused and enlivened by the sorts of questions I'm working with in my Buddhist practice. I see life itself as a question, not as a fact. This question can be articulated in a number of phrases: 'What is the meaning of life?', 'Who am I?', 'What is this?'. Beneath those verbal articulations is a recognition of life as an unfolding mystery. We find ourselves in this world, we wake up to the fact that we have been born and that at a certain point in the future, we don't know when, we will die. To me that is utterly mysterious. Why should that be the case and what does it mean? I see the task in many ways as never to lose sight of the fact that we're living in such an utterly mysterious and at times extremely beautiful form of being. For me Buddhist practice is continuously being alive to and responding to life in that way, trying to live most fully.

I find it amazing that people think that Buddhism is nihilistic and pessimistic. To me it's quite incomprehensible. It's a very common view due largely, I think, to the way Buddhism has been represented in the West since the middle of the nineteenth century. The Buddha never said life is suffering but that is something we see again and again in Western books on Buddhism. The Buddha said that the first truth is simply *dukkha*—the unsatisfactory nature of conditioned existence. The other view widely propagated is that to end suffering one must somehow extinguish the life force itself in Nirvana. There are quite a number of Buddhists who believe that—but that's only one view of many. The later Mahayana Buddhists have a very different vision which recognizes that you *can* live in the world in the midst of all the difficulties and problems in a way that doesn't keep you trapped. Instead the problems actually become a context for a sense of freedom. That freedom is about not being tied to the deep assumptions that keep you locked in repetition.

So, the Buddha Dharma gives me a framework within which to respond to life as question in its various guises, intellectually, emotionally, creatively. This is ongoing. There are points where I get frustrated with Buddhism, certainly; particularly when it becomes institutionalized and when it becomes an arena for people wanting to gain power, where politics come into it. I find that very tiresome. But I also see that there is a part of myself which is also a political animal, and I get caught up in it as much as anyone else. That's the nature of mind. If you believe in something and you regard it as valuable, you're going to want to make some effort to preserve what you think really matters and be critical of ways others have which you feel are not helpful. That's politics. If you're a writer, if you have any kind of public personality then it does have a political dimension. I don't think one can escape the social dimensions of any statement one makes in the public domain. It's going to have an effect which you can't predict. That's a responsibility one cannot escape.

I'm not convinced the Buddha was terribly interested in

trying to describe the nature of reality in some philosophical and ontological sense—in other words describing 'what is'. The Buddha was concerned with showing people how to be free from certain misconceptions of reality which cause pain. For example, the Buddha continuously emphasized impermanence. Now impermanence is not something we have much difficulty with intellectually—we know that everything changes, that we're going to die. The Buddha emphasized this not to provide some revelatory piece of information but to encourage a way of looking at and being in the world so that we pay continuous attention to that dimension of change. The understanding of impermanence thus becomes something that liberates us from those deep-seated assumptions which believe that at the heart of things or myself, nothing will change. He's reminding us to pay attention continuously to the transitory nature of things.

Of course impermanence *is* part of the nature of reality, but it's not being taught by the Buddha as the final philosophical answer to the great questions of life and death. It's being taught really as a didactic device. By following it we can begin to be in the world in another way. If we can really take this idea of impermanence to heart, we'll live in the world in a lighter vein. We're less likely to be so strongly invested in fixed ideas about ourselves, other people and society. The other fantastic thing about impermanence is that it recognizes that everything is going to grow into something else. Thus it becomes a way of seeing life which is far more creative. It recognizes that every circumstance is one out of which something new can grow. The classic Buddhist philosophy says everything that is an effect is also a cause. A circumstance, whatever it is, is the result of previous circumstances, but it's also the cause for what is going to follow. It has both a resultant and potential aspect. It's going to change into something else. So, with all changing situations (which can be stressful, like moving house or divorce) we have the freedom to make it into something that is going to cause us an awful lot of misery or not. It empowers the individual to be able to work with this continuously changing sensuous fabric of reality. At a deeper level the idea of Emptiness or selflessness comes in. Impermanence is the recognition of the fundamental continuity of a thing—the relativity. That is the core liberating idea.

Transformation is tied in with the whole idea of impermanence. It's taking responsibility in creating one's life. To me Buddhist practice is about treating one's body–mind processes as a kind of raw material for a quasi-artistic expression. Our lives can become something beautiful and aspiring. We have the freedom to do that. If we live our lives under the dictates of habit and conditioning, we are just going to keep on reiterating what's there anyway. The real challenge of Buddhist practice is to seek as deep a change as possible to the way we are in the world—both subjectively and in the social domain.

Meditation is essential to this process. Meditation is a

feature of Buddhist practice that marks it very distinctively from the many other religious traditions. The diversity of approaches in Buddhist meditation is extremely impressive, and meditation is a highly developed culture in Buddhist societies. There are two ways of looking at meditation. You can view it as a series of techniques that different traditions have developed. You can follow a series of instructions and sit for an hour a day and do it. That is utterly crucial for grounding your practice. But it can also become a routine, a habit, a kind of repetitive behaviour too. In this way it can become consoling but not terribly transformative. I feel that if meditation is to be effective, the qualities that you might cultivate in a formal meditation period have to be translated into your everyday experience—otherwise it becomes just a pleasant escape from the problems of life. For meditation to become effective your life has to become more meditative and your sensibility has to be infused with those meditative qualities. At that point the formal hour-a-day meditation session may not be so necessary. It's more a question that your work, your relationship with others, your ongoing self-awareness of your acts, thoughts and speech all become a continual 'meditative' process.

Of course you cannot achieve awareness simply by wanting it. You have to train. Discipline is very central to any Buddhist tradition. And it is hard work. A lot of what Buddhism is suggesting, however attractive it might sound, is for most people deeply counter-intuitive. Like impermanence—we don't intuitively feel we are going to die. We don't intuitively feel that everything is connected. Meditative practice is very much about training oneself to look at the world in a way which we know is more realistic but which we aren't attuned to. The Tibetan word for meditation is *gom*, meaning to familiarize or to get used to— through the process of getting used to these 'counter-intuitive' ideas you find they then become second nature. They stop being ideas that you crank up on your meditation cushion— they become the way you see and respond to things in a quite unselfconscious way. That's when the practice begins to have a transformative effect on your life because it's at work in every situation—even when you do something that you know is morally doubtful you cannot escape from an awareness of that. You can't gloss over it any more. You know it does matter.

This sort of practice is not just about seeing, hearing, touching things in a way that is informed by such insights, but also knowing that those insights have consequences on how we make moral judgements. You begin to recognize the consequences of things you say and do, on others and on yourself. You become more attuned to that causal process.

Causal process is 'karma' which in the standard Buddhist view means intention. To many Buddhists that automatically affirms the belief in reincarnation [because it is mooted that one's present circumstances are a result of actions conducted in the past, including previous lifetimes], although it is strange that it does. I have no trouble believing in the fact that every action has a consequence, but I don't believe for that consequence to be 'carried over in time' it need be embedded in some sort of psychic entity that survives death and that is reborn. That may be the case—I just don't know. I have a totally agnostic view on reincarnation. I've struggled with it for many years. I was taught as a monk that if I didn't believe these things then I couldn't really be a practicing Buddhist. Since I really wanted to be a Buddhist then, I bent over backwards trying to persuade myself this was the truth of the matter. The Tibetan tradition claims to have proof and reasons why one has to believe this, but I never found any of them convincing. The turning point came for me one day when I woke up and realized that even if it turns out that after death there is a big, blank void it wouldn't make the slightest bit of difference to my commitment to the practice now. In many Buddhist traditions, particularly the Tibetan and the Theravadan, there is a sense that you are only morally motivated to do good because of the consequences of future lifetimes. To me that has never been a reason for doing good.

The whole issue of reincarnation is a matter of supreme indifference to me. If anything I find it an enormous distraction. And a number of people I speak to say this is the idea that puts them off Buddhism. They say, 'I'm very drawn to the meditation, to the Emptiness, etc., but I could never bring myself to believe in something like reincarnation'. It goes against those elements in Buddhism which are pragmatic, direct, experiential and about transforming one's life here and now, about wisdom and compassion. What has reincarnation got to do with it?

To my mind reincarnation is simply part of the world view that the Buddha lived in. There's nowhere in the early or the later canon where the Buddha has to go out of his way to say what rebirth is, because everyone knew it was the case. I think he did believe in it. In the West, however, it has become a world view that I feel has become suffocating in some ways. The idea is central in the Tibetan and Theravadan traditions which are Indian-based, but if you train in Zen it's not such a big deal. The Zen Buddhists will go along with the idea but it's not in any way central to the practice. Someone like Thich Nat Hahn doesn't emphasize it—and he's supposed to be an authority in the field!

One of the problems when we say 'Why Buddhism?' is that people are often unaware of the considerable differences between the different approaches. The Tibetan view has a certain prominence at the moment and the big movies of recent times, *Little Buddha*, *Seven Years in Tibet* and *Kundun*, all focus on this idea of reincarnation. This mythos of reincarnation is always going to draw people to the movies. It's an immensely seductive idea.

In my view reincarnation severely limits the map. It gives you a metaphysical conception of what happens after death, which to me is a denial of death. Death is experientially something that is the most profound mystery of them all.

What I have made up my mind about is the fact that we stop. But what that is and what that means, I don't know. And I don't know what happens after death. If one lives one's life to the full, seeking to embody the ethical and spiritual values of Buddhism, then if there is a life afterwards then that is surely one of the best preparations you can have for it, but if there's not it doesn't matter either. I find having theoretical explanations for an afterlife slightly repellent in the sense that they try to envisage within the extremely limited confines of the human mind–brain something which by definition occurs after the human mind–brain has died. I think it's a human attempt to try to control the uncontrollable. I find death is enhanced in terms of its mysteriousness if we are able to confront it with totally open eyes and heart.

So, yes, I believe in continuation, karma and that what we do bears results, but do I have to believe in a little entity that hops from one body into another? I don't find the idea of this little individualized entity terribly useful.

Buddhists say, 'The full realization of Enlightenment is going to take far longer than a single human lifetime', but one can draw very different conclusions from that. One could say that therefore we need to create a culture in which the emergence and development of these values, their substantiation in the structure of our society, is a project to be carried over for many generations. It is something we need to work at for the sake of our children, for those who come after us, for the environment. One can draw a perfect non-reincarnation-based view of continuation. By abnegating the idea of 'my' continuity, 'my' coming back, you create the conditions whereby these values will flourish. Whether individuals will come back as Lama X and Lama Y is beside the point.

The real challenge for Buddhism in our times is to be able to find a communal and collective response to the various kinds of suffering that beset life on this earth, and that is something which needs more than my personal efforts. It requires the emergence of a culture of awakening —in politics, environment, culture, everything. That is the vital point.

We find ourselves in a time when the traditional religions of many cultures (the institutions of Christianity, Judaism, Islam and to some extent Buddhism too) have not really come to terms with the complex world that's been opened up in the twentieth century—what we now know about the nature of the cosmos, evolution, genetics and so on. Many are having a very hard time responding. Mostly they simply deny it. The challenge is to learn how this world view can be spiritualized. Where can we find ideas, insights, practices that are quite consonant with such a view of the world and which can be an integral part of this culture of awakening? Buddhism is in a very strong position to respond to this challenge. That's one of its principal attractions. Buddhism is the only world religion which has no theological objections to the discoveries of science. Strangely, the views of the universe and so on that scientists come up with are often strikingly resonant with traditional Buddhist ideas.

Take, for example, the idea of interdependence—the recognition of the world as an utterly interdependent, inter-related process in which every organism is somehow dependent on all others in an evolving, self-sustaining, self-healing process. That idea is so compellingly Buddhist it barely needs comment. The premise that there is no central governing agency making the thing tick is also very, very Buddhist. These scientific discoveries reinforce my confidence in what the Buddha was teaching. At the same time, though, it offers a challenge as to how we actually give rise to a system of ethics founded on complexity and unfindability, because traditional ethics, particularly in the West, have been premised on the certainty that there is some kind of god that underlies everything. I think Buddhism is in a position to work towards figuring that out. I find that very attractive, although I can't say much about it.

I think it will also entail considerable rethinking on the part of Buddhists as to what they do believe. One of the reasons why I find Buddhism attractive is because it is in a transitional stage. The institutions of Buddhism are still strong but there's also a recognition that one can't just preserve the past. It's a matter of considerably transforming what we know as Buddhism. It's early days. It's utterly impossible to predict what kind of Buddhism will emerge out of the meeting between science and a 2500-year-old tradition. We just don't know. It's very dangerous to approach this with any foregone conclusions. All we can do is to practice in the most sincere way we can and trust what will come out of that. It's about being quite radically honest with one's experience and also having a heartfelt confidence in the Dharma. 🙰

Being in the gateway

INTA McKIMM
A dying person full of joy

*T*he call was urgent: 'Get up here quickly! We don't think she has much time left'. Inta McKimm, a 71-year-old long-time Tibetan Buddhist practitioner from Brisbane, Queensland, was dying. A week previously I had heard that she was seriously ill, and had asked if she would share her thoughts on how her Buddhist faith was helping her at this significant time of her life. She had graciously agreed to be interviewed and said she was happy to share the insights that she was now experiencing. It was a golden opportunity. Death and dying are something of a speciality in Tibetan Buddhism. From the very beginning, followers are encouraged to look death squarely in the face through a series of graphic teachings and meditations, accepting the fact that death is definite but the time and place of death indefinite. The idea is to lessen the primal fear of our demise and to encourage us to live our lives with meaning. Inta would also be thoroughly familiar with the Buddhist description of the actual death process, which delineates in precise technical detail the sensations the dying person experiences as the mind or consciousness leaves the body, the visions that occur in the Bardo (the Between state) and the workings of rebirth. It is every Buddhist's wish to die with a peaceful mind, that state being deemed most beneficial to secure a happy future life. The more advanced meditator, however, actually trains to use the dying process, with the extremely subtle and clear mind that arises at that time, to achieve unparalleled levels of spiritual evolution. Whatever the level of advancement, all Buddhists agree on one thing—that we die as we have lived.

Within hours of getting the message, I had jumped on a plane and arrived at her Newmarket home, a 1920s wooden house built on stilts in the Queensland manner, surrounded by lush sub-tropical trees and bushes. I was curious but apprehensive about what I might find inside. When I walked into her bedroom, I thought there had been a mistake.

Inta McKimm, small, green-eyed and red-haired, was sitting up in bed glowing. Her eyes were clear and sparkling, her skin luminous, and her face bore an expression of puckish amusement. She was wearing dangly earrings, an elaborate necklace, gold eye-shadow and some exotic perfume. She looked like a young woman ready to go to a party, rather than someone preparing to meet the Grim Reaper. All around her was evidence of her faith. An altar beside her bed held water bowls, statues and flowers. There were photographs of various lamas around the room, and above her bed hung a painting of the Buddha.

In spite of appearances, the prognosis was indeed serious. Inta had been diagnosed with lung cancer, and two secondary tumours had appeared on her brain. Just four days earlier, a Tibetan lama from a nearby affiliated center had been summoned in the middle of the night to administer the Buddhist last rites. She had rallied but knew she did not have long. She was using the reprieve, she said, to learn her last lessons and to tie up all loose ends. 'The house was getting smaller and smaller and I was wondering how I could reduce myself further. Now, I've found a way,' she joked.

The atmosphere in the house was joyful. Since 1980 her home had doubled as the Langri Tangpa Center, a place for Buddhist teachings and meditations and now her students were treating Inta's pending death as a celebration. Under the supervision of her daughter Miffi, they were cheerfully going about getting her meals, administering her medicine, answering the telephone, taking in flowers and organizing the care roster. More significantly, they were also quietly and lovingly administering to her every spiritual need day and night: reading her prayers, leading her in various meditations, sitting cross-legged in the large shrine room outside her bedroom and dedicating their spiritual endeavors to Inta's successful death and rebirth. The topic of death was clearly not taboo, as the large printed message pinned over the dining-room table indicated:

Inta says she is beginning to die now. Try as much as possible not to be upset, so as not to disturb Inta's mind. People sitting in the house, please talk quietly and rejoice.

Inta had led a colorful, difficult life. Born in Latvia to a musicologist father and a socialite mother, she had run away after World War II both from an unhappy family life and an avenging Russian army by jumping on a ship headed for Australia. She was then aged sixteen. After a lonely and displaced start in her new country, Inta went on to train as a psychologist and then an acupuncturist. She specialized in Jungian psychotherapy and pioneered a Jungian/Buddhist technique called 'waking, dreaming' whereby she attempted to bridge Western and Eastern approaches to spiritual well-being. Always creative, Inta designed and made jewellery and clothes, and frequented Melbourne's avant-garde theatre and music scene. Her first marriage to a fellow Latvian ended in divorce. Alcohol and abuse were a factor. Her daughter by that marriage was taken by her husband's family. After the marriage break-up, Inta saw her only once when the daughter was thirteen. Her second marriage to jazz trumpeter Barry McKimm, fifteen years younger, lasted thirteen years and produced her second daughter, Miffi.

It was Buddhism, however, which she encountered in 1974 when the Tibetan lamas made their first visit to Australia, which was the strongest single influence in her life. She was so convinced of its message that she started the first meditation group in Melbourne, and went on to become the director of the Langri Tangpa Center in Brisbane, part of a worldwide network of Tibetan Buddhist centers under the umbrella title of the FPMT (the Foundation for the Preservation of the Mahayana Tradition). As a pioneer in bringing Tibetan Buddhism to Australia, Inta met and hosted many high-ranking lamas including the Gyuto tantric monks, from Dharamsala whose massed reverberating tones 'almost took the roof of my house off'.

By the time I met her, Inta had been a sincere Buddhist for more than 25 years, having attended numerous courses, taken several initiations and conducted various retreats. Her guru, Lama Zopa Rinpoche, a Sherpa from the Mount Everest region of Nepal whom she had met on her first course, was pivotal in her Buddhist education. Within the Tibetan Buddhist tradition the role of the guru is regarded as paramount in guiding the disciple through the rapids of life and death. On hearing of Inta's illness, Lama Zopa had duly responded in his own inimitable way. His letter to her was now a source of great comfort and inspiration:

My very dear Inta,
    I don't know how to say how sorry I am and how

fantastic it is that you have found this disease. As a Dharma practitioner it may be good to study the thought transformation of how to utilize sickness as a means for causing happiness to all sentient beings including bringing them to Enlightenment. In this way you use your sickness to practice Bodhicitta, which means experiencing the illness on behalf of all sentient beings.

So you can do these things to make basic preparation. These are the most important. Think, this is your best retreat, 100 times more powerful than years of doing Vajrasattva [the Buddha of Purification] retreat with a self-centered mind, with a comfortable life, and so forth. Because here the fundamental practice is that you give your life to other sentient beings. You give your happiness to others and experience their sufferings yourself. Like the earth, the fundamental practice is Bodhicitta, exchanging oneself with others.

Lama Zopa went on to tell several stories of famous Buddhists of the past, including the Buddha, who had carried out supremely selfless acts. He also gave detailed instructions on specific mantras and visualization practices Inta could do. He ended his letter thus:

Then, when it is time, maybe it is better for you to lie down like Guru Shakyamuni Buddha did, in the lion position [on the right side, with the right hand under the head, the little finger blocking the right nostril] when passing away in the sorrowless state. That helps the mind to be transferred into virtue more easily. It reminds you of Buddha, and so also leaves a positive imprint. It is easier to stop attachment, anger and so forth. Unless you would prefer the sitting position. But generally it is better to die in the lion position as the Buddha did.

Like this, go ahead. Enjoy your death. Make the best use of it; take the greatest profit from it. Like the most successful business person in the world, become a billionaire. I will pray for you. Don't worry. You met His Holiness the Dalai Lama, Lama Yeshe and many other great Bodhisattvas. You met the Mahayana [the 'great vehicle' of Buddhism practiced in Tibet], heard complete teachings on the complete path, specialized in the quickest path to Enlightenment. So you have prepared so much, done lots of meditation on the Lam Rim [the graduated path to Enlightenment], benefited lots of people. Rejoice in this many times every day.

I want to say thank you very much for everything. Your own practice and your help have benefited so many people and the organization. Since there has been much karmic connection, we may meet somewhere. Please enjoy. Good luck. With much love and prayers, Lama Zopa.

The interviews were conducted over a period of three days and nights. They were interspersed with many breaks for tea, coffee, packaged soup and marzipan (Inta's favorite fare), as well as make-up sessions and lots of laughter.

❀

"*I* am as well now as I ever have been. Life is happy, ecstatically happy. I never imagined it would be like this at the end. It's an incredible surprise. I thought death would be a drab experience, a bleaching out. But it's not at all! Everything I ever wished for is arriving in abundance. It is all becoming simpler, clearer and much more beautiful.

It's ridiculous really. Quite crazy! I'm dying, there's no denying it. When I get out of bed I wobble all over the place. The tumours that are pressing on my brain mean I can't see properly. The cancer in my lung, which doctors tell me is the size of a large apple, is creating pressure all around my body and if it weren't for the medication I'd cough myself to death in two minutes flat. There is a little pain, not much, but pain is no big thing. Dying is such a celebration. I'm freeing myself from all the things that cluttered me up. I wish everyone could experience what I'm going through. I wouldn't want anyone to miss out on death!

The happiness is coming from the guru and the guru's teaching. Most definitely. It started when I let go of the illusion that I could extend my life, the moment I recognized that, 'Yes, I am going to die and I am going to die very soon. I am mortal and nothing can change that. It's the universal law'. That was the big breakthrough, the freeing agent, because I could no longer magic up a map of unreality with all the frustrations that come from that continuous fabrication. There was nothing for it but to pull out all attachments to this life, and that is basic Buddhism. Lama Zopa, my guru, has said over and over again that to be happy we have to break the attachment to this life. Before now, however, it has all been academic!

Of course, the first instant of that knowledge really hurts. It is like the pain of breaking up with a lover that you really care for; the same sort of anguish. But when you have cut the clinging, the pain disappears. And when the pain disappears there is nothing left to fear. All that is left then is pure love and compassion for the suffering of others, Bodhicitta as it is called, because that same fear and anguish is what everyone entertains. Bodhicitta is the only thing that makes sense and it has to be generated within because no one else can give it to us. I now know that I have to feel Bodhicitta towards every living particle, without discrimination, including those things we deem imperfect. I have to love even my cancer cells, because they need love as much as anything else.

Knowing I was ill came fairly quickly in one way, but in another sense I had known it for years, without it disturbing me. It was simply something that was happening which I didn't need to jiggle with or try to fix up. Then last September, when the Dalai Lama came to Sydney to give the Kalachakra Initiation, I knew that something was seriously wrong. Now, I am an amateur painter and for some reason I was urged to paint the Kalachakra deity, which is extremely complicated, with many different faces all having different expressions. I knew it was a matter of time as to who would get there first, death or the painting, so I made a pact with Kalachakra himself to allow me to finish the work. He kept his side of the bargain. At the end of January the painting was completed and I was diagnosed with cancer and given two to three months to live. I believe that the Kalachakra painting was something really worthwhile that I had to do before I died.

When I think about dying I am not afraid, not at all. How could I be? I have never been so happy. And the happiness is growing. I am dropping all the loads. I've recently become especially interested in the film *Wings of Desire*, which is about angels hovering all around us ready to help. I never used to believe in angels but I do now, although I hate the term! Jung talked about a collective unconscious, but I now know with absolute confidence that there is a collective conscious which is basic goodness, and it's there all the time for everyone. Until I began to experience dying I never knew goodness like this existed or that it was the reality of life. It is so unexpected. Before I got only glimpses of it through the lamas' teachings, but the closer I get to finishing up, the clearer it becomes. I now know that suffering is a myth, a complete untruth, it's a glimmer in the light. We seem to have to go through the business of suffering in order to try to understand it—but it's a non-existent thing in its ultimate reality. It has no substantial cause. I really want to tell people how incredibly beautiful, happy and full of love life really is, but it's becoming difficult to communicate. Being in the gateway, as it were, my perceptions are now coming very fast, and the words often can't keep up.

It's strange I've seen all this only as the end of this life is approaching. If only I could have known it sooner, but I suppose that's not the way. I have done countless death meditations which are aimed at making us realize that death is a reality, that we only have 'now' and to drop all the nonsense. But we don't do it. We think death is going to happen in the next ten or twenty years, so the immediacy that could propel us into direct understanding isn't there. We're still lulling ourselves with false hopes—buying a new dress, getting a new car, going on holiday, whatever we think is going to make us happy.

Before it happens I am using the time left to prepare. Lama Zopa has told me to enjoy my death and I'm trying to do just that. I lie here looking at beautiful pictures of the Buddhas, seeing beyond their representations. I watch videos of the Dalai Lama and the young reincarnate lamas who have been reborn to teach others the way out of suffering. I'm enjoying the incredible goodwill of all the people who come to see me. I am bathing in the happiness of all the little things that are around me. I turn on the bathroom tap and the water has a pure quality I've never heard before. Even the noise of the traffic has become like music. It's as though all sounds have become pure sounds. My home has become a pure abode.

All the meetings I have with people now have become so meaningful. It's like an exchange of gifts. I try to say something significant to each one of them—an insight into their lives, a helpful hint, a guideline. It seems that my intuitive understanding is coming more to the fore now, and I no longer fear what I have to say, so long as it's based in goodness and not malice. Even with people I have no particular affinity with, I find there is a warmth there and something useful to exchange. It's as if all the bits of my life are now being used for positive purposes.

It is not continuously like this, of course. I am not a Buddha! There are moments when my energy sinks, usually in the middle of the night. I call these times my 'little Bardos', my little between-states, and use them as mini-previews of my death. They give me the chance to rework something in the right way, another opportunity 'to transform the problem into the path of Enlightenment' as the teachings instruct us to do. Instead of being bowed down by difficulties that confront you, you learn to utilize them for positive ends. It's the way of transformation, which no one can ever take away from you. It goes on for ever.

I say prayers every day and do specific tantric practices which I've been initiated into. I can't do the extended versions because the physical symptoms of my illness make it hard for me to be as concentrated as I used to be. But it doesn't matter, there's nothing like years of familiarization, and I've discovered the trick of going fast, which helps convey the meaning very well. Actually, at one stage I became quite disoriented and confused which was frightening. The last bastion of security, my identity, was threatened. It was good that it happened, because then I had to come to terms with it. My personal identity was one more thing that I could hook onto. I had to let it go too. Now I have medication to keep the disorientation at bay.

I am also following a wonderful practice called the Five Powers at Death. In it you start by giving things away. I made up a list of who was going to get what, spent a little time refining it, and then did it. It has been a wonderful freedom. There is nothing to clutter up my mind any more. My mother, who is 94, is in turmoil because she can't send me her tea service and is worried that all the relatives are going to try to appropriate it. She doesn't realize that the tea service is the last thing I want! I have also planned my funeral service. I have a couple of outrageous pieces that I want performed, including Nick Cave's 'Mack the Knife', which represents to me the epitome of the suffering of this life—Samsara, as it's called in Buddhism. It's where we all start from. The service will end with a tape of Lama Zopa reciting an esoteric prayer—the Praises to Palden Lhamo, a female tantric deity— which will be a pacifying agent and a resolution. The order of the funeral service I hope will represent the journey we all make from suffering to peace and happiness.

The Five Powers at Death also teach you not to be attached to any person, especially your friends and family, because it will only hinder you when you have to part. Buddhism maintains it's best to go forward into death as freely as possible. It's argued that we are doing this constant leaving anyway, from one life to the next, and so there is no need to get overly sad about our present departure. For me this lesson has been quite easy. I learnt non-attachment fairly early on in the piece.

I hear the sounds of the students having their meetings outside my bedroom door, and hearing their voices is a delightful habit, but it's not something I need. It is like having a lovely cup to drink out of. You enjoy it but you do not have to go on doing it for ever. Even Miffi, my daughter, I'm not sad to leave. Although we have many interests in common, we have always been able to live happily without one another. Frankly, that's a help at this time. When I was giving out pieces of advice to my students I got this nagging feeling that I had forgotten someone. It was quite a shock to realize it was my own daughter. Now I understand there was a reason why she had to be left to last. At the beginning mothers have to learn to let their children go, and at the end of life the roles are reversed and children (and students in my case) have to let the mother or teacher go. It is very important for my peace of mind that they are not clinging, but allowing me to move on.

Why Buddhism? In Buddhism I found all the answers I was looking for. I tried and tested many different avenues in life. In that respect I was a bit of a hedonist. I wanted to be aware of as many diverse aspects of life as I could. I've had various careers and numerous interests, many of which have been intellectual and brilliant. Whatever I tried, however, I always felt there was something missing. I had a sense of frustration and I kept wondering what it was. Even Jungian psychology, which I had a very good grasp of, did not have everything. In Buddhism, however, everything was there. Whatever question cropped up I found that if I applied the method, Buddhism always delivered the goods.

To my mind Buddhism is the most advanced spiritual psychology imaginable. I don't know if anything will ever catch up. Its potency is tremendous. The more you look into it the more it reveals. It is a never ending source.

On a personal level I would have been a total wreck in many ways if I hadn't had Buddhism. It has been quite a rotten life in some respects! The teachings have given me a method of dealing with, and releasing, all the harsh things that have happened to me.

To start with, my childhood was really traumatic. My parents were cold and extremely ambitious in a social sense. There wasn't much space for me at all. In fact, the feeling of neglect and personal misery was so strong that I often wondered if I were an orphan. I can remember several incidents which totally broke my heart and once I cried for six hours non-stop. Sometimes I wonder if all the sadness I experienced then wasn't the nucleus for cancer. The lungs, after all, have to do with emotion.

My best memories of my childhood are about the times when my parents were absent. They used to go out to parties and then I was free. Then my life began. My grandmother, my uncle and I would get together and have a terrific time. My uncle would play Chopin's 'Funeral March', which was the only piano piece he knew apart from 'Chopsticks', and I would do what they called my 'elephant lily dance'. I was a chubby little girl and was born partially deaf, so I wasn't very graceful at all! I would stomp all over the flat, making the floorboards shake. It was great fun. For a short time I could do something without being criticized for not being perfect. I suppose my parents thought success in all things would bring me happiness, but it was the bane of my life.

My grandmother was the only person I have trusted in my life, apart from Lama Zopa. It was my grandmother who taught me that I could curl up in bed at night and get rid of the fears of the day through saying prayers. My parents were atheists but my grandmother was a Christian of a rather unorthodox sort. That was extremely precious, and I am extremely grateful to her for it.

After that there was the unhappiness of being a young migrant in Australia. When I first arrived I couldn't speak the language and so was very lonely and felt extremely displaced. There were many things I had to go through to rehabilitate myself both in my own eyes and in the eyes of society. There have also been personal disappointments—several unhappy relationships, including two broken marriages and being separated from my first daughter; the pain of wanting control over relationships, and never getting it. There was lack of recognition, the feeling that everyone can have a good time except me!—you know, all the sufferings that everyone has. The same old story.

The trigger which started me off on the Buddhist path was the book *The Third Eye* by Lobsang Rampa. I was absolutely fascinated by it. It changed my life quite forcibly for about a fortnight and left a strong imprint. The next landmark, although I did not realize it at the time, occurred when I was doing Hatha Yoga for health reasons. I had a vision of a beautiful, youthful green woman, who I later discovered was Tara, the female Buddha of compassionate action. What particularly captivated me, however, was the exquisite and interesting jewellery she was wearing! Nothing else. I looked at it really closely and hurried off to copy it. I've still got the necklace hanging over there on the bedroom wall.

Shortly after I started looking for gurus, because everyone had one. It was the early 1970s, and gurus were coming in droves to Melbourne, where I lived. As usual I felt I was missing out because I didn't have one! I came across a swami from Sri Lanka actually by going to a 'wrong' address. He laughed and told me it wasn't a mistake at all but a 'divine accident'. I invited him to teach at my house for a while and he was instrumental in putting me in touch with the basic Buddhist view of things, including vegetarianism.

The biggest turning point, however, happened less than

a year after I met the swami, in 1974, when I went to Diamond Valley in Queensland to attend a meditation course given by two Tibetan lamas, Lama Thubten Yeshe and his heart disciple Lama Zopa Rinpoche. After that it was all set. I knew as soon as I set eyes on Lama Zopa that this was something I had hoped and longed for all my life—and it was happening now. Meeting Lama Zopa was like a homecoming. Before me I saw a person who I could trust completely. And then the teachings! I would cry every day as soon as I walked into the gompa [shrine room] out of sheer relief. People thought I was having a terrible time on that first meditation course but it was one of my happiest times ever.

The Buddhist idea of guru devotion started then, quite spontaneously, and has been developing ever since. Before me I saw this kind, kind being, who was enabling me to understand that the things that were lacking in my life weren't lacking in me, which I thought was the case. They were just lacking. Lama Zopa subsequently stayed at my house (which I turned over to a Buddhist center) a few times, and he has shown me what a human being can be. He embodies unconditional love with a lot of outrageous fun. Lama Zopa is very capable of having a good time, in a very natural, playful way. Every insight, every piece of happiness and wisdom that's happened to me since has been through the kindness of the guru.

Having a guru when you are dying is an indescribable

blessing. Although he's not physically present, I feel he is with me all the time. Whenever I need reassurance he is here instantly, giving me strength. At the beginning I had to have his image before me to remind myself how he looked and how I related to him. Like the teachings, Lama Zopa was external. Now he and the teachings have become an inner reality, a source that doesn't end. At the same time there is still this outer being to whom I have infinite gratitude because without him it would not have happened.

His letter to me shocked me into viewing my death as an opportunity. That first line he wrote was startling: 'My very dear Inta, I don't know how to say how sorry I am and how fantastic it is that you have found this disease'. Then I saw the reality of what he has said. His shock tactics woke me up, and brought clarity beyond my normal level of functioning. Because what he had said was true, I couldn't ignore it.

The cat lying here beside me shows me so much. In one sense it is a limited being insofar as it does not have much understanding. It's just doing what it needs to do. But in that act of being what it is, it has perfect goodness, and the perfect reason for existing. We don't have to do all this striving. We don't have to keep fixing things up. In essence we are OK as we are. In all this doing we have forgotten how to be.

When I actually begin to die I feel absolutely confident that Lama Zopa will be with me, to help and guide. The connection has been established and it will never cease. Even now when I have an important issue to work out he appears in my dreams, compassionate and even-minded, giving me advice, telling me where I am going wrong. I trust in him because he has the bigger picture, which I haven't.

Death itself is the biggest adventure. How successful I am is a matter of how well I can sustain the mind I have now. It is all in the mind—it's nowhere else. What will happen is a question of my spiritual development. Tibetan Buddhism has a very scientific approach to the death process. I've been trained in that I hope I can take note of what's happening rather than being overwhelmed or submerged in the experience. I've tried to memorize the major guidelines so that they are really encoded in my mind, for me to rely on. I don't know whether I am adept enough to be able to meditate on the clear light that appears at the end of the death process, but what I hope to do is to try as much as possible to have a non-contrived awareness. If I could drop all expectations, intellectually acquired and otherwise, there would be no problem. If I can stay in as natural a state as possible, that would be ideal. I don't want to wish or will myself to do anything because what I am aiming for is to leave myself out of the picture completely. Letting go of my identity is the big one. I hope I can do it!

I'm going into the unknown, certainly, but don't we always? There is no need to be afraid. Lama Zopa has said I have been a good Buddhist, and I think I have become quite a good person at the end of my life. I have done a lot of practices, heard many teachings, and done quite a few retreats during the past 25 years and I trust in all of that. I have complete confidence and reliance on the teachings. In all my 71 years the teaching is the only thing that hasn't deceived me and I can't see that is going to change now.

There is a lot of talk of the hell realms in Buddhism, but personally I'm not scared. I have done a lot of purification practices to help eliminate the negative imprints on my mind stream, which is the best protection technique you could have. Of course, it is possible that when my energy gets weaker the negativities will come up, but I don't think they will be gross nor a real threat. Beside, I've been taught that whatever visions appear, be they peaceful or wrathful, are all illusory, a dream, so I feel I am well armored.

I don't actually know what is going to happen to me after death. Buddhism teaches Rebirth—that our mind or consciousness, which is not material, separates from the body at death and continues. The mind, they say, is a continuum changing from moment to moment. It makes perfect sense to me. You can observe it in daily life, the flow of consciousness continually changing, it is not fragmented. Nothing suddenly stops and starts. Where I end up, however, is in my hands. From my dreams and my own life experience I have a feeling where this continuity might be heading, although I don't think about it obsessively. Since I was a child I wanted to be a doctor and some sort of a preacher, and I managed to fulfil those two strands by studying

acupuncture and teaching Buddhism and Jungian psychology.
I feel those characteristics will continue and be more
developed in the next life.

Most of all I hope to meet up with Buddhism again, to
be reconnected to my spiritual lineage so that I can get the
true Dharma. That's the most important thing. It is only
through meeting the teachings, wherever that may be, that
my own spiritual evolution can progress.

Yes it would be very nice to go to a pure land, and maybe
I could learn faster there. But what I want more than anything
at this point is to return here. There are so many things to
do, so many areas where help is necessary, from insects
upwards. I really hope that I can carry through all the
wonderful things that I have understood in these past few
weeks and come back to show that suffering is an illusion
and that life is fundamentally good. I must put this
understanding to good use, it's my obligation. Otherwise what
have all these valuable insights at the end of my life been for?

I really hope, however, that I am going to be more
materially comfortable. In this life I thought there was some
kind of virtue in being hard up and I definitely want to modify
that. Computers also fascinate me so I hope to steer myself
towards doing something with them.

Every day it feels as if the little doors of my life are
opening, like in the Christmas cards. When they are all open,
this life will be complete and the mandala of my life will
be revealed. ”

MIFFI MAXMILLION
Inta McKimm's daughter

Inta's daughter, Miffi Maxmillion, a couturier for stage artists, rushed up from Melbourne when she heard of her mother's illness. As a child who was brought up 'bouncing on the knees of visiting lamas', Miffi is a first-generation Buddhist. Somewhere in her hectic schedule of taking care of Inta and running the center, she found time to talk about how Buddhism was helping her deal with her mother's imminent death.

*It was on my birthday, the 26th of April, that the telephone rang with the news that Inta had terminal lung cancer. I found myself very inappropriately excited. This was the big gig! We had had all the rehearsals with the death meditations for years and years, now the show was on. Furthermore, it was Inta's show! My job in all of this is being the stagehand. I've got to make it as easy for her as possible.

Although I've taken over running the center which is extremely hectic, planning the details of Inta's death and dying has been easy. It's both a privilege and a joyful experience. When I came up we got the giggles for the whole of the first day. I spend a lot of time with her going through the photograph albums, plucking her eyebrows, putting on her make-up, doing her hair. We crack very bad-taste death jokes and laugh a lot, finding plenty of humor and ridiculousness in our situation. Sometimes it feels as if Inta and I are the two happiest people at the center!

When I was young I was very committed. I did retreats and daily meditations. I guess something must have gone in. I have always loved the gompa [shrine room] with all the ritual that goes on there. I could sit in all-night pujas [prayer ceremonies] with the candles, the gongs and trumpets for ever! I remember when I went to my first disco I was completely nonplussed. It just didn't compare. It didn't make me go 'Wow!' like the pujas did. To me as a kid, they were the ultimate party. When you're a child you don't have to think about a puja or what it means, you just go for it. Being brought up in Buddhism, I of course rebelled against it as a teenager. I desperately wanted to be a nun at ten, but when I turned twelve I changed my mind. I put the whole lot on the back burner and after a while took it out to see what was left. I reckoned that whatever the philosophy was, the lamas were great. My belief in them was unshakeable. Then two things happened. I got the guts to argue with the teachers on points I disagreed with. And I got into physics, maths and things like the chaos theory. Suddenly I saw what the lamas were getting at when they talked about everything being impermanent and there being a non-existent 'I'. Buddhism then became a checklist for all the things I got enthusiastic about in physics. If it happened in Buddhism and physics, then it was obviously true. The two strands of thought were coming from different directions and if they joined up I'd accept them. Buddhism now has to be put in Western terms for it to be relevant to me.

I believe we are all traveling through different bodies and Inta's death is like a send-off of your best friend to a very special place. It is not a horrific instant death, she is not in a coma. She has time to prepare and the road map is there. It's perfect, the most fortuitous circumstances ever. Inta is totally prepared. She has studied the teachings and meditations on the inevitability of death and the death process. She has 100 per cent guru devotion. Lama Zopa asks after her every day, sends her cards, and phones from time to time. She is surrounded by incredible love.

The idea of her not being here doesn't upset me at all. I'm a bit astonished at how un-sad I am. Just because someone isn't physically present, it doesn't mean they are not close. It's factual. Inta is old and she is going to die. I'm her attendant in this. Inta brought me into this life and I am helping her out of it. It's really very easy for me. I'm only 30 and it will only take a few weeks or a few months. It's nothing. Around the center I've gone into practical mode. One of my main aims is to ensure that people rejoice at this time. I've been quite strict about people not being upset around Inta. It's just self-indulgent, dramatic, romantic and brings no results. This is Inta's show—she comes first and is not to be bogged down with heavy emotion!

To my mind death is like dreaming. Sometimes it scares

me. The trick of it is not to be attached to going unconscious, but to dip into another type of consciousness. I think Inta's willpower, tenacity and good heart will get her there. I observe that she is dying as she has lived. As the big project gets closer, she is becoming faster and faster, getting into a flap about details that I have to try to talk her out of. But out of what looks like superficial chaos, everything magically works out. It always has. I am also waiting for the twist just before the end! **99**

Inta McKimm died at 11 a.m. on 2 August 1997. Her breathing remained strong until the last, when she suddenly opened her eyes very wide and clear. An Australian nun, who was in the room, Yeshe Khadro (a director of a Buddhist hospice), rushed to her side and spoke the name of her guru and her preferred mantra into her ear. That was it. Inta remained fearless until the end. Miffi reported that the atmosphere in the room was 'amazingly strong and very gentle'. Prayers and mantras had been said by her bedside around the clock in the day preceding her death, and they were continued for several hours afterwards. Contrary to all civil customs in a Western culture (and exhortations from medics), Miffi did not move Inta's body until she felt the death process was truly over and Inta's meditation was complete. On Monday, 4 August at 9.30 a.m. a trickle of blood and fluid came from Inta's nostril—the classic Buddhist sign that the subtle consciousness had finally left the body. The lama who presided over the funeral commented that Inta had had an excellent death and was clearly a special practitioner.

Unencumbered by guilt

CLIVE ARROWSMITH
Photographer

Some years ago rumour reached me that famous fashion photographer Clive Arrowsmith could be spotted in a London Buddhist center doing prostrations and saying prayers. I was intrigued. 'The Arrow', as he's known in the trade, is one of the brilliant British photographers of the David Bailey circle, known as much for their flamboyant lifestyle as their talent. All were pretty much *enfants terribles*. Born in North Wales and trained in art, Clive has photographed more models than he can possibly remember, been featured in glossy magazines on both sides of the Atlantic, been the only photographer to shoot the prestigious Pirelli Calendar twice in succession, and was appointed the official photographer of Prince Charles's fiftieth birthday celebration. He boasts umpteen smart advertizing clients, has been married four times and has seven children (he thinks). Top of the list of celebrities that he's photographed and that he names on his CV, however, is the Dalai Lama.

I interviewed Clive one Saturday morning in his large flat, one of several in what looked like a converted stately home, in the unlikely south London suburb of Clapham. In the center of his sitting room stood a large Buddha statue, in front of which Clive had set up his altar, complete with pictures of various Tibetan deities, rows of water-bowl offerings, and personal spiritual memorabilia. On his mantelpiece were photographs of several Tibetan lamas, including his guru, Rato Rinpoche. On the wall was a sign: 'Don't be frightened, get enlightened'. And against the back wall, rather incongruously amid all this unabashed Buddhism, was a life-size antique statue of Christ revealing the sacred heart.

Clive himself beamed warmth and welcome. A large man with long gray hair and blue eyes, he was sporting tracksuit trousers, trainers, two days' growth and a wrist rosary for counting mantras. The interview can only be described as a romp. Clive was funny, self-deprecating, spontaneous and refreshingly frank, particularly about his former fondness for drugs and alcohol and his relationships with women, whom he openly adores. He also spoke as fast as a camera motor drive, whirring out ideas, flashes of insight and witty asides at a rate which was most alarming for an interviewer trying to keep track of the conversation and any thread of argument which might be in existence. Every now and again he would leap up to show me something or to display the latest photograph he had on his computer, playing around with the technology, giving Prince Charles a third eye in the middle of his forehead. All the time his fourteen-year-old son, Paris, also a Buddhist, read quietly in the background. They were clearly very close.

For all his flamboyance, after several hours of talking I was left with the impression that for Clive Arrowsmith Buddhism was no fashionable faith. 'It is more important than my career. Without it, life is ridiculous,' he stated quietly. As I walked away his words came echoing down the hall after me: 'Buddha's blessings,' he shouted.

❋

"*T*he moment I saw Rato Rinpoche, I knew I was home. That was it. I had always wanted to be a Buddhist ever since I first heard the name 'Buddha'. When I was eight I looked into the mirror in the wardrobe at my grandma's house and thought, 'Who are you?' I thought, 'That's not you'. At the time it was an extraordinary revelation. When I was older I realized this was the quest of Shakyamuni Buddha—the search to find out who and what we really are, the discovery of our true nature. But Buddhism, especially Tibetan Buddhism, had always fascinated me, and books such as *The Tantras of Great Liberation* and the biography of Tibet's famous eleventh-century yogi, Milarepa, were perpetually by my bed.

I was brought up as a very Welsh Methodist in a family which had been steeped in religion for hundreds of years. There was Arrowsmith's Chapel in the town (my grandfather and my great-grandfather were preachers), and my religious education consisted of having to wear black on Sunday, not playing ball, not doing this, not doing that. But I never liked God very much. He was always so vengeful, smiting people down, and doing dreadful things. I once heard His Holiness the Dalai Lama say that any path that does any harm to the practitioner, or indeed anybody in any way, could not be a true path. That was a great comfort. Getting rid of God was a tremendous relief because Buddhism posits that the very notion of a first principle is illogical. If you believe in a Creator you come down to the question 'Who creates the creator?' It doesn't make sense. Letting God go was a little frightening at first, but I wasn't struck by a meteorite or anything.

As I was growing up I had lots of experiences which could be described as mystical. When I was about twenty I opened a book about the Andromeda Spiral, the spiral galaxy, and as I was looking at it it seemed to rush at me sucking me into it. I wasn't stoned or drunk in those days, so it was rather scary. There was this sense of not having control of anything, of being 'got' but at the same time realizing I was still there and that everything was all right. (Rather like getting a bank statement that says you're vastly overdrawn and feeling you're going to be killed instantly and then realizing a split second later, 'No, it's OK, I'm still alive'.) I think it was similar to the Emptiness experience that Buddhism talks about. You realize that you are the one who's receiving and conceiving all these different stimuli in your mind stream. In the most normal, basic sense the mind manufactures the Universe as it goes along. The mind modifies and transforms itself. We make our own heaven and our own hell. It is all imputation. Some people hate the stink of whisky, others can't live without it. Some people adore football, personally I cannot stand it nor the mentality that goes with it, but it has to be tolerated. It's all imputation. Nothing has any inherent quality of its own.

In the 1970s I had other experiences brought on by various potions, which showed me that my mind was not as I normally perceived it to be. There were visions of being above the Earth, of feeling overwhelmed by the beauty and vastness of the Universe, things like that.

I wanted to be like a mystic. I used to sit upstairs in front of a blank wall in a Japanese way and try to meditate. It was terribly pretentious. I didn't have a clue what Zen was about, although I was interested in that too. I also had various Indian teachings and read people like Sri Ramakrishna. Then, through knowing the Beatles (I had been at art college with John Lennon), I got involved with the Hare Krishnas. I was taking a picture of Phil Spector for his albums *Back to Mono* and *A Christmas Gift for You* and George Harrison was sitting there being very peaceful and chanting Hare Krishna. I thought it was very beautiful and tranquil and told him so.

The next thing I knew he had sent the old white Beatles limo around with intructions on how to chant, 'Hare is like Hare, Krishna is like Krishna'. So I began to do that.

And then thirteen years ago, I was going through this traumatic divorce with my third wife Annie (who had given up her career as a top model to follow the Maharishi) when a special thing happened. A book came through the post— it was *Transforming Problems*, by someone called Lama Zopa Rinpoche. The title jumped out at me and as I was willing to try anything to pull the marriage together, I rang the publisher and asked if there was a Buddhist center in London. They directed me to Jamyang Meditation center, which was then in Finsbury Park but is now in Kennington. I went there with my son Paris, who was about one, and as we walked through the door I was told that on that particular day a lama called Rato Rinpoche was visiting from New York. I knew from my reading that Rinpoche meant 'precious one', so I went in and that was it. Phew. As soon as I saw him I knew that here was something very genuine, very extraordinary and very special. The very next day I photographed him. I don't want to sound like a Hollywood movie, but my eyes filled with tears and I thought, 'Well, there we are!' I didn't have to think about it, analyze it.

The fact was that when I saw Rato Rinpoche I knew all other paths were gone. What I saw in him was the truth of a man in the phenomenal world existing and interfacing with all different situations. In a flash I knew that this was my guide—this was my salvation. There it was, straightaway, there, at that moment in time. I now know that Rato Rinpoche has always been there and that I've been gradually getting closer and closer like a guided missile. I believe there is a spark of light within everybody which is there constantly and which is in fact their root guru, their teacher—whether they have met him or not. Initially I was rather tentative about admitting Rato Rinpoche was my master. The first time I did, I got goose pimples. Once I addressed him publicly as 'Master' and he quietly reprimanded me. 'Don't call me that', he said. A true master is very unassuming. He's like the air you breathe; he's in every pore.

It was synchronicity. It all came together. There was so much that appealed. I always instinctively felt that Buddhism was a clear path unencumbered by guilt. To me the past was past, the future was yet to come and there was no point in repressing your defects because if you repress anything it will explode and you'll end up in a ward. When I heard that was a Buddhist teaching, I thought it was great. The Buddha said we just have to transform and purify all that we've done in our past and constantly, every day try to rectify our negativities. Eventually, when you become good at meditation, you enter a pure realm where everything is transformed. Then the mind becomes so tranquil you are able to see things as they really are.

As I began to practice I thought, 'This is exactly as I always believed things should be'. Besides Dharma is so beautiful. It grows and grows, but you've got to persevere. It's like learning to play the guitar. At first you're not very good at it but you lumber on doing the best you can and you get more proficient until one day you can actually play the most beautiful piece of music. And that music will inspire you. That's what happens with the Dharma.

It's not some peace, love, dove, groovy, freak, crashpad, incense-burning thing. Buddhism is real, otherwise I wouldn't do it. I'm a very busy photographer. I haven't got time for anything that doesn't work. If I buy a camera, like a Hasselblad, I buy it because it is efficient. You can replace the cogs—it works. If I buy a car, I buy a Mercedes because I have faith in it as a reliable machine. In the Adamantine Vehicle [the Diamond Path of Tibetan Buddhism] you will find the most reliable, perfect machine which enables you to endure all situations that arise and which allows you to enter dimensions that your mind has not even conceived of at this stage of development.

Buddhism has made a huge difference to my work. Before I was a bit out of it, to say the least. I used to shout at everyone, including fashion editors, tell them to bugger off, and be absolutely awful, crazed out from various substances. I was very offhand and arrogant, and I've suffered from that negative karma. I've had to claw my way back to working with some of the major companies again. Now I try to develop patience as the Buddha said you should, especially when shoots are going badly, and as a result things work much better. The ego is still there, of course (this is a creative profession), but if someone says, 'No, we don't want the picture like that, we want it like this', I now look to the Dharma for a matrix to be able to make it work. In the old days I would have said, 'I don't do those kind of pictures', and the whole thing would have collapsed in a mass of contention. Now I'll say to the client, 'Can I show you how I would like to see it?' and I give them my view. I try not to be dictatorial, because I've learnt that we're all potential Buddhas. And because of my attitude, they calm down and the miraculous thing can happen where we'll meld our views together without it being homogenized to the point where it's watered down. Instead it emerges as a new thing. That is what Buddhism is trying to do—foster co-operation and understanding. When you look at the history of Planet Earth, all contentions have been to no avail. In the end, sound, gentle, kindness works over a longer period of time.

My photography has improved. It's expanded. I'm more competent than I've ever been and will get something out of the most dreadful circumstances—even a thunderstorm. Before, I was a bit frantic (still am), rather like a gunfighter shooting and randomly hitting the target. Buddhism has given me the application so that I get all the techniques right without losing the verve and inspiration, I now lay the ground out carefully and from that planning I get a better picture. It's applying yourself to a situation and not being distracted. Buddhism says you have to make the preparation if you want the best result. It's so totally practical and methodical. Now when I take the picture it's like the mongoose and cobra, we move together. Me and the sitter are in union, as in yoga, and from that union you get a picture which has 'moment'.

'Moment' is hard to explain but it's what I've always admired in artists like Leonardo da Vinci and Caravaggio. People queue up to see the *Mona Lisa*, which I know is a corny picture because it's been seen so many times, but it still has tremendous 'moment' about it. A picture is just marks on film or paper—but a great picture lifts you to somewhere else. The marks have been put there in such a way that they elevate you to another state. That's due to the techniques and skill of the artist and it's what I'm trying to do. I don't agree at all with the Christian adage that you must not create any graven image. In pictures I can create other universes for people. I think the visions of artists have inspired people down the ages. I'm not saying that I'm a great artist, but I used to be a painter and when I turned to photography I used classical kind of lighting and I've never strayed from that. For me every job, even if I don't get it right, is still a Sistine Chapel. I am so obsessed by making it fantastic. So photography is right for me and there's no discrepancy between it and Buddhism. It is how it should be because the practice should permeate your health, your social life, your work—everything. A lama gave me a large white crystal on which he wrote, 'May you go to the land of Heruka [a tantric Buddha] and be a photographer there'.

When I first encountered Buddhism, I used to go all the time to get teachings at the Jamyang Buddhist Center. I concentrated on the basic map of Buddhism, the Lam Rim, also known as the graduated path to Enlightenment. Now I don't have any time so I concentrate on doing my practice instead. I don't miss a day. I do it no matter where in the world I am—on planes, in hospital having an operation, wherever. It's far too beautiful for me to forsake, ever. If I'm doing a commercial and need to start shooting at six in the morning I'll get up at four, even if I haven't stopped working until midnight and crashed into bed at two. That sometimes goes on for days and days. And I say to my poor dear darling girlfriend when I get back, 'I can't come out because I'm so tired'. I don't do it to get pats on the back—it's just the way it is.

In the morning I do a whole stream of things. I do prostrations to the Buddha, Dharma and Sangha [religious community]. I set out small bowls filled with water in front of the altar which represent offerings of light, water for drinking and washing, food, music, perfume, flowers, the traditional gifts presented to honored guests in the East. I then go through a series of rituals which include making offerings to the Buddhas, saying mantras, reciting texts, and saying prayers for the path to be made clear and for blessings to flow to the center, my master, and His Holiness, the Dalai Lama.

At night I do prostrations and offerings to my master, Rato Rinpoche, recite more texts, repeat all the opening prayers, say mantras to the Buddhas and recite all the points one should observe on the Bodhisattva path. I also pay homage to Padmasambhava, the founder of Tibetan Buddhism and say yet more prayers to Rato Rinpoche. On Sunday, as well as doing the above, I recite the King of Prayers—the Prayer of Ways High and Sublime. There are 57 verses, which begin:

> *O lions amongst humans,*
> *Buddhas past, present and future,*
> *To as many of you as exist in the ten directions*
> *I bow down with my body, speech and mind.*

(I read this to my father just after he died. I never thought I would be able to see my father dead, but afterwards I felt quite uplifted. It was wonderful to have the lifeboat of Buddhism at such a time, because it had taught me about the transitoriness of things.)

Constantly speaking at great speed (because I'm always in a rush), my prayers take me 60 minutes non-stop—morning and night. If I did them slowly it would take about two hours. Sometimes I'm going so fast the words come out wrong—'goodhas' instead of Buddhas, say, or a rude word by mistake like 'Bumisattvas'. I burst out laughing. I think that's the teachers keeping me awake and stopping me from becoming too heavy or paranoid. But because I'm Welsh and get frightened, I make sure I do everything. I overheard my girlfriend say, 'One thing about Clive, he may be mad but he's inspired me to do my own meditation'. I was very touched by that. She's a kind-hearted, beautiful girl and a Satsangi, a follower of the Path of the Masters. Even though I rush through them all and am often worried or stressed, I find that afterwards there is a 'peace which passeth all understanding', as Jesus Christ said. It lies within you. It *is* all right. The problem is we're trapped by our mind stream so we're constantly disturbed.

Because of the Dharma, I now see beauty where I did not see it before. I see it everywhere. Recently I had to photograph children at a cancer hospital and I opened the door to their ward and my first human reaction was one of wanting to run. Then I remembered compassion and went in and hugged them all. Like that.

I now view my relationships and women differently. One of my main deities is Tara, the female Buddha representing compassion in action, who is extremely powerful. I talk to her all the time. I used to think women were people with whom you got into bed. Now I'm much more respectful because I recognize that all women are potential Buddhas. Ironically, the more you treat women as goddesses the more attractive you become to them! I've just done a casting of 300 women for one big ad, and I tried to see the most positive in each one of them. Buddhism teaches that behind the delusions there is the Buddha nature and that's visible in every human at some stage of their development. Even Hitler was a beautiful baby. But I just adore women—and that's it. They're wonderful, aren't they? Beauty beyond conception. I've been in the present relationship for seven years—it's turbulent because we're both quite crazy people, both quite excited by life and want everything to be perfect.

There's a lot of debate within Buddhist circles these days about whether drugs and alcohol damage or enhance spiritual insight. About whether they matter. Of course they do! It's just common sense. I used to drink every day. I'd have a glass of champagne in the studio, then I'd come home and take drugs and various things like that—it was an escape to get away from the worry of all the jobs and because I was quite nervous and shy. Before I went to photograph someone famous I thought, 'I'll just have a glass of champagne'!

I haven't taken drugs or had a drink or smoked for thirteen years now. I can't stand it. I wish I'd never wasted my time. And life is so much better. The relief! I could take off but I could not land. I believe everyone should have a good time and be happy, but permanent happiness does not exist in things like drugs and drink. Permanent happiness only exists when the mind is freed from any attachment. Strangely, I haven't had any difficulties stopping taking intoxicants; not at all. I know it's all due to the grace and blessings of my teacher. He's given me more strength than anyone could possibly imagine. Three months after quitting I went to the Buddhist Center and was walking in the garden with my teacher and he turned to me and said, 'Life is better without arrack'. He just knew.

I see my teacher at exactly the right times. He is coming to stay with me next Tuesday. He will sleep in my bed and I will bring him tea in the morning at six and I will do my practice upstairs and he will do his downstairs. Every time you meet your teacher there is some purification. The last time I saw him I got sick, I had some trouble with my lungs. I met one lama who had throat cancer but who wasn't doing anything about it because he viewed it as a purification.

The greatest thing that has ever happened to me has been to photograph the lamas, especially the Dalai Lama. I've not spoken to him, I've just been there. It's what the Indians call *darshan*, receiving the grace of the guru's presence. It's just so extraordinary—unlike anything else. For example, I was once setting up in a London apartment where His Holiness was staying, and my van driver came in and sat in the corner wearing sunglasses. I was sure the lights were going to bounce off them and wreck the session. In came His Holiness, I prostrated, he sat on this chair and there was no reflection at all. Nothing. It was just fabulous. Everything looked fine. There was no logical explanation. At another time I was photographing the opening of the Tibet Office in London, standing in the corner, and after cutting the ribbon His Holiness came over, got hold of my head and started laughing. Everything went. I was there but I had a brief flash of Emptiness. It was quite extraordinary. Then I had to rush upstairs and try to photograph His Holiness with tears in my eyes. Over the years I have taken many photographs of him which have been made into postcards and posters. I never take any money for them. I couldn't. I regard it as a great blessing because they're sold all over the place, which must help the Dharma. I'm not proud of it and I'm not not proud of it. It's just the way it is, and I wouldn't have it any other way.

Taking pictures of the lamas is just so easy. I set up and they exude this supreme energy and quality. It's what I would like to attain. That's why they are in the world—they return to us as Bodhisattvas to show us the way. We see them and say, 'He's good' or 'She's good', 'I'd like to be more like that'. We learn because we want to emulate them. That's why they make a vow to come back. The lamas are so amazing. I was wondering whether to change to a new agent or stay with the old one and from another country I got the advice from a lama to appoint the new one. When I went to meet the agent in his office there was a picture of him sitting on a rock in Tibet as a small boy. His grandfather had gone to Tibet with Younghusband, who invaded Tibet at the head of the British forces in 1904. I didn't know that. I took Rato Rinpoche to meet him and my agent said to my teacher, 'Everything seems so happy when you're here'.

If our minds were perfectly clear, our understanding and our concentration perfect, we could achieve liberation in a moment. My son Paris asks, 'Why are we bowing?' And I say, 'We're prostrating to what we're going to become, which is awakened, and to men and women on this planet who have achieved control over their mind'. We are lost in our emotions, aren't we? Up one moment, down the next. Hating, loving—sometimes within days. It's said the Buddha is being beaten on one side, kissed and caressed on the other, but feels the same towards both parties. It's very hard for us to have equanimity.

What the Dharma keeps telling us is to persevere, to have patience, to realize that you do not know everything and that all will be revealed to you when you are ready— when the mind is sufficiently open. I always thought Einstein's theory of relativity, that the object goes towards the speed of light and is multiplied by its velocity, was a good example of Buddhism. As you go along, the mind receives what it is ready to receive and expands to that level, so that you understand on deeper and wider levels as you progress. Tibetan Buddhism is really techniques repeated over and over to enhance the mind's positive aspects—leading to your being able to play the guitar or compose huge Buddha worlds and do whatever you want. You are able, by the power of the wisdom methods.

We practice so that we can be reborn into a life of leisure and ease (rather than being a head-hunter in New Guinea and going around with a skull on top of a stick), so that we can keep on practicing in order to free ourselves from the cycle of birth and death. We're all imprisoned by our emotions; lust, greed, ignorance and the 'I want, I want'. I remember seeing a film with Humphrey Bogart and Edward G. Robinson, who played a terrible vicious monster who had all these people trapped in his house. There was a shot of him taken underneath looking like a huge frog and Bogart said, 'Whadya want, Rocco?' And Edward G. Robinson took the cigar out of his mouth, the cigar juice dribbled down his chin and he said, 'More. Yeah, that's what I want. More'. That's what we're all trapped in.

Although I didn't like God, I've been in love with Jesus all my life. He was the safety valve amidst all the Methodism. To me Jesus is a Bodhisattva, because his message was 'Do unto others as you would have them do unto you', the kingdom of heaven is at hand. You are it, it is you. That's Buddhism. I found this fourteenth-century statue revealing his sacred heart one day when I was walking in the Kings Road in the pouring rain. I saw it in a shop window, recognized it was important to me and knew I had to have it. To me it represents the Heart Sutra, the Buddhist teachings of Emptiness that I read every day, and is a great locus of beauty and refuge. I've often thrown my arms around it. They say many rivers flow to the mighty ocean. It doesn't matter what path it is, so long as it leads to liberation. The thing about Buddhism, however, is that you actually achieve the completion stage and become a Buddha. It's the only path that does that. What that actually means is beyond my conception. I know it means one can handle any situation. Even on drugs I used to think 'I'm stoned, I'm high, I'm in

Los Angeles, I just wish I had control'. I don't think there is any Enlightenment without a great deal of suffering. It could be the suffering of the mind losing certain things it has clung to which have given a false sense of security.

What I know is that Buddhism has saved me—no matter what happens from now on. I've got to a certain point with it so that if I fall down I can jump back to the same level. It's a practical way of life which gives you ethics without sentimentality. And from that practicality it blossoms through the darkness of Samsara [suffering] into the most beautiful thing, like the seasons now and again blossom in your mind. You do rise through the dark waters of life and experience that there is a blue sky above—and that you are it. **99**

A deep shift inside me

LAMA PALDEN DROLMA
Teacher, mother and psychotherapist

$\mathcal{A}$t first glance, Caroline Alioto has all the marks of a regular modern American woman. She lives in California, eats health food, has been married several times (with two children from different husbands), and is a practicing psychotherapist with all the language that goes with it. A second, longer look, however, reveals that she is a most unusual person indeed. To begin with she is a lady lama—a title bestowed by the Kagyu school of Tibetan Buddhism on certain meditators who have undergone a strict three-year retreat—with robes to match her status. Then there is her exotic past. She has ventured far geographically as well as mentally, intrepidly breaking down barriers of habit and culture as she goes. One of her husbands was a Rinpoche from the remote and largely unknown Himalayan kingdom of Bhutan, where she lived for two years as one of only a handful of Westerners. Perhaps most significant is the fact that she is rapidly becoming a highly respected teacher with an ever-increasing group of students both at her own center, Sukkhasiddhi in San Rafael (north of San Francisco), and at nearby Spirit Rock, founded by well-known author and teacher pair, Jack Kornfield and Sylvia Borstein.

I first encountered Lama Palden Drolma (to use her Tibetan ordination name) in 1996, when I was doing research for a book, and she graciously invited me to stay in her house, even though she had never seen me before in her life. I met a tall, slim, brown-eyed, 40-something woman with a stylish air and an infectious giggle. I was struck by the way she managed to do umpteen tasks (cook food, answer the telephone, supervize her ten-year-old daughter, feed the cat, chat to friends, organize Buddhist teachings) simultaneously and at vast speed. She was also extremely unassuming. It was only after I had known her for some time that the extent of her training and the profundity of her spiritual expertize emerged. I wondered whether this lack of self-publicity was due to her personality or her gender. Whatever the reason, I found it an attractive trait.

Lama Palden's journey into Buddhism illustrates many points. During our conversation she used the words 'practice' and 'realization' many times. The two are inter-connected, and pivotal for those who seriously want to follow the Buddha's path. That the Buddha maintained that spiritual evolution is something everyone can achieve since we all have Buddha nature, but the responsibility and the effort is in our own hands. In this context the Buddhist does not wait for a moment of 'grace' to fall on her or him, nor hope for a blinding light on a road to Damascus, but sets about working on his/her own inner transformation according to spiritual maps plotted by those who have gone before. The Buddhist practices to reach awakening just as a concert pianist practices to play a sonata. On this journey the markers along the way are 'realizations'—moments when the subject of meditation stops being a mental pursuit and becomes felt or real; moments when the meditation drops from head to heart. Realizations are the difference between dogma and true wisdom. You know when a teacher has realizations because they teach from their own experience rather than mere book learning, and because their actions do not differ from their words.

During the conversation Lama Palden also revealed (somewhat bravely) that as a child she had had memories of past lives. This is the business of reincarnation. While some Western Buddhists regard reincarnation as an unnecessary tenet (see the interview with Stephen Batchelor) many, like Lama Palden, accept it completely. Certainly reincarnation or rebirth is totally feasible, expected even, within Tibetan Buddhism; consciousness is said to leave the body at death and move on to another form, carrying its propensities with it. Thus consciousness moves from life to life in a continuous stream, bringing with it habits, predilections and predispositions laid down in previous existences. For Lama Palden reincarnation explains precisely why she is a Buddhist and led the life she has.

This interview was conducted in Lama Palden's study in Marin, California, a small room into which she had managed to fit a desk, sofa, many fascinating books and an altar filled with Buddha statues, flowers and an ever-flickering candle. It reflected the many facets of her life. Her conversation was frank, serious and punctuated by the occasional giggle.

"What I was looking for was what you would call 'mystical union'. I had had mystical experiences as a child in church. I used to sing in the choir, and during the devotional singing and chanting I would often have a very strong sense of coming into the divine presence. All along I loved church—there really wasn't any dogma in the Episcopalian Church I was raised in. But it didn't go far enough. I was yearning to purify and in some way transform what I experienced as my own neuroses, my own suffering, so that I could come into a deep state of peace and grace. I had felt them at times but they weren't always there. As a teenager I was keenly aware of a lot of emotional turmoil. What I wanted was to become a vehicle for blessings and healing to come through me to other people—to be able to benefit humanity somehow. I had had that concern from early on. With the Church it got to the point of 'When do we go to the desert to do the Retreat?' In those days that part was never forthcoming.

In the early 1970s I started exploring comparative mysticism in different traditions like Sufi and Zen, studying and learning from various teachers in the San Francisco Bay area. Then a Sufi friend dragged me to see Kalu Rinpoche, an elderly lama from Tibet. He had done a total of around 25 years retreat himself and was a highly revered teacher. It was only Kalu Rinpoche's third trip to the West. I didn't know all this, of course, but as soon as I saw him I knew he was my teacher in a very fundamental sense. I had been practicing these other traditions sincerely for about six years, all the time praying to meet my actual, true teacher. I just saw him and sensed an authentic presence and an embodiment of truth. He was a pure being and something rang so deeply inside of me. I just knew this was the person I'd been looking for, who could provide the profound spiritual practice I wanted. I took Refuge with him the night I met him. It was the full moon of September 1977.

Four months later I sold everything I had and went over to his monastery in Darjeeling to study with him. I was 25 and I had a five-year-old son who was going to come with me but he ended up staying at home with my mom. She took care of him, which she did twice over the course of my training. Once I began studying with Kalu Rinpoche and some of the other lamas, I began to have a profound appreciation for Buddhism and the tradition. I found it met everything that I had been longing for. As soon as I started doing the practices I felt a deep shift take place inside me.

In the Buddhist practices I found the way of transforming myself which I had been looking for.

Kalu Rinpoche had a rather funky monastery. It's been built up a lot more since. He had a little tiny house attached to it, right above the road on the way to Darjeeling. He gave me and my traveling companion a room to stay in that belonged to two monks who were on holiday, so we lived right in the monastery itself for the entire four months we were there. Kalu Rinpoche was incredibly gracious. He taught us himself at least three times a week quite extensively. There were a handful of Westerners and he had a translator. We had other teachers as well, including Bokar Rinpoche (who became Kalu Rinpoche's successor). All in all we had teachings just about every day.

We were also meditating right from the very beginning and doing a series of traditional Tibetan foundation practices called Nyondro. These include established rituals for purification, taking Refuge in the Buddha, Dharma and Sangha. I was also learning to dedicate all my spiritual practice to the benefit of all beings. It consisted of saying a very simple little four-line prayer, but it was a very important prayer. I found that it radically altered my experience of spiritual practice. Along with this I was meditating on the Bodhisattva of compassion.

So I was there with Kalu Rinpoche and he didn't disappoint me at all. In fact I was filled with a deep happiness and felt a tremendous sense of blessing. At one point I had a really remarkable experience. When I was 22 I had seen a therapist for a short time, and she had mentioned to me that I should work on self-love. It was the first time I'd ever heard of such a term. I thought, 'Self-love, what's that?' For about three years it had become like a koan [Zen riddle given to students to meditate on] for me. 'Self-love—how do you do that?' One day in Sonada (near Darjeeling), Bokar Rinpoche had been teaching us and we came out of the tiny temple and Bokar Rinpoche looked at me. I actually saw gold light coming out of his heart and into my heart—and something turned inside me. It was an experience of somebody loving me so much but impartially so that somehow my own love was awakened in a way that it never had been. From that day on, something clicked inside me and I felt an experience of self-love. Over the years it has stayed with me and grown.

Five years later I did a three-year retreat on Salt Spring Island in British Columbia, during which time the work I'd done on self-love was very helpful. It was so hard—I had to have a lot of compassion for myself then! There were twenty of us altogether, ten men and ten women, in separate compounds. I had prayed for years to be able to do a long retreat, and Kalu Rinpoche was very keen on the idea. Afterwards I felt that I had done at least one thing that was meaningful in this life. It was extraordinarily worthwhile. My practice changed night and day after that retreat.

It was a really intense training period. We got teachings

constantly from a Canadian monk who was a lama. And Dezchung Rinpoche, a high lama, came twice for extended periods. (I really felt a tremendous blessing in his presence. He gave a boost to my practice.) We were also sitting on the cushion twelve or thirteen hours a day. We practiced all day long, and during our break we studied Tibetan texts. All our texts were in Tibetan, so we had to learn to read Tibetan. I had learnt a little bit before, but I learnt mainly in retreat.

It's extremely hard work doing intensive practice. To put it into perspective, later I went back to college and then went to graduate school, and I felt as if I was on vacation the whole time. It was so simple compared to doing a three-year retreat, because to discipline one's mind and to work directly with one's mind is probably the hardest thing you can do. That is where the self-love was useful. In that retreat my imperfections were in my face all the time. I saw what I considered my own obscurations [negative tendencies obscuring progress towards Enlightenment]. Since I was a teenager I had been very aware that my discipline wasn't perfect. I would think that it would be excellent to be able to meditate perfectly all day long, but in that retreat I saw that my mind would run around and think about all kinds of different things and get distracted. I had to face that and work with it. In a sense it's easier to face those challenges in retreat because that's all you are doing. The day is so structured that it gives you a situation where you can really attend to your spiritual practice without the outside distractions. I've never really had a problem with self-discipline since my three-year retreat.

Deep emotional needs also came up for me, and there was no outer means of fulfilling them. Needs for a companion, personal love, that sort of thing. Also when I went into retreat my son was ten—so every day I was aware of not being there for him. Once again he was with my mom. It wasn't that I was guilty, but I was feeling a great deal of concern about him. Even though he was only ten, I asked for his permission before I went into retreat. And he gave it. And Kalu Rinpoche had told me it was very beneficial for mothers to go on retreat if the child were in a situation where they were well taken care of—and if the practice were really good then it would justify the separation. That really made me devote myself as ardently as possible to the retreat and the practice.

Still, my parents and siblings certainly felt that I was being irresponsible. They were always very supportive of the spiritual path but they felt that going away for three years and leaving my son was over the line. My father thought it was hugely selfish. Nevertheless, they still helped me. I think my parents are wonderful people and I'm deeply, deeply grateful to them, especially my mother. She's been incredibly loving. But it weighed on me the whole time. I really truly believed that if I could realize some of the teachings it would make it worthwhile, because I felt the blessings that emanate from touching upon the truth would make up for the sacrifice my son and family were making. This retreat, however, was much more than an investment. From the start my motivation was to do it for others. I always knew that I wouldn't really be able to help sentient beings until I had deeper realizations. As a teenager I had volunteered in political movements (my family were very politically motivated), including joining an anti-war movement. Within two months I realized that the anger that fuels wars was inside each of us, and that until I learnt how to deal with my own anger and defects, there really wasn't much use my trying to change the world. From then on I saw that the way to progress was to go inside to resolve my own negativities and then from a place of inner peace to try to benefit the world. That was the path that I decided on.

Although in the short term my going away was difficult for both of us, I thought I would have more to give to my son and that ultimately he would benefit through my retreat. In the end I think it paid off. We had to work through getting back together and him being able to trust that I was going to be there and that I really cared. He knew that, but he had to understand on a deep emotional level. It was very difficult for him, but he always maintained afterwards that he was very proud of me and very happy I'd done it. Now he's 26 and has done periods of retreat himself including a five-month one with Pema Chodron in Nova Scotia. [Pema Chodron, a Canadian grandmother and ordained Tibetan Buddhist nun, is one of the West's most prominent teachers and practitioners.]

In the January of the last year of the retreat my younger brother died, which was excruciating for the whole family, especially his young wife. I was due to finish the retreat in October. Not being with them was very painful, especially since I knew my son would be feeling the loss greatly as my brother had been an important role model for him. My family very much wanted me to be there, but Kalu Rinpoche reminded me by phone through our lama that while I could do whatever I liked, I had agreed to be there for three years. With that I knew that I had to stay, because I had understood when I went into retreat that you set aside all concerns for family and worldly things during that period. It's not that you don't pray for your family, friends and people every day, but you don't go running out to fix things. So I had to face all the pain with my sitting practice and try to help the situation in every way I could through prayer. I went through tremendous grief, but ultimately that brought me to a huge turning point in my own practice. Everything in me was screaming to go to be with my child and my family, and through not acting on it I was forced into an experience of my true self—true self in the sense of that which is beyond all time and place, beyond death. It was as though I set myself free from loads of conditioning. It didn't mean my compassion was less (I think my love and compassion for my family has deepened), but somehow it burnt up a lot of my limitations.

Put in more Buddhist terms, I realized absolute reality

through that experience. What I felt happened was that I agreed to deal with things from an absolute point of view. I had to jump off the cliff of my conditioning into the abyss of the totally unknown, unconditioned Emptiness. I knew that Kalu Rinpoche's mind would hold me and it did. Even though he was thousands of miles away, I felt his presence. I jumped and what I contacted was a sense of the absolute true *vajra* [diamond-like] nature in myself which I have never lost. Through that I was able to go through the grief and ultimately come into a sense of deep joy.

The other piece of the story is when I came out of retreat my parents both independently told me they felt it was good that I had stayed and finished. They said in the depth of their own grief they had wanted me there but later they realized that fundamentally there was nothing I could have done because he was already dead and they realized it was important I complete my training. I found that very moving, because even though I had had a realization of the absolute true nature of mind, that didn't mean I no longer had any emotions and feelings nor was I invulnerable to what people thought and said. I had not let go of all attachments either. Those continued to surface. I still have my obscurations.

I have no fear of death. To me death is a transition. I feel that it's going to be a wonderful opportunity to open up and deepen. The Buddhist tenet that consciousness continues is not a belief, it's a fundamental experience, although obviously in this life I haven't died yet. For me it is not such a far leap because I remembered other lives when I was a child. I remembered living in other countries like Peru, China and some kind of Arabian country and wondering how I got to this place. It felt unfamiliar. I had those memories as far back as I could remember. I just knew I had been in other places in other times, although I never talked about it. And I always felt that there was something that I had to do. In fact, when I was two I ran away from home because I thought I was being so lazy not accomplishing my mission. I thought I'd been dilly-dallying letting my parents take care of me and it was time I embarked upon my serious work. I knew I was young but I thought I had enough of the basics. I really felt guilty. My mom found me at the train station. She somehow made me understand that it was OK for me to stay at home and that there was a lot I still had to learn.

When I was 26 I married a Bhutanese Rinpoche who was the incarnation of a Tibetan teacher and went to live in Bhutan, the Himalayan kingdom which has been a stronghold of Buddhism for centuries. Then it was even more cut off than it is now. There were only a handful of Westerners there and I was the first American who had ever been married to a Bhutanese. We lived with the royal family part of the time, but then we lived in His Holiness the Karmapa's house, which he wanted us to use. [The Karmapa is head of the Kagyu school and one of the most eminent figures in Tibetan Buddhism. His reincarnations can be traced back further than the Dalai Lama's.] I loved it there. I was very happy and it was extremely relaxing for me in a very fundamental way. We'd visit with people, go out a bit, I'd go and see Kalu Rinpoche and take teachings, but most of the time I just did spiritual practice. I think that it's really valuable to see a religion in its own culture. Often I've noticed that when people take up Buddhism in the West they do it in a rather uptight way: it has a rigid quality—it has to be done just so, and everything is very quiet and serious. When you see Buddhism in its own country it's a very natural outflow of daily life. There are children in the temple, people just pop in to make offerings and it's all really relaxed. It was very helpful to me to see this. I also noticed the embodiment of compassion in the people—compassion for me and for each other. That was extremely nurturing. I was there for two years.

The Bhutanese are very devoted to all their lamas. They have this system in Bhutan that whatever is offered the recipient is obligated to give back double (because they are richer). We spent quite a lot of time with His Holiness the Karmapa in his monastery in Rumtek, Sikkim. I was profoundly affected by him. His compassion and loving-kindness was just phenomenal, and so was the field of Shunyata [Emptiness] that you felt in his presence. Any ideas based in ego that I had were completely exposed when I was with him. They were so obvious it wasn't even worthwhile voicing them. We would spend a lot of time with him just chatting and while we were with him he'd receive visitors and letters from the many centers all around the world which were under his direction. Sometimes he would get upset at the behaviour of the lamas or monks in his monasteries and to me he seemed like a mother with her teenage children saying, 'Oh no, what am I going to do now? Lama So-and-So has run off with all the money from the center. Lama So-and-So has disrobed and now there's a big commotion'. Or he'd say, 'This center isn't going right', or 'This Lama isn't behaving properly, now I have to figure out what I'm going to do about this situation'. So, it was very obvious to me from early on that the lamas were not infallible. Even though they had a high degree of training and some of them had realization, they clearly were human beings who had their own imperfections as well. And I knew it because of being married to a Rinpoche too—he was quite open with me about his own shortcomings. We would talk over these things and try to support each other in our Dharma practice.

In the West we tend to be dazzled by lamas and sometimes we can be hurt by them. In the Vajrayana texts [the esoteric tantric teachings of Tibet] there's a very clear message about seeing your lama as the Buddha. I think the key here is that if you are going to see your main teacher as your guru, he or she needs to be capable of fulfilling that role. In my mind, people like Kalu Rinpoche and the Dalai Lama are very developed beings in whom we can place that kind of ultimate trust. I did that with Kalu Rinpoche and I never felt my trust was ill-placed. What we Westerners have to understand is that there are many different levels of realization in somebody who is a lama. [A lama simply means a teacher.] At one level an ordinary lama is like a parish priest: he's someone who has studied and done a great deal of practice and one hopes is very sincere in what he is doing, but nevertheless is still a student. He is still on the path along with his students. Basically a lama is a spiritual friend who can help share what he knows to guide one further along. There should be a sense of us all being Sangha [spiritual brethren] and spiritual practitioners together on the path. Now there are some lamas who are highly realized, but they are very rare. It's more common among the Rinpoches to have high degrees of realization and some of the lamas are very realized, but both lamas and Rinpoches keep working on their own practice throughout their lifetime. They may be aged 30 or 40 and become heads of monasteries, but they still keep developing their spiritual growth. Many of them do come to deeper states of realization and hopefully all of us practitioners will as our lives keep unfolding.

Speaking from my own position as teacher, I want to share what I have been given. I have had a lot of experience and training and so I can help people by giving instruction and practicing with them, but I am not a fully realized person. We can't expect people who aren't fully realized to be infallible. All of us are in process. Even the Dalai Lama says he's just a humble monk. Obviously anybody who looks at his life, listens to him speak or goes into his presence knows immediately he's far beyond what most ordinary monks are. To be like him ultimately is something all we Buddhist practitioners can aspire to. For me, however, it's very much an aspiration, not an actualized reality.

Apart from teaching Buddhism, I'm also a psychotherapist in private practice. I chose this line of work because I didn't want to be dependent on earning my living from the Dharma, because as a lama I was already doing some counseling and because Buddhism and psychotherapy are closely related. Both are working with the human mind and psyche. In actuality there is no way to separate them. Buddha and the many teachers of the lineages who came after him have taught the way to liberation, yet often we as human beings fall short of being able to fully accomplish what we have been taught. We all have neuroses, and psychological obscurations—East and West alike. Anger, greed, jealousy, desire and pride are endemic to the human condition. Psychological work can help us to unravel some of the unskilful behavior that we can indulge in, which in turn helps improve our capacity to practice. Now the Dharma does that too but basically the Dharma says, 'Do this and don't do that'. Well, that's fine, but some people find that they can't stop the compulsion to act out in negative ways. Even if they practice very devotedly for years they can't stop their compulsion to act out of greed or pride or anger. That's where counseling can be helpful. Buddhism can help but it doesn't necessarily stop the compulsions—and this is where the idea of the subconscious comes in.

Buddhist practice doesn't necessarily deal with deep psychological issues because the human mind has a way of sealing off certain aspects of our personality or experience that we don't want to deal with—that's why it's called the shadow, because we block it off and aren't aware of it. We can practice for a long time without facing what we don't want to look at. This is where a skilful teacher can come in—he or she can point out, 'OK, you're missing such and such. You need to address yourself to looking at so and so'. For example, the teachings over and over again emphasize that we should be kind and loving but why aren't we always like that? Some of this stems from psychological causes and working on the blockages and processing the issues can actually open up our compassion.

I think Buddhism has not been fully translated into our culture. That's what is happening now. I believe everything that is needed is included in the Buddha's teachings, but they have not been culturally transmitted to the point where we can readily access them. Our language, our education system and our conceptual thinking processes are different.

Some people might think that there is a conflict between Buddhist views on karma and Western ideas of psychotherapy. Karma says that if you are unhappy, or in a poor situation, it is due to actions that you yourself have committed in the past [including previous lifetimes]. Psychotherapy, on the other hand, works on the principle that your upbringing and conditioning are mainly responsible. And personally I don't have any conflict because I have always felt completely responsible for everything that's happened to me. It's all due to my own obscurations. These two different approaches are reconciled through compassion. We fundamentally have to have profound compassion for ourselves and others. People do things to other people out of their own suffering and ignorance and we need to have great compassion for them, as well as for the people who experience pain through the acts of another person. The whole question of karma is exceedingly complex and has been totally over-simplified in the West. My experience of Tibetans and Indian Himalayan people who practice Vajrayana Buddhism is that they have a profound compassion for all human beings in the situations they find themselves in. And it's all interconnected. All of us who aren't fully realized have certain degrees of ignorance and obscurations that we sometimes act out upon others and ourselves. We have all caused suffering and experienced suffering. We should all take responsibility for our own healing. Whatever has happened to us is what has happened. How we relate to that is our own responsibility and our opportunity for growth and healing. All of us have the opportunity to take what has happened to us in our lives and use it for our own transformation. We can't change what has happened. We can change how we relate to it. We can relate with hatred or with forgiveness and love, to ourselves in the first place and to others in the second, in the understanding that this is all part of the cycle of ignorance.

I set up the Sukkasiddhi Center here in Marin County two years ago in order to have a place where the teachings of Kalu Rinpoche, the Kagyu lineage and Tibetan Buddhism in general could be made available to people who aren't able to travel to the East. I want to translate the essence and principles of these teachings into modern American daily life. My view is that we honor all religions and all religious traditions and feel that they're all a deep enrichment for humanity. My particular bent has been for Tibetan Buddhism but I have a great love and respect for all religious traditions. I teach two to three times a week and lead some retreats. I have been giving Refuge for some time—recently 20 people took it. Some of the students had taken Refuge back in the 1970s but the seeds of Vajrayana practice had lain dormant. They're now sprouting. The youngest Refuge taker was aged three. It was her own idea. We also have day-long retreats and special events. My vision also includes building a place a little removed from town where people can do long- and short-term retreats. That dream is coming closer. There is already a group of women who want to do a three-year retreat. One of my main motivations was to help build a community of people who could practice deeply together.

I'm really interested in teaching meditation because I believe it is the profound means for Awakening as well as an important aid in daily life. I have emphasized teaching practices which lead to the realization of Emptiness or openness—and simultaneously teaching practices which engender loving-kindness and compassion. Learning to meditate and having a daily practice leads to a more satisfying life as it gives us a way to unhook from daily stresses and learn to come to a place of peace and presence within the self. Meditation calms the mind so one has the possibility of making choices from a settled, peaceful state. In the beginning meditation can help us become better human beings through being happier in our lives. It gives more contentment. Ultimately, however, meditation can lead to full realization. This is where the teachings on Emptiness come in. We don't really have a word in English which adequately expresses what Emptiness means. Realizing Emptiness fundamentally means coming into the experience that who we really are is not our personality, not our conditioning, but a magnificent divine being. The teachings on Emptiness refer to the fact that an actual substantial self cannot be found. Nevertheless there is a stream of consciousness. Who we really are is beyond life and death. If realization has occurred, then it doesn't matter whether we are dying, healthy, poor, rich, famous or unknown, because who we really are isn't affected by changing conditions. Buddhist meditation and teachings can help us to realize and come into that experience. That is very liberating, because if we take ourselves to be only our conditioned or constructed self, the ego personality, we're fundamentally never going to be liberated.

I teach beginners and advanced students too. There are many people around here who have devoted a great deal of time and sincerity to their practice and study so that it's actually bearing fruit. People are able to start going into deeper levels of practice now. Still, I am completely amazed how quickly people are progressing and coming to this level of maturity. I can only think it's the blessing of the teachers and the practices. What's happening is very exciting. I never expected the opening that I'm seeing in myself and others.

I've devoted all my adult life to studying and practicing Buddhism. If I had not had a second child I would have gone back into retreat. That's what I really would like to do at some point in my life. In a sense the three-year retreat was really tilling the ground and I feel I'm at the point where my practice could go deeper. Right now I have a lot of responsibilities but I hope to be able to spend a few months a year really practicing. The profound nature is still untapped. **99**

Pie in the sky
in your fridge

PHILIP GLASS
Composer

*P*hilip Glass, the American composer, is an original and undoubtedly brilliant figure. This is the man who stunned the music world with his 4½-hour single-act opera *Einstein on the Beach*, who withdrew all his published work after working with Ravi Shankar in Paris (on the grounds that his style had changed fundamentally) and who created a new film genre, the 'film opera', when he removed the entire soundtrack of Cocteau's 1950s film *La Belle et la Bête*, replacing it with his own opera. He never repeated the experiment. 'I don't mind repeating failures until I get them right, but I am not interested in repeating successes,' he was quoted as saying. Not surprisingly over the years he has gained a formidable reputation. 'He's an enigmatic figure with a steely stare whose music is too harsh, too formulaic,' said one critic. 'He's a minimalist, a modernist, an experimental, avant-garde composer whose music is too inaccessible', was the opinion of another. Recently, however, these somewhat harsh words have given way to praise. His score for *Kundun*, Martin Scorsese's powerful, moving film about the early life of the Dalai Lama, gained him an Oscar nomination and applause around the movie-going world (wherever the film was allowed to be shown). And his new score for the re-release of 1931 classic *Dracula* has been credited with resurrecting the nineteenth-century art form of melodrama.

Apart from his musical fame, it was known among the cognoscenti that he was also a committed Buddhist whose sustained support of various Tibetan groups has helped establish Tibetan Buddhism in the USA.

I made my way to his home in the lower East side of Manhattan one cold March evening, wending my way through the Chinese restaurants to the rather unimposing tall, gray house where he lives. Philip led me down the passage past the bicycles leaning against the wall and down into the basement, to his kitchen, where the interview took place. It was large and 'minimalist', with no visible signs of usual culinary chaos nor any 'soft' touches like tablecloths and curtains. The man himself had a mop of thick hair, a large nose, rather sad down-turned eyes, big bony hands and an expression of sensitive angst. As the interview progressed it became clear that Philip Glass was serious, kind—and intensely private. He was also rather elusive. It was almost impossible to glean any details about his personal experience of Buddhism, but occasionally he let slip a piece from a text or teaching that revealed he's studied well. Similarly, he was so reluctant to declare any knowledge of spiritual teachers that he referred to them as Tibetan 'friends' or sometimes just as 'people'. It was only when he was three sentences in that you realized he was referring to some high lama he knew. Rather than reveal his own insights into Buddhism, Philip preferred instead to focus on what he found valuable within Tibetan culture and society as they reflected Buddhist teachings. It was an original and useful tack. One of the most significant aspects of Buddhism is the way in which it has informed the social and ethical morés of the country it has settled in. This was particularly striking in Tibet where there was no differentiation between 'church' and 'state' and where even the language was invented for the sole purpose of translating Buddhist texts. Thus Buddhist principles had firmly infiltrated the very psyche of the Tibetan people, whether they were actively practicing the religion or not.

Like many of his generation Philip Glass's association with Buddhists started when he met the first wave of Tibetan refugees in Darjeeling in 1965. From that time, signs of Buddhism could be seen in his work. His three operas, *Einstein on the Beach*, *Satyagraha* and *Akhnaten*, all contain an essentially Buddhist theme—social change through non-violence—and his later works are centered on transcendence. He has also stated that making music has certain parallels with meditation in that both require laying the foundations, paying attention, effort, and the patience to repeat the same 'exercise' over and over again until you *become* the object of your attention.

It is in his personal rather than professional life, however, that he claims Buddhism has had the biggest influence. As he told the Buddhist magazine, *Tricycle*:

> The real impact of Buddhist practice affects how you live on a daily basis, not how you do your art. How you live day by day, moment by moment. The impact of Buddhism is not theoretical, as in how you paint or how you write a novel. That's hardly as interesting as how you live your life on a daily basis, don't you think? Aspects of Buddhist studies, such as the development of compassion, equanimity and mindfulness, are the practical aspects of daily life. Funny isn't it? It turns out that the pie in the sky is the same pie that's in your refrigerator.

66 *I* first came across the Tibetans in 1966 in the refugee Tibetan community in and around Darjeeling. There were about 200,000 of them living in tents. At that stage they were still pouring out of Tibet, and the community was far from settled. I had worked with Ravi

Shankar and had met people in the Hindu tradition, which was why I was traveling in India, but knew very little about Tibetans. I found out very quickly. Firstly I was astonished that Tibet had been invaded by another country—I had no idea. In the mid-1960s very few people knew what had happened. I came back to New York and was directed to a man, Rato Rinpoche, who had just come over. In 1967 there were about four Tibetans living in New York. There were that few. In New Jersey there was Geshe Wangyal, who was actually Mongolian. He had studied in Lhasa, like many of the Mongolians, and had become a Geshe. He was the teacher of that first generation of translators—Robert Thurman, Alex Berzin, Geoffrey Hopkins, men who are all in their mid-fifties and sixties now. Geshe Wangyal had arrived in the late 1940s and had set up a little monastery in Freehold, New Jersey and had been more or less discovered by these fellows. That's when I met them.

I also met the people at the Office of Tibet, including the Dalai Lama's representative and his wife. He became my language teacher for a number of years. Then I met another lama, and he wanted to start a teaching center. I decided to help him the best I could. We got a lawyer to help organize it and I began doing concerts to help raise money. I did that for about ten years. At a certain point he had established himself fairly well and I kept in touch with him. I'm technically still on the board of the Tibet Center, although I do not have much contact, to be truthful.

Later, in 1987 Allen Ginsberg* and I began working with another center, Jewel Heart. Now they're spread out all over— Ann Arbor, Cleveland, Nebraska, Chicago, New York, Malaysia and Holland. By that time I had been through the process of helping people set up teaching and cultural organizations several times and was almost an expert. In the USA it is always helpful when public people get involved in projects because then others get interested. I don't know why that should be, but there it is.

Over the years there have been many things to do, including helping lamas who have just come out of prison. At a certain point the Tibetans themselves became well organized. There are now organizations in this country just for helping with refugee problems.

Initially it was the culture and the plight of the Tibetans that interested me rather than the religion. But it all comes together, doesn't it? If you get interested in one aspect you learn a little bit about the others. I don't know very much about the religion, but I've met a lot of teachers and people from the community. I never got very good at the rest of the stuff.

---

* Poet-songwriter Allen Ginsberg, of Beat Generation fame, was also a committed Buddhist, as his death in his New York loft on 5 April 1997 exemplified. Hearing that he had terminal cancer and sensing he did not have long to live, he tidied up his business and sat down and wrote his funeral poem, *Gone Gone Gone*. His teacher, Gelek Rinpoche, and a group of Tibetan monks were at his side when he took his last breath and they stayed with his body for almost 24 hours, saying prayers, chanting, and doing rituals.

The thing that's so striking about the culture of Tibet is that its spiritual wisdom tradition is the most important part. It became the identifying and defining characteristic. We have scarcely anything in recent Western culture like that. We have pockets of it, artists who are dedicated to culture in a certain way, people involved in humanitarian, scholarly and philosophical work. But in Tibet it's all integrated into one wisdom tradition. The highest point of this culture is the development of the Bodhi mind [the altruistic intention to seek Enlightenment in order to relieve all sentient beings of suffering]. In a way that pre-dates and goes far beyond what most people even think of as social responsibility. It's a commitment that is very profound. And that goes throughout the entire population, percolating from the top to the bottom and from the bottom to the top. For many of us coming across the Tibetan culture, the first thing we see is the unfailing kindness and open-heartedness of people from every level of society. We have to remember that the Dalai Lama himself came from a peasant family, so we're not just talking about an elite upper class. It's an upper class that becomes renewed periodically through these appearances which come from all over society. [The Tibetan Buddhist system revolves around finding the reincarnations of high spiritual teachers so that they may continue fulfilling their pledge to help ease the anguish of living beings.]

What I am saying is that in Tibet all the aspects of culture —the philosophy, religion, science, history, art, humanitarian social service—became integrated into one single vision. In contrast, the West is so fragmented. Someone like Allen Ginsberg, whom I was very close to, was considered an extreme outsider most of his life because he represented ideas like this. He was not even considered a normal person in many ways. Normal people in this society may espouse values of this kind to a certain degree, but they're never required to live by them. Nor are they expected to. When you discover, for example, that a friend has given a large sum of money to a hospital, you probably will be surprised and pleased, no doubt. I was talking to a young person in California recently and she mentioned that on the weekends she worked in a refuge for homeless people. 'I just do it for five or six hours a week,' she told me. That's not common. I said to her, 'Why do you do it?' and what was interesting was that she gave me an answer which I don't believe was truthful. 'Well, I don't know many people and it's a way of passing the time,' she replied. I believe the real answer was that she was motivated to help others and that it made her feel good to do so. I was impressed by a rather obvious diversion from what her real feelings might be and realized that the answer she gave was one that people would understand.

In order to keep in touch with these people in the beginning I regularly went to India—I've probably gone there sixteen to eighteen times. That was the way to do it. As the Tibetans became more settled in the West it became clear that theirs was not a temporary situation. The Tibetans don't talk about going back to Tibet any more as they did in the 1960s and 1970s. Now we're looking at a culture which is trying to find its way outside its place of origin. What is especially important to remember is that there is a second and third generation of people who have never seen Tibet.

I got involved with the Tibetans not simply because I liked them. There was much more to it than that. You have to ask, 'What do they represent?' The people are part of and are connected to a way of life that is continuous, coherent and which represents a profound way of looking at the world. Of course the people are nice, but people are nice in Africa, and South America and Alaska. You can find good people everywhere. The Tibetans' real difficulty now is to maintain that coherence. Before the Chinese invaded, Tibetans grew up in a culture which totally supported a way of life—there was nothing in the culture that didn't support it. That same community transplanted to India is basically now a fragment of a culture existing in a larger culture which has very little connection to what they are a part of. Instead of having a country, tradition and history which nurtured this identity you have a culture which is struggling to hold onto its lifeline. It's quite, quite different. It's very interesting to be witnessing it.

It's also important to remember that the teachers who were born in Tibet, taught there and came over here in their late teens and early twenties, will also be gone in ten years.

We are the last generation to witness that kind of lineage and the ability to transmit it in that pure form. And that's the truth. These are the lamas who can trace themselves back to Tsong Ka Pa [founder of the Gelugpa School or 'Yellow Hats', the largest sect of Tibetan Buddhism] and beyond that to Milaprepa [Tibet's most famous yogi, who transformed himself from an arch-rogue to an Enlightened being in one lifetime and whose hauntingly beautiful poems are recited to this day] and beyond that to Padmasambhava [the founding father of Tibetan Buddhism, who sublimated the wild Tibetan 'heathens' through a series of sensational supernatural feats and who is revered as a Buddha by his followers]. They're talking about pure lineages which can be traced way back. I am very conscious of the uniqueness of this historical moment. Whatever degree it can transplant itself is happening right now. Fifteen years from now these teachers will not be available; from then on we'll be dealing with teachers born in India or very intelligent and well-trained Western people. That's not a bad thing, but that kind of continuity will be gone. Anyone who is born today will meet Tibetans who grew up in India (which has its own value and qualities), but they won't meet a teacher who can tell them Tibetan ghost stories (which are hilariously funny and amazing). It's a great privilege to have met these great lamas from Tibet but it's also very sad that no one else will ever know people like that. They are disappearing from view.

The Tibetan lamas I have known certainly have wisdom,

kindness and strength, but I've seen that among Catholic priests. The best people in all religious traditions will have that. The thing that sets the Tibetans apart is how transparent the tradition appears within their person. They have an open-mindedness that you don't find almost anywhere else.

I'll tell you a fascinating story. A few weeks ago I was talking to a Tibetan friend of mine [read lama] who is aged around 60 now, and I said, 'When you were in the monastery, what did you know about geography?' He replied, 'Well, we knew the center of the earth was Mount Meru' [a mythical mountain]. I said, 'Do you mean you thought the earth was flat?' He said, 'Yes, we thought the earth was flat'. I was astonished. 'When did you see it as round?' I asked. 'In 1959, when I was twenty,' he replied. 'In my own lifetime I went from flat to round.'

Stop a minute and think about what that means. It occurred to me I didn't know anybody who could have said that. I realized it wasn't just him that this had happened to— it had happened to hundreds and thousands of Tibetans. I looked at him. He wasn't proud of it, he was just stating it. I repeated what he had told me: 'You went from flat to round'. He said again, 'Yes'. This to me is the most amazing thing. What kind of mind is it that's so flexible, so versatile, so grounded in inner strength that can suddenly see the whole world differently—without having a problem with it? These people were not having emotional breakdowns. We weren't sending teams of psychologists to help them readjust.

That's what we do in this country when the slightest thing happens—if there's a train wreck we send in teams of psychologists to give counseling. In comparison we're talking about fairly common mishaps. Then they all sue each other for psychological problems. This man had had his universe turned upside-down and was not only coping, he swallowed it whole. I've met open-heartedness and kindness, but this flexibility of mind is something I've never seen. And he has all the other qualities too—all the attributes you would expect from someone brought up in the Four Noble Truths and the Eightfold Path [the fundamental tenets of Buddhism].

This same ability to cope applies to the Tibetan people who were imprisoned by the Chinese for a number of years. I was talking to a man [read high lama] not so long ago who had been in jail over twenty years. I said, 'What was it like?' He said in a breezy tone, 'It was OK'. I asked him, 'Was there a lot of suffering?' He thought a bit and said, 'No'. I pressed him for details: 'What about the food?' I couldn't get him to complain. I'm sure there were people who did complain and who had terrible things happen to them, but you were not going to find out from this man. He'd been in jail for a long long time. What you have to ask is, was he oblivious or did he have a world view which didn't project blame on things outside himself? This man did not have any bitterness or resentment, and it wasn't just a freak accident that made him what he is. It was his Buddhist training which got him through. The point is these lamas believe in taking on responsibility for their own happiness—that's why they don't blame other people.

One of the precepts in the Seven Point Mind Training [a teaching said to be the ultimate instruction in cherishing others more than oneself] is 'to want very little'. If you want very little then you'll always be happy. Of course it's an obvious thing to say, isn't it, but the fact is that they live by it. If you take that idea and you actually practice it, then it turns out to be true; or at least it seems to be. I have no personal experience of it, I can only go by what I've seen and what I've heard expressed. What impresses me about Tibetan Buddhists is the unfailing practice of putting the teachings into their life—so that the tenets are not merely theoretical. The way they live and their practice come out of the teachings. There is no separation. The teaching and the practice are identical.

The thing I've become best known for [in the Tibetan community] was the music for the *Kundun* film. I had known Marty [Martin Scorsese] before but by the time it came up (1996–97), I had been in touch with the Tibetan community for 30 years in a fairly continuous way. I knew the history— I had met the Dalai Lama numerous times, so that to work on *Kundun* was very easy and a natural thing to do. More than we could ever have hoped for, *Kundun* provided a document of what a world that no longer exists looked like, a world which is not recoverable. For me the most surprising thing was to see that world come to life. I have many, many books of still photographs of Tibet, but I had never seen people actually walking around in costume, nor anyone on a horse wearing these clothes. You got the feeling of what it was like. Marty told me that they had Tibetans on the set who replicated exactly the kind of clothes that were worn in Tibet. They knew how the clothes looked, how to wear the hats and how to make it all. He told me a story about how one day a young Tibetan was watching the filming and she turned to a friend and asked, 'Did it really look like that?' And the friend said, 'Yes it did'. She replied, 'Do you mean our culture was that rich?' and he said, 'Yes, it was'. Then she began to cry.

Marty himself was passionate about the film—he cared deeply about trying to represent the situation of the Tibetans, especially vis-à-vis the Chinese. He said to me on many occasions, 'This is a story that has to be told. People need to know about this'. That was the reason he went to so much trouble and incurred the displeasure of the studio. He threw himself heart and soul into it because he wanted this movie to make a difference. It was a brave decision to go with unknown people to give it that authenticity. There are only Tibetans in the movie. There are no box-office stars. There was no attempt to get a 'star' to play the Dalai Lama. Marty said there were no performances—it was their story. It was real.

Because of the political implications, the fear we had was that Marty would make the movie and somehow it would never even come out—that they wouldn't distribute it at all. And here in the USA the studios were warned off. In America it was whisked off very quickly—many people never got to see it. Still, it got two or three Oscar nominations and we all went to the Oscars and the film got a lot of attention. At a certain point Disney lost control of it in a certain way. I'm sure it wasn't what Disney had in mind. They were looking for a quieter exit than that. We thought we weren't going to get anything, so we were pleased with what we got.

For me, however, the most interesting thing about the film was during the screenings when we invited people in the Tibetan community including government officials as well as Rinpoches to see the end result. I never take at face value what people say to me about my work because it's hard to get a frank response. However, on many of these occasions the reactions were emotional and spontaneous. These people were obviously very moved. *Kundun* is as good a record as you're going to get. "

A vision of personal evolution

ROBERT THURMAN
Professor with presence

An interview with Bob Thurman beckons like a night at the theatre. There's the drama, the powerful presence, the booming voice, the brilliant utterances, the fascinating glass eye and the witty, fast humour. It would be wrong, however, to think of Bob Thurman merely as a stage event. His academic credentials are impeccable. Dr Robert Thurman, to give him his full title, is Professor of Indo-Tibetan studies at Columbia University, New York where students flock to hear him. He is the author and translator of several widely acclaimed academic and popular books—including *The Tibetan Book of the Dead, Inner Revolution, Essential Tibetan Buddhism*, and many more. And long before his daughter Uma became famous as an actress, he was hailed as one of the most influential and provocative spiritual thinkers of our time. It is not just his scholarship and his own meditational insights that have gained him this reputation, but his ability to put complex, esoteric and often dry Buddhist concepts into brilliant modern-day speke.

Bob has led a colorful, somewhat dashing life. Born to an actress mother and newspaper editor father, he gained his flair for verbal delivery from the Shakespearean evenings his parents used to hold in New York, at which the young Robert would be encouraged to read alongside such luminaries as Sir Laurence Olivier. Prone to romantic gestures, he got kicked out of his smart school for running away in the spring of 1958 to join Fidel Castro's guerrilla army, but got into Harvard anyway with brilliant grades. By the end of the first term, aged eighteen, he'd fallen in love, married a French heiress and had a child with her; they divorced the next year. His wife for the last 33 years has been 'soulmate' Nena von Schlebrugge, a former Swedish model who was previously married to counter-culture guru Timothy Leary. With her he has five children now in their twenties and thirties, all with Indo-Tibetan names—Taya, Ganden, Uma, Dechen and Mipam. In this household all the children were encouraged to find their own answers. 'We were raised in a free-thinking environment, to be individuals and to question authority,' said Uma in a recent magazine.

As the very first Westerner to be ordained as a Tibetan Buddhist monk, back in 1964 (when the Tibetans had just arrived in exile in India), Bob experienced privileges afforded to few today. The Tibetans, fascinated and delighted that a 'barbarian' was actively seeking Enlightenment, threw open the doors. The Dalai Lama personally oversaw his studies and checked his spiritual progress, also arranging for some of the highest lamas from old Tibet, including his own senior tutor Ling Rinpoche, to coach Bob in all aspects of Tibetan Buddhism. During the course of their weekly meetings they became close friends, Bob asking questions about Buddhist philosophy, the Dalai Lama quizzing Bob on all aspects of Western culture and beliefs, including Freud, nuclear physics, Plato, Jefferson, democracy, airplanes and cars. Returning to the USA, Bob found no support for his life as a monk and no way to share with his contemporaries the joy and clarity he had found among the Tibetans in India. He disrobed. The friendship with the Dalai Lama continues to this day, however. In 1979 Bob helped organize the Dalai Lama's first visit to the USA so that he could publicize the tragedy of Tibet.

It was hard to get an appointment with Bob Thurman because of his extremely hectic schedule, but eventually he agreed to squeeze me in before the launch of his book *Circling the Sacred Mountain*, an account of his pilgrimage to Mount Kailash in Tibet, revered by Buddhists and Hindus alike as the abode of the gods. The interview took place in Manhattan in a small room in Tibet House, which he founded with Richard Gere to preserve Tibetan culture. The interview was somewhat chaotic. Bob talked while eating take-away noodles, his dog was running around his feet and people were constantly popping in and out of the room asking him questions. He still managed not only to keep the thread of the interview going but to keep ahead of me so that I would be only halfway through my question when he would say, 'Right, right', and answer. His brain works exceedingly quickly.

I asked Bob what he considered Buddhism most had to offer contemporary Western society. His answer in one word was 'meaning'. He also gave a pithy account of the philosophical core of Buddhism—the stuff that absorbs and excites the 'thinking' seekers in the West. It's a rich feast, deeply satisfying to those who do not want glib answers to the Big Questions.

66 *I* was looking for better teachings in philosophy than I was getting in Harvard. I wanted to know how the mind works and how really to live what you understand. I was after a living philosophy—a yoga. In 1961 I lost my left eye. I was fixing a flat tyre and the tyre iron slipped and went into my eye. I encountered my own mortality. I gave up Harvard and decided to go on a vision quest. I was already interested in Gurdjieff, Sufism and Hinduism as well as Buddhism, and I went on a pilgrimage through the Middle East to India, looking. It wasn't until

I met the Tibetans in India that my progress was arrested. That was coming home.

It was not a specific thing or person, it was everything. I loved the language. I couldn't speak Tibetan but I started learning immediately. I loved the teachings: the Four Noble Truths, the foundation of Buddhism; Shunyata, the teachings on Emptiness; Lam Rim, the Graduated Path to Enlightenment; Nagarjuna, the Indian master who expounded so brilliantly on Emptiness. It all completely made sense to me, like ABC. It was fabulous beyond belief. I remember chanting prayers for two days and almost leaving the universe.

I was twenty and wanted to become a monk then and there, but then I got news of my father's death (which only made me more determined to find myself), so I left India meaning to return. Back in New York for the funeral, I met Geshe Wangyal, a Mongolian monk who lived in New Jersey. Mongolians practice the same style of Buddhism as the Tibetans. He really had a big impact on me. He was something. In his presence I was weak-kneed and almost speechless, and yet the amazing thing was that Geshe Wangyal himself seemed as if he were not there—he seemed fully content and unconcerned for himself. When I couldn't find 'him' I was forced to ask myself, 'Who is this "me" I've been pursuing?'

In *Inner Revolution* Bob Thurman adds to the story of Geshe Wangyal:

As a teenage monk Geshe Wangyal had almost died of typhoid in the hot Black Sea summer. His mother heard that the monks had given him up for dead, so she came to the monastery and spent three days sucking the pus and phlegm out of his throat and lungs to keep him from suffocating. When he awoke, the first thing he was told was that she had succumbed to the disease she saved him from and died on the very day he recovered. He was appalled when he observed that though he felt grief at the news, another current in his mind would not let him think of anything else except his overwhelming thirst after his ten-day fever. Noting this dreadful degree of selfishness, he resolved then and there to give his last ounce of effort to freeing himself and others from such involuntarily selfish impulses. I had never encountered directly such unconditional compassion in my entire life. I was hooked.

The glory of Buddhism is that it is a presentation of the meaning and the purpose of life, supported by a lot of verification. It is a system that provides reasonable proof, demonstration, persuasive argumentation and a spiritual outcome. It does not demand that you shut down your own thinking processes. It does not ask you to believe something. Even the Buddha said, 'Don't believe in me particularly'. In fact, individual teachers do have an impact on one, but then they say, 'Don't follow us blindly and slavishly'. (At least the

good ones do, the naughty ones try to create dependency.)
We come from a culture where all meaning has been
suppressed and where there is no point to the whole thing.
On the one hand, science is supposed to be controlling the
physical environment. The other option is to say that reason
is limited and to go back and believe in some non-rational
theology, to have faith and feel good about that. But many
people find those choices unsatisfactory. They don't want to
go with either the reality thing or the faith, feel-good thing.
Buddhism, however, is a mediating approach. It affords a
tremendous fruition to the purpose of life, a vision of personal
evolution *and* it is spiritual.

I live in the middle of New York where most people are
thoroughly caught up in having a partner, a family, a
comfortable existence, and trying to emulate the lifestyle of
film stars. That's what they are preoccupied with because
they believe there is no meaning to life. They think, 'It will
come to nothing whether you enjoy life or not, so you might
as well enjoy it'. They have no idea there's an amazing higher
level of enjoyment. They don't know that you can have bliss,
so they just have fun. People who are strongly theistic, of
course, get their meaning by wanting to go to heaven, but I
think most of them do that when they get near to dying, on
Sundays and holy days. The majority don't *viscerally* live for
the future life because the 'reality teaching', science, teaches
that this is a delusion. The reductionists say that the idea
of a future existence is a 'feel-good' thing that belongs to

pre-modern people and that while it may make you feel better, in actuality it's pretty silly.

Buddhism teaches future (and past) lives. Science teaches evolution from Darwin and most people think that's sensible. They have this story of the monkey, the hunter, the Neanderthal and so on. However, the evolution principle is not personal because it's your genes or your species that's doing the evolving and you are just a link in the chain. You can say that that meaning grips you to some degree because you care about your children. But clearly people don't care about their children or their grandchildren enough to really change their way of life and stop destroying everything on the planet. That's because they don't feel they are personally going to be involved in the future. So the theory of evolution is only temporarily meaningful for them. Ultimately it is meaningless.

Buddhism also has a chain of being (humans can become animals, animals can become humans, there are heavenly realms and hellish ones), but the big difference is that you personally are involved in it, and so it carries enormous meaning. You know that if you screw up you are going to have a really nasty future time because you are going to work your way into a form that is going to be very very unpleasant. (Within Buddhist philosophy, however, this is not a permanent state and it doesn't happen that some arbitrary judge dooms you on the grounds that he doesn't like you or because you believe in the wrong thing.) Obviously it's not in your comfort zone to be living in the Nile being munched by crocodiles, or being some fish being chased around by a bigger fish! That's a negative cautionary meaning, but it's a meaning for sure. If you feel you are bound into the continuity of nature *personally*, it mobilizes your natural self-preservation instinct not to have some horrible future time. That is the first reaction before the great altruism of Buddhism to save all sentient beings from a similar fate is mobilized.

The positive meaning is that, within this Buddhist chain you can become a glorious being who can fly around from universe to universe without a spaceship, who loves all beings, is only blissful and who can help others become blissful too. That's Buddhahood, which we are all capable of attaining. It's a totally magnificent prospect. Beyond Star Trek! You personally can be God. To me, that's very meaningful. I personally do believe these things. To me they seem sensible. They relate to the fact that within the infinite anything is possible. We observe continuity in everything. Why should human subjectivity (and animal subjectivity too) be the one exception, the things selected to be illusory when matter is not, genes are not, species are not, gases are not. Why should human and animal subjectivity be the one thing that absolutely doesn't exist? That is asinine, in my view. To me the idea that you can either come from nothing or can become nothing does not make sense.

Bob Thurman expands on his understanding of Enlightenment in *Inner Revolution:*

We tend to think of enlightenment as a distant cognitive state, either an intensely stressful intellectual comprehension of a huge number of physical facts that a computer could handle just as well, or a semi-obliterated state of mystical transcendence better left to denizens of the margins of society... We become enlightened when we see through our blinding misperception. Through examination we see the once rigid ego dissolve into fiction, and the solidity of our world turns fluid. In that lightness of the transparent self, we feel a new connectedness with the world. Freedom from enslavement to the ego as center of the universe becomes the bliss of union with the free-flowing energy of the world. Beyond the tense pacts, conflicts or standoffs between 'I' and 'you', 'they' or 'it' there is a liberated 'we' flexibly interacting on the field of total freedom.

The word 'enlightenment' is a good equivalent for 'Buddhahood' because it is both the intellectual accomplishment and the spiritual experience of complete awakening. Enlightenment is more than cognitive; it is emotional and moral, since the openness of wisdom brings happiness which automatically releases the most positive emotions and generates benevolent actions.

I often debate with Christians, and one of the things I delight in is explaining to them that they also believe in former life. First of all, in Christ's time reincarnation was common knowledge and part of the cultural view. Everyone believed in it, including the Jews, Pythagoras, Plato and Socrates. It was like 'Where's your uncle, where has he been reborn?' It still exists in the Jewish tradition although it's kept a little esoteric. So, historically Christianity co-existed perfectly well with the idea of the multiplicity of life. Jesus never banned the idea. It was banned by the Council of Nicea in 543 when the Church decided it wanted to gain more control over people by telling them there was only one life, consequently this was their only chance so they had better belong to the Church and pay allegiance to it. It was not in the Church's interest to have someone trying again.

Interestingly, in these debates none of the Christians will say they came from nothing or that there was a time before God thought of them. According to their belief, God creates the soul, and the soul has infinite pre-existence in God. Well what was it doing in God? Was it lying on a shelf? Was it in a jar of Vaseline? Where was it? They don't think about that. They just cover the idea of infinite pasts by saying it co-existed with God. I enjoy that argument. I think it's very important for people to expand their sense of boundary and their sense of being.

Buddhism also provides extraordinary meaning with its teachings on Emptiness or *Shunyata*. It's really a great thing that *Shunyata* can be proven, verified and experienced. What *Shunyata* does is to open one up. With that, one definitely cheers up! The Tibetans in particular and Buddhist philosophers in general tend to over-mystify *Shunyata* and make it all so high-fallutin', technical and scholastic. That's because lamas worry in case you might have some existential experience of nothingness, or think everything is meaningless and become lost. So, Nagarjuna in the Buddhist literature describes *Shunyata* almost as 'a secret teaching'. I contend, though, that people who are brought up today in a materialist civilization are already bitten by the poisonous snake of nihilism—they're already completely swimming in the poison of it. Therefore *Shunyata* should be openly and simply talked about as a challenge to nihilism.

Emptiness only means there is no non-relative thing. In the inter-relational world everything is inter-related. You may have a very deep visceral feeling of that, which is a knowledge of *Shunyata*, right there.

Dr Thurman expands on this theme eloquently in *Inner Revolution*:

> Each person can go on interminably laboring under the delusion of being separately one against all, each loving only his or her self and feeling the focus of the hate of every other. Or we can realize our relatedness to all, that we are made up of one another's molecules, we breathe them in, we absorb them in our food, we are recycled and physically affected by everything around us. My self, empty of separate self, is no different from someone else's

emptiness of self. In a world where each person is all for all, each may find no separate self to love, but each has everyone else on his or her side, and each becomes the focus of infinite love. Thus in the universe of boundless lives in space and time, every being finds ultimate release from the prison of self-concern in the energy of universal responsibility for others.

Some people have the idea that when you realize Emptiness it makes everything seem more light. That's not accurate. It can mean that the weighty things in your life become less weighty because your perceptions are not so absolute. On the other hand, it can also mean that they are even more important. Because there's no escaping the consequences of everything—good or bad behavior, insight or confusion—these things have infinite consequences. It's like Nietzsche's doctrine of the eternal recurrence. You end up where you don't want to do anything you wouldn't be willing to do for ever. That makes it quite weighty. In one way it makes everything dreamlike, if you want to emphasize that side of it. Tsong Ka Pa (1357–1419), the brilliant yogi scholar who reformed Tibetan Buddhism and founded the Gelugpa or Yellow Hat sect, says that some people, after realizing selflessness, experience a sort of haze where everything looks kind of fuzzy and wuzzy—as though they were stoned or something. He emphasized that's not at all what it means. Tsong Ka Pa stated that things look just as solid as they ever did, but now you know that solidity is illusory, so that's what makes it dreamlike. It looks just as weighty and solid as it ever did but now you know simultaneously that it's all interconnected, and it's only relative.

Likewise the ego might lessen, but you might also want to make it stronger, actually. You are free. Once you realize Emptiness is empty, it *is* your creation. In tantra the Buddha says, 'I have the self that is the diamond of the knowledge of emptiness'. Diamond is quite a hard thing. It's unbreakable. It is a common misunderstanding that Buddhism makes you into some kind of wishy-washy person. It's a mistake to present Buddhism like that. For example, women in Western modern society who are trying to come out from millennia of being suppressed and bossed around rightly get nervous if they think that egolessness, or selflessness, means you should go and be a martyr and let everyone trample all over you. It shouldn't be interpreted to mean that at all, because it would be very bad for the tramplers if the tramplees were to revert to saying, 'I'm a Buddhist, so trample on me'. It would hurt the tramplees and the tramplers a lot. This is a very important issue.

Over the course of my 35-year involvement with Buddhism I think I've become more tolerant. Buddhism continues to fail with me. It fails with everybody because we're still ego-centric pains. I'm still self-seeking, still have problems, still get unhappy sometimes, still have worries. So it continues to fail, which means that it's not its fault, but that I continue not to use it well enough. Even an exceptional person like the Dalai Lama admits he still has to keep working at it. He reshapes his motivation and watches out for vanity in case he gets proud when people praise him too much. The Dalai Lama is constantly working with his mind. And I try to as well, although I am much less of a success than him. But there's been enough of what Geshe Wangyal would call 'a slight increase in jollity'. If I keep trying, in some lifetime or another, Buddhism will succeed with me. I can say there's a little incremental progress, definitely, and a lot of intellectual satisfaction—absolutely. **"**

Unfolding to new experience

SISTER KOVIDA
Alms pilgrim

When I learnt that there were some Western monks and nuns going on alms rounds through villages in the English countryside, I was fascinated. Here was tangible proof that Buddhism had taken root in Western soil. After several phone calls, I tracked down a nun who was willing to talk to me. Sister Kovida was to be found at the Amaravati Buddhist Monastery, one of the four 'forest monasteries' of the Thai Buddhist tradition established in Britain since 1977 by the renowned American monk, the Venerable Sumedho. Amaravati is located in Great Gaddesden, Hertfordshire, a small village about 50 kilometres north-west of London in the beautiful Chiltern Hills. From the train station I took a taxi up the tiny winding lanes, passing the ruined castle where once the barons of England had offered the crown to William the Conqueror and the grand Ashridge House, a former royal hunting lodge and medieval monastery, now an international management college.

Sister Kovida could not have found a more idyllic place to live. The temple at Amaravati ('Deathless Realm') is an aesthetic and architectural masterpiece. As you enter you find yourself in an exciting, palpably sacred space with its stone and tile floor (heated from below), its web of rustic timbered beams and columns reaching into the vaulted ceiling and the one great gilded Buddha statue sitting serenely against a stark white wall. Wood is a deliberately dominant feature, symbolizing the fact that the Buddha attained Enlightenment under a tree and then asked his acolytes to follow him into the forest. Behind the golden Buddha is a small chapel dominated by a five-metre-long hanging glass panel etched with a figure of the reclining Buddha. Here, the bodies of the deceased are brought in for prayers and deeper contemplation on the impermanence of all phenomena. Outside are cloisters, Christian-style, for Buddhist circumnambulation, and all around are the woods and hills of the Hertfordshire countryside.

Sister Kovida and I talked in the sitting room of the nuns' quarters, one of the many separate buildings dotted around the grounds occupied not just by the residents but by visitors who come for courses and retreats. Like so many of the nuns and monks encountered during my journey through Buddhism, Sister Kovida was full of laughter and lightness of being, in spite of a heavy cold. Aged in her late thirties, she was slight with sparkling blue eyes and was wearing brown robes. Her shaved head was covered with a woolly hat to ward off the cold December draughts. She had been called Laura Bridgman before being ordained as Kovida, a name which, she explained, has the connotation of 'one who sees'. 'It means seeing things clearly, not being deluded by projections and superficial appearance. It's a good name for me to reflect on,' she said.

Buddhism first entered her life when she saw a TV documentary on Tibetan monks. 'There were a lot of tensions in my family and the image of the monks struck me very strongly. It wasn't a thought, simply an impression. They were beautiful, full of lightness and clarity. There was a rightness about them, a quality that made sense. I had not felt that in any career or worldly endeavor.' After that Sister Kovida endeavored to find out more about Buddhism. In 1983, aged 22, she attended a Buddhist Festival (Wesaka Puja) presided over by Ajahn Sucitto (the British abbot of Chithurst, Sussex, the first of the four forest monasteries to be opened in England). He led a guided meditation, and for her it was revelatory. 'Because I was completely naive and open, I just went into a blissful state. I floated in and out of it. Ajahn Sucitto remarked to my friend that he thought I would be back!'

The world, however, beckoned for a few more years. There were relationships, travel, a career as a qualified psychiatric nurse in a clinic for people with drinking problems and a job in an arts and crafts center for the unemployed. She dipped in and out of meditation courses. And then came the seminal retreat at Amaravati in 1990, led by the same Ajahn Sucitto and Ajahn Anando (another Western monk) who talked about the key Buddhist themes of cultivating loving-kindness, compassion, equanimity and karma. 'It was like a window opening. I was very impressed by both of them so I decided to come and live here and be ordained,' she said simply.

I talked to Sister Kovida about her unusual lifestyle. Thai Buddhism (the 'Theravada'), is notoriously austere and the monastic discipline (the 'Vinaya') strict. Those who become monks or nuns vow not to handle money, not to store food and to eat one main meal a day out of the alms bowl before noon. There are particularly rigid rules concerning the monks' behavior towards women and vice versa. A monk is never to touch a woman and a nun must never have an intimate conversation with a monk unless there is another man present. The tough training is designed to help the adherent 'let go' of attachment and develop inner strength and patience. Specifically, I wanted to ask Sister Kovida what it is like to be a mendicant nun in rural England.

❀

66 *T*he first time I went on alms round I accompanied another sister to Midhurst, which is the nearest town to Chithurst, in Sussex. It's real stockbroker

belt. It was the first time she'd been as well. Since we are not allowed to ask for anything, we simply make ourselves available without being too obtrusive. So we try not to stand right in front of the supermarket door, nor outside a pub. We try to pick a spot where people can choose whether or not to approach us—where they can easily walk past without feeling awkward or embarrassed. According to English laws we can't stay in one place for more than ten minutes, otherwise it's considered to be begging. We stand a little bit back, keep our eyes lowered, and try not to look too austere. We hold the alms bowl close to us with the lid slightly open and we just wait.

On that first time I felt incredibly selfconscious and uncomfortable. In our practice you watch what comes up in your mind and I noticed I was trying to justify why I was there. It touched a lot of pride buttons about status and people looking down on me, thinking I'm strange. I kept thinking, 'I've always paid my own way'. Also I was hungry and wanted something to eat. After a while I found myself watching a person coming towards me to see if they would give me something. I noticed that whole acquisitive mind and the agitation created by desire. I felt hungry and insecure. I attempted to balance that by thinking, 'I'll be fine if I don't eat. I'm well fed most of the time. I'll probably be fed tomorrow. I'm not going to die if I don't eat today'. I learnt to physically ground myself by remembering, 'I'm OK doing this'.

What often happens is that people pop money in the bowl. But if that happens we are not allowed to receive money, only food. We're making ourselves available to collect food for that day. So if people put money in, we very gently offer it back. We don't want to offend. Then if they ask us what we are collecting, we explain we're collecting food to sustain us for the day. People generally respect that we're not asking for money, and quite often they'll go and buy something for us. We are given all sorts of things—biscuits, sandwiches, fruit, cakes, bread rolls. I never look in the bowl and think, 'I've got four packets of chocolate biscuits, and I really fancy something savoury'. You're so grateful for whatever you get—especially filling things. A packet of biscuits is great because you're walking and burning up a lot of carbohydrates. Usually we get a very strange diet, but we're just pleased to get anything.

If you do get a yearning for something specific, say a piece of cheese or whatever, you learn to feel the experience of craving and if you fully open to it without repressing or following it you discover it's just a natural energy of the body. It simply arises, and then it goes. That's what the Buddha taught about craving and it's absolutely true. When you can do that fully the result is a deep feeling of peace. If you follow your craving you will never find true satiation. According to the Buddha, craving is one of our main causes of suffering. Within our tradition we have what is called the Four Requisites: robes, alms food, lodging and medicinal support.

We reflect on the use of alms food 'not for fun, not for pleasure, not for fattening, not for beautification, only for the maintenance and nourishment of this body for keeping it healthy for the holy life'. It's a really helpful reminder to know that the absolute basics are good enough. I'm quite fortunate in that I don't eat very much anyway. I can survive on small amounts so it's not such a testing thing for me. It's harder for the monks because they need more.

The point of doing alms round is so that the monks and nuns can live in direct relationship with lay people (although it is more unusual for women to be supported as alms mendicants in the East). That's why the Buddha set it up. The idea is we can only live where lay people have invited us and offered to support us. They directly support our lifestyle and our aspiration and they, in turn, may benefit from our presence, our guidance in the teachings of the Buddha and also by the very act of giving, which itself can engender a sense of joy and self-respect. It's a relationship of reciprocity. An economy of generosity.

Although this is an Eastern custom, somehow people in the West seem to understand it. Perhaps it's because they have seen Buddhists such as the Dalai Lama on the television. I don't know how they know, but people give. The only time I haven't received anything was on that first alms round. Every time since then I've received enough to eat. I've been on alms round many times now; sometimes we just go walkabout, going to villages where they've never seen us.

Last year we walked through the Cotswolds (the hills around Oxford) and I'm planning to go to Scotland next year. Over the years I've become much more confident about what I'm doing and the rightness of my life for me. The more I'm in that space, the more people relax with who I am and what I represent. Last year I went on a walking pilgrimage with one of the novices. Novices still use money so I would do the alms round by myself.

I've never had any hostility, only kindness. I remember one New Zealand man coming up and saying how brave we were and what a radical thing it was for us to do. He asked us lots of questions. But most English people are quite shy and don't say very much. They like to make their offering quietly and quickly and then disappear.

Once or twice we have been asked to pray for someone, not then and there but to bear somebody in mind when we chant back at the monastery. That's nice. And sometimes people start to talk about a difficulty they are experiencing. I remember an elderly lady, an Austrian immigrant, who told me about a misunderstanding with her daughter. I think she was quite lonely and needed someone to talk to. Often older people come up—they're not so intimidated by the difference. Because we are women I think people are rather protective of us. We don't deliberately conjure that up, but they are.

We don't go on alms round every day, in fact it's quite rare. Instead the lay people who are visiting or doing retreat at Amaravati make food offerings to the monastery and cook it. Again we try to think of it as food to sustain us just for that day. At this monastery we have the most amazing food—if anything, we ask that our meals be simplified. We have been provided for in that way every day for the past 15 years. We eat whatever is served and that can be meat. Today we had rice and different types of stews. Some Buddhist orders are vegetarian but we go by what the Buddha did. The Buddha maintained that being a vegetarian is not necessarily going to liberate you, so he did not set that as a basis for his training. He said that diet, yoga and physical means have their own merit but they are not the ultimate refuge or source of purification.

When we go on alms pilgrimages, not only do we not know what we are going to eat that day, we also do not know where we are going to sleep at night. At seven or eight in the evening, when it begins to get dark, we'll look for a village or a farm and we'll go up and ask if there's a corner of a field we can stay in, or a barn. We see what happens. We don't expect anything more than a roof over our heads at night, but as alms mendicants we can't demand or expect that. Our side of the bargain is to make ourselves very easy to look after. The minimal standard is all that we require. People always offer us somewhere—I've slept in feather beds, in fields (we have sleeping bags and tents), barns, woods, back gardens, summerhouses, garden sheds, outhouses. Once we stayed on a narrowboat (the long barges that navigate the canals). We were also offered a bed in a beautiful, country estate but we chose to go to the barn instead—we laid out our sleeping bags on the straw. But usually we sleep in fields and copses. It's really nice.

The first time I knocked on someone's door and asked for somewhere to sleep, I was fearful. But when you do it you discover it's OK. Our training discipline is very supportive. We have guidelines and boundaries to maintain the integrity of the situation. You learn how to receive with dignity and without compromising either yourself (because I represent not just myself but the Sangha, the Community of monks and nuns) or the giver. They should not be put in a position where they feel obliged to offer more than they are happy to offer. This is helped by recollecting what you do actually need, and not being too limiting with yourself so that it is OK to knock on someone's door and say, 'Do you have anywhere we could stay for one night? We are Buddhist nuns and we are traveling through here'.

Their first reaction is surprise. Then they usually say they have to go and check with their partner or spouse. You can hear them talking it over. They say, 'There's no harm in it, why not?' Then next morning they'll be a little bit braver and maybe ask a bit about us or invite us to breakfast. We wouldn't expect breakfast, but it is appreciated if it is offered.

Sometimes, it does cross your mind what might lie on the other side of the door. There have been occasions when I have sensed an atmosphere about a place that doesn't feel right. You tend to trust that. But I figure I'm always with somebody else, and since my intention is good I feel it's unlikely I'll come to any harm. Even if I did, I hope I would be able to deal with it skilfully. As a psychiatric nurse I've had plenty of practice appeasing aggressive people. In fact people are very sweet. We hear so much about awful people, but the majority of those we meet are extremely kind.

I love going on alms pilgrimages because you have to let go of any planning and control. I am quite an organizer and have many responsibilities, so there is something very freeing and relaxed about pilgrimages. If I can see two or three free days, then I pack my things and go. It's refreshing mentally not having to think much. I never imagined I would be standing with an alms bowl and knocking on strangers' doors, but it encompasses qualities that I wanted to be part of my life, which I was reaching out for: faith, opening to the unknown, a life that was not regulated and predictable. It is rather radical, but that is why I became a nun. I wanted to break through conditioning and limitations. I'd like to do it more often and in places other than England.

None of the nuns and monks are allowed to handle money. Our lodgings and bills are paid for by people who act as stewards. It's a charitable body and the trustees take care of it. We're like children, in a way. If there is anything we need we can tell any lay person who has offered support to the monastery—otherwise we have to go without. Actually, we're incredibly well supported. We share with other monasteries when we have an excess and keep what we have to a minimum standard. If we need to go anywhere we can make a request to be taken in the monastery's car. For rail we use vouchers. The bus is difficult—we have to have someone come and buy the ticket. But if I just want to go into our nearest town, Berkhamstead, I generally walk.

I thought it was another type of person who became a nun, but there was only one way to find out. I thought, 'I'll just try, and see what happens'. Once I made the decision I stuck to it. That was seven years ago. The idea came to me in a retreat lead by Ajahn Sucitto after a discourse he had given on karma. I remember there were several aspects to the teaching: I am the owner of my karma, heir to my karma, born of my karma, related to my karma, supported by my karma, whatever karma I shall do for good or for ill I will be the heir. Karma is like habit. I'd always been (and still am) someone with a strong tendency to try and fix it 'out there'. I feel that if I can mend the world, then my heart will be at peace. That's why I did so much social work and nursing, but there was always a sense of futility because no matter how much I did (or anyone else did), there was always more. It wasn't an intellectual dilemma, more an internal struggle. There was something in what Ajahn Sucitto said about karma, or the way he said it, that made me see through that struggle. For a moment I managed to drop it. I saw that I really needed to work on my own heart, my own needs and cravings, my own need to help and resolve. I saw that if I did this I would have more ability to help. Also I was very inspired by the people I met at the monastery. It was a gut feeling that this was something of real value to offer the world.

I had been on retreat here for three months and was sewing my white novice robes when I learnt my brother was getting married. I had special permission to go out to attend the wedding, and there I met up with my mother and discovered she was seriously ill. She hadn't said anything to me about it. She was diagnosed with motor neurone disease and so I left the monastery to look after her. She and I lived together for eighteen months until she died. After that I came to live here, and was ordained six months later.

In my daily life there's a continuous endeavor to understand where suffering is really coming from and to take responsibility for it both in myself and in my environment. I try to be more clear about how I affect others, how I am affected, how I can be more true in my way of living in the world. I see it as a continual unraveling of karmic predicament or habit. As the clearing happens there's a sense of opening and unfolding to new experience. There's an inherent experience of change, the possibility of life having a more creative dynamic and more wholesome qualities.

I get up at 4 a.m., shower, do some stretches and tai chi. At 5 a.m. it's morning chanting, reflection on the Buddha's teaching and silent meditation for an hour. For 45 minutes we have 'chore time' when the monastery gets cleaned. We each have a designated area. I'm responsible for cleaning the bathroom, toilet, corridor and office of the section where

I live. I quite enjoy cleaning. I'm very thorough. At 8.15, as the 'work nun', I organize taking care of the grounds. It's a middle-management position which involves a whole variety of jobs. I work in conjunction with the work monk. At 11 there's the meal offering. Eating for me is a way of relaxing, so I take my time. Then I rest. In the afternoon we have time for meditation and study. Tea is offered at 5 p.m.—a drink, not biscuits and cake! At 7.30 there's evening puja (worship). We begin by chanting praises to the Buddha, Dharma and Sangha, a passage asking forgiveness for the day's negative actions of body, speech and mind, and an hour of meditation. Then we do a chant called 'the sharing of blessings'—any good karma we've accrued from the day we share with all beings. After that I read a bit. I'm currently reading a commentary on the Supreme Net of Views, the first sutra in the whole of the Pali scriptures (the canonical language of the Buddha's teaching), which describes all the different views about self and the world that were current at the time of the Buddha. Its function is to help one recognize and discern the difference between them and those of the Buddha. I usually go to bed between 9.30 and 10.

There are some things I miss from my former life. Occasionally I miss dancing. I'm not allowed to dance or play music. I miss music too. Sometimes I just get the urge to be very free-flowing. I'm not very self-contained. We're not supposed to gesticulate while we're talking, and I gesticulate a lot when I speak. I also feel like being anonymous at times. Most people go home from work—I never go home. I never have a separate public and private life. Sometimes I feel the pressure of that. We're public when we eat (we share our meals with the lay people who come here), public when we meditate, we're public a lot of the time. There's a longing to be reclusive, sometimes.

I also miss intimacy, physical intimacy. That's probably the biggest renunciation. Sexual intimacy is only a part of it. Really it's not being able to express one's love and affection for somebody by a hug or a kiss. That's one of the strongest urges of human expression, and there's a lot of energy in our natures to do that. Because I have had to stand back and try to understand the meaning of the rule concerning this I have come to appreciate its value. I see how a lot of the impetus for physical intimacy comes from feelings of insecurity, wanting to be understood, reaffirmed or connected to somebody else. I realize I was quite hooked on relationships but they didn't really fulfil me. It's the same thing as being able to go into a shop and buy whatever you want to eat and discovering it doesn't fully satisfy you. You can argue that 'relationship' is a form of giving, and is therefore virtuous, but it is much more fulfilling for the other person if you are not wanting something from them in return. The more I've come to understand that, the more touching and being connected is not so relevant. I find I can have a very, very deep connection with someone at the distance you and I are sitting. I chant in the mornings and evenings, and that's a powerful form of expression too. And I love living in the country, in such a beautiful part of the world. We have these huge open spaces where I can go out and see the stars at night.

My relationship with my siblings has changed over the years. Both my parents have died and I'm the youngest of six children. Most of them respect me for becoming a nun because they see the integrity of what I'm doing. Initially they were afraid there would be a separation—a double grief—losing their mother and me simultaneously; but I maintain close contact. I never had any intention to break the connection, and so we visit each other regularly. In one way I am not the person that I was. I don't have the same patterns and way of being and yet I am more accepting of them—more open. We've become closer, which is great. They don't like me eating out of my alms bowl when I'm having lunch with them, however!

Thai Buddhism is traditionally hierarchical, with nuns having a lower status than the monks. They are meant to sit behind the monks, not eat at the same level, not touch even the mats the monks sit on and never make eye contact with their teachers. When I first came here this was very alien to me. Now I see that form is one thing and where people are in their hearts is another. None of the monks here has assumed an inherent superiority. I have accepted it. I'm quite strong in myself and you can't dismiss the fact that sexism is endemic to the entire world. If something isn't clear, one has to learn how to hold that without opposing it or being antagonistic. There have been a lot of adjustments here. They have been done in a gradual way. We don't want to snub Thai values. A key change is that we sit at the same height as the monks and in parallel lines although the monks are still served first at meals. For the West that's normal, in Thailand it would be radical. The women would be outside! I also make eye contact with my teacher.

Within Thai Buddhism it is possible for women to become Enlightened. There definitely have been Thai women who have realized nirvana, who are acknowledged and respected. In Thailand they value spiritual attainment above all else. I tend to see nirvana as a gradual clearing away of the encrustations, until they are all cleared away. Nirvana is not a matter of gaining, but losing. I feel that our inherent quality is basically goodness. There's just confusion and ignorance covering it up. The more I can manifest that inherent quality the more I can enable others to find their way through as well. 99

The vastness and power of the mind

YVONNE RAND
Zen priest and teacher/student

Going to interview Yvonne Rand, one of the foremost Zen teachers in the USA, was like entering a Japanese silk screen. As the car wound round the mountain bends on the way to Muir Beach, just north of San Francisco, the mist rolled in from the Pacific in huge swirling waves covering the entire landscape in an ethereal, evocative shroud. By the time I reached the Goat in the Road Meditation Center, where she lives with her husband Bill, a young Tibetan reincarnate lama, his attendant, and various retreaters, you could only just discern the exquisitely laid out garden with its white rose bushes, apple trees and strategically placed paths for 'walking meditation'. In the middle of the garden stood a fine meditation hall, with its warm wooden walls, polished floor, beautiful lighting and multitude of

Buddha statues that Yvonne had rescued from various shops intent on selling them for commercial profit only.

Yvonne greeted me at the gate—a statuesque woman in her early sixties with short gray hair, blue eyes, and a round, kind face. She was wearing a purple skirt and a dark red shawl, although whether this was the mark of being an ordained Zen priest was not clear. I was interested in talking to Yvonne as she had been there at the very beginning of the present great surge of 'American' Buddhism. She had been at Stanford in the mid-1950s when characters like Richard Alpert and his fellow faculty members became interested in meditation and Eastern religions. Alpert went on to Harvard where he met Timothy Leary and later changed his name to Ram Das. She had also been among the first students to sit at the feet of Shunryu Suzuki, one of the most influential Zen masters of his time (and renowned internationally for his book *Zen Mind, Beginner's Mind*). Suzuki had come to the USA from Japan in 1958 for a visit but was so impressed by the openness of mind he found there that he stayed on and established the San Francisco Zen Center. Yvonne became chairman of the board until she left to set up her own center.

Yvonne also exemplified the way Buddhism in America was heading, with her easy mixing of different Buddhist traditions. Although firmly based in Zen, she also embraces Tibetan Buddhism, finding no conflict between the chaste lines of the former and what she calls the 'baroque' beauty of the latter.

After 32 years of sustained Buddhist practice and study, Yvonne's portfolio is broad and encompassing. She teaches at her center and at university, she conducts weddings and funerals, she leads retreats, she is in constant demand as a speaker, she sits with the dying, and not least, she is a wife and mother.

Yvonne told me about her journey into Buddhism in a charming, tiny room situated in a corner of her garden. It was big enough to hold just two chairs, a table and a lamp. She spoke in an unusually clear, measured way, choosing her words with enormous care—a reflection of her belief that 'right speech' is a vital component of the Buddhist path. She began as dusk drew in and when she had ended it was night and too late to drive back over the mountain. The chairs were taken out, a futon laid down. In that tiny room where many had done retreat, my dreams were spectacularly vivid.

❊

66 *I* didn't see Buddhism as a live, viable path until I met my first teacher, Shunryu Suzuki. It was one Wednesday evening, in the late summer of 1966 and I had gone to hear him lecture. Immediately I realized: here is someone who is an actual practitioner of the tradition that I have read about. About ten years previously, at Stanford University, I had done an intensive year's seminar on Buddhism, reading a lot about Buddhism in China, taking an

historical interest. But I had no idea that Buddhism was a tradition that I, as an American, could practice. Initially I was as drawn to the people who were practicing as I was to Suzuki as a teacher. There was a degree of relationship, a connectedness, that I was not used to and I was very intrigued. It took me a while to recognize that this sense of connectedness was the compass point of a shared meditation practice.

At first I was both fascinated and a little fearful around Zen meditation. I kind of walked around my meditation seat for a while. I had done some meditation in the Christian context at Stanford and had become quite involved in a group studying the teachings of Jesus according to contemporary translations of the New Testament. That meditation was really more contemplation and prayer, focusing on Jesus's teachings about how to live one's life and various qualities of the heart. There was nothing about the yogic side of meditation which is so emphasized in Buddhism. When I was first given instructions by Suzuki Roshi in Zen-style meditation, it was an enormous relief. The specific detail, what to do—how to sit with the back straight with the head, the heart and the lower part of the belly aligned, paying attention to the breath—it immediately felt right. It was what had been missing in Christian meditation.

What I very quickly realized, experientially, was when I sat in that way with that kind of centeredness and groundedness, the physical posture affected my state of mind.

And through paying attention to the breath, following each inhalation and exhalation without a lot of ideas about why I was doing it, I began to discover the relationship between breath, physical posture and state of mind. I also very quickly began to experience the consequences of being quiet and collecting myself in the way that meditation allows—in enhanced awareness of what was going on around me both during meditation and the rest of the day. Within a very short time I discovered a real difference in the tone of the day—experientially—depending on whether I meditated or not.

By the time I met Suzuki Roshi I was married, had two children and was teaching mathematics at high school. Within a year my husband was quite threatened by my interest in Buddhism and meditation. It can happen in any religion where one partner begins to follow a spiritual path and the other doesn't. He had a sense of my going away and he didn't quite know where to. There were other factors. We were very different people. While our kids were pre-school and our whole world was contained within the sphere of being a young family, those differences were not so apparent. Once I began to step back into the world, those differences were more noticeable. Since childhood I'd had quite a strong inner life and so it made sense that it should manifest in religious or spiritual activity. Anyway, my husband became quite fearful. Authentic spiritual life has everything to do with intimacy—intimacy with oneself, intimacy with others, intimacy with every aspect of the world and that was not a route that he was drawn to. I didn't understand the increasing sense of separateness, difference and misunderstanding between him and me, but there was a way in which Buddhism and meditation gave me something positive to move towards. What I do regret is not staying in the marriage long enough to do the emotional and psychological work which would have made our separating kinder. I did that later.

I was left as a single parent with two young kids in a spiritual community where there were few people with children. In many ways the center and Buddhism became a substitute for being married. Suzuki Roshi encouraged me to move to an apartment which was next to the temple at that time. He'd look out of his window and wave at me. I had a sense that he was taking me under his wing. The meditation helped me with my parenting, although my kids were aware of it more than myself. Once when my daughter was visiting a schoolmate the mother asked, 'Why does your mother meditate?' and my daughter's response was, 'Well, she's nicer to be around and it looks like she feels better'. It was quite accurate. One of the effects for me was like waking up after being for a long time in a slumber state. I began to see how much I'd been on automatic. I also felt I'd found home.

But because I was a single mom and my kids were little I was not able to go to the meditation room at five in the morning as the rest of the community did. So very early on I had to find ways of translating what I was exposed to into the situation I was in. Although at the time I saw this as a liability, it ended up as being a real asset. For instance, it was very clear to me that given the experiences I had had with my own mother, who was very possessive and held on tight, I could well do the same thing, but I knew how harmful that could be. I remember one of the first practices I took on was to be willing to do whatever I was doing with my own children with any other child who was around. I was consciously counteracting my tendencies for possessiveness by being as inclusive as possible, and not giving any preference to 'my' children.

My mother was also given to terrible rages (she was an alcoholic and although not a practicing one until she was much, much older, all the patterns were there). So when my kids were young, if I got frightened I would express it as anger, and then I would feel just terrible. One of the very significant consequences of meditation for me was to learn how to deal with that strong negative emotion—neither suppressing nor expressing it. I saw there was a third option which was to be able to be present with it, not denying it, nor stuffing it down, nor letting it out. If you get angry and upset you can pay attention to what you are feeling in your body, in your stomach, the tightness in your throat, whether your chest feels constricted—you can even acknowledge that there is a lot of anger coming up. It's one thing to describe and acknowledge it and another to act it out. I soon realized that whatever emotion was coming up would dissipate extremely quickly. With my children it was very useful. It became abundantly clear to me that if my relationship with my children was not consistent with what I was studying in Buddhism then in some way I was being a fraud. I was interested in using my relationship with my children as an opportunity for studying my own mind stream, and cultivating self-awareness. I could see that my state of mind had a big effect on my kids.

Within six months of beginning my practice, I began to work for the Zen Center as secretary. It was an exciting time. We were trying to buy the Mountain Center and raise funds. No one thought we would pull it off. I threw myself in. It was one of the ways of dealing with my life falling apart. In my role as secretary I had an unusual amount of contact with Suzuki Roshi in many varied situations which were just not in the meditation hall, and we got very close. I took him shopping, to appointments and I would drive him to Tassajara Mountain Center and back. So from 1967 until he died in 1971, in a curious way I had a kind of domestic relationship with him. I think I was very blessed.

Physically, he was shorter than I and rather slight, with a very fluid face. In meditation he would have down-turned lips and be very serious, but then he would bloom with this wonderful smile. He loved a lot of the things I loved, like rocks. He was mad about rocks. In Tassajara and also at the site where eventually his ashes were placed he did some of the most beautiful stonework I have ever seen. He loved stones. We used to give each other stones, which was very dear.

He exemplified Buddhism. He had an extraordinary capacity to be present, a remarkable ability to make whoever was around him feel special—as though he wanted to be just with that person. At the same time you understood that everyone else in the room had exactly that same experience, which was quite marvelous. He was both tough and very kind. I remember long conversations with him of a sort that no one else had been open enough to have with me. One Thanksgiving we had driven back to the temple and were sitting in the car in the car park when he began to talk about trust. At that point in my life, trust was a real issue. Having grown up in an alcoholic family, I knew only how to trust blindly or not at all and had little idea about the ground in between. I remember being quite startled when he said, 'I don't trust anyone'. For him to make a statement like that after I'd seen him always giving people lots of room and fundamentally being very trusting puzzled me for a long time, until I eventually began to understand what he was pointing to was untested trust. A good teacher, and Suzuki Roshi was certainly a good teacher, would say things to a person that were very particular to that person.

And so I constantly found myself in situations which were incredible opportunities for being taught. I only realized this later. He was very patient with me, which I appreciated enormously. He could also be very troublesome, especially if people got stuck on a certain way of being. There was one student who was making a big issue about being a vegetarian and one day as Suzuki Roshi and this student were driving out of Tassajara they stopped for lunch and while the student was going to the bathroom he ordered two hamburgers and transferred his meat into the student's bun. He'd do things like that.

The most important experience of my time with him, however, was helping his wife look after him in the last months of his life. He had cancer of the gall bladder. I spent huge amounts of time every day sitting with him, taking care of him, massaging his arms, giving him drinks of water, reading him letters, writing his letters for him—just being with him as he got sicker. Watching him as he met his own dying was a huge, powerful experience for me. He was utterly present, moment by moment, he didn't turn away from anything, he was very calm and at ease, not in the least bit afraid. There was this gradual unfolding and dissolving. It was a time of enormous clarity and ease. It showed me how it is possible to die. I sat with his body afterwards and helped to prepare it for the funeral.

Within a year people began asking me to sit with them while they died, and it's been a major practice ever since. When people ask my advice about what is the best thing to do, I say, 'Just keep them company. Understand that sitting with a dying person is a great opportunity to stay with whatever you are accustomed to turn away from. It could be fear of pain, whatever. In being with the dying you meet your own edge'. In the USA, where the emphasis is all on doing, just hanging out with someone is much more challenging. I've really seen how people consistently die the way they have lived. That's very clear. On the other hand, I've been completely amazed how many people who have had hard lives, if they have some clear intention in the way they meet their dying, can die well, without fear and agitation.

I don't think much about what comes after death. In Japanese Buddhism there is acceptance of past and future lives, although Suzuki Roshi didn't talk much about it—he thought there were more important subjects. One of the things I like about Buddhism is that I'm not asked to believe in anything. The great emphasis on inquiry, investigation, examination, checking things out, analyzing has always been very compelling for me. I believe in bringing one's common sense into the meditation room. For Westerners with their strong philosophical foundation in materialism, the whole notion of past and future lives is very troubling. It can be an obstacle to a lot in Buddhism which is accessible, effective and useful. Having said that, I consistently get the feeling when sitting with a dying person and then with the body that there is a 'presence' or 'consciousness', if not located in the corpse then in the room. After two or two-and-a-half days that quality goes. So, it makes sense to me that there is some continuum. There's a way from this morning to this evening. This morning seems very much past, and the future life might be when I get into bed tonight or wake up tomorrow morning. At that level I know there are past and future lives continuously.

I was ordained as a Zen priest in 1973 by Dainin Katagiri Roshi, and then in 1985 I went on a pilgrimage to Bodhgaya, India, where the Buddha attained Enlightenment, to hear the Dalai Lama give teachings. At that time I was heartbroken. It was a time of great turmoil within the Zen Center. I didn't know where I fitted in. I had real discouragement about Zen in the West and about my own Zen community that I had devoted most of my adult life to. I went with Bob Thurman, who introduced me to the Tibetans. I had been very close to Lama Govinda (author of *Way of the White Clouds*), but of course he was German and this was my first exposure to the Tibetans in any big way. Two hundred thousand people had gathered in that little village to hear the Dalai Lama. Thirty thousand Tibetans stood on the backs of trucks—they'd come from Tibet any way they could. My heart just burst open with His Holiness the Dalai Lama and with one lama I met, the late Tara Tulku. Tara Tulku completely inspired me. In him I saw the Bodhisattva vow realized, and so it became possible for me. I could actually imagine the possibility of full awakening for the benefit of all beings, because here was someone who was doing it in front of me. It's one thing to have the idea of loving-kindness and another thing entirely to see it manifest. And there's no substitute for that. Long-time Zen practitioners, if they're really authentic, have developed loving-kindness but it's not named. There are no practices overtly designed for that cultivation. And we need it. It's one of the weaknesses in the Zen school. Each school has its own strengths and limitations.

During the breaks I sat in a corner of Tara Tulku's room and just watched him. People would come and pay their respects and during the break he'd sneak me a little bit of hard cheese or fruit. He invited us to take our meals in the monastery. The joyfulness, the open-heartedness and warmth was just balm for my soul. Much of my unhappiness at that time was due to the fact that for several years I had felt a failure because I wasn't really a monastic (I looked a monastic but I was really a householder). In Bodhgaya, where there were Buddhists from every possible tradition and culture, I finally got it: 'I'm a lay, householder priest'. I felt an alignment. It was a big relief.

I invited Tara Tulku to San Francisco to teach. It was a very exciting, wonderful week. Bob Thurman translated for him. At that point Tara Tulku could have been teaching shoemaking and I would have studied with him. Tara Tulku became my heart teacher—more than Suzuki, because I was really ready. I studied with Tara Tulku formally, took initiations from him, and did long retreats with him both in Bodhgaya and here. He was really interested in training me as a teacher. He consistently wanted to know what I was teaching and studying and made a lot of suggestions. He also encouraged me to go through the formal initiations involved in authorization to teach in the Zen tradition. He completely honored Zen as my home path and was adamant that I should never leave it, even though I was also doing Tibetan Vajrayana practice. It was through practicing with him that I began to see the elements of Tibetan Vajrayana Buddhism in Soto Zen.

Fundamentally, I still think of myself as a Zen teacher and the meditation that goes on in this meditation hall is Zen. What I get from Tibetan Buddhism is a very full articulation about loving-kindness centered mainly around the Tibetan deity practices. Their depiction in statues and wall hangings (tankas) is baroque loving-kindness. I find the sacred art in Vajrayana entirely inspiring and beautiful. My experience is that people's hearts open in an environment which is beautiful. When it's appropriate I introduce my students to it and suggest they receive formal initiations if they do want to practice it for a prolonged period of time. The practices to do with Vajrasattva (purification), Tara (compassionate action), and the Medicine Buddha are the three that come up the most. The meditation on the Buddha as healer is very important as a vehicle of prayers not just for oneself but for others.

I also love the sparseness of Zen, that stripped-down quality. I will periodically empty the meditation room. I've also become more conservative over the years. I've built a little house for the tantric altar because I wanted a place that was a little less public. Some of the iconography is too easily misunderstood. It's not helpful (which is why it was hidden in the first place). I love the aesthetics of Zen.

Over the years I have watched Buddhism in America change. The cultural encasement of Buddhism has been a challenge, especially for women. When I first met Suzuki Roshi I would do sitting meditation in the bedroom with the children before they woke up in the morning. That was unusual. In fact I was criticized for not being a very good practitioner. The emphasis was on everyone meditating together in the meditation hall, but that has much more to do with Japanese culture than it does with Buddhism. It takes a while to make those kind of distinctions.

In fact the whole situation was quite patriarchal, although I didn't let myself know this for a long time. There was this odd situation where Suzuki, coming from his culture, didn't have much confidence in training women and yet he was very open to both his men and women students. There was tension there. In Japan men had the highest roles in the hierarchy and the role of women was, and still is to a large extent, that of second-class citizens. You rarely find a Zen master who would be teaching men and women students. It wasn't long before Suzuki Roshi's time that a Zen priest was allowed to marry and then mainly on the grounds that he needed a wife to run the temple. So the whole role of women in his context was a bit unusual. But he was unusual—from an early age he had wanted to come to the USA, and he was remarkably free from cultural conditioning.

He was greatly inspired by the seriousness of his students: he said we were not exactly monks and nuns and not exactly lay people but a little of both. Just before he died he apologized to me for not ordaining me, and confessed that he didn't have the confidence to know how to train women students. He also acknowledged that he didn't recognize how serious a practitioner I was. I've always been very grateful to him for expressing that to me.

Today there are certainly more women teachers than there were twenty years ago. One of the biggest factors in Buddhism coming to the West is that half the practitioners are women, but I think the patriarchal mode is more long-lasting than we want it to be. It's easy right now to get too enthusiastic and hopeful about the support of women as significant teachers and practitioners. Maybe it will happen and maybe it won't. Western Buddhism is still too young to say.

Over the years I have seen the interest in and legitimacy of Buddhism change enormously. As well as teaching at Buddhist centers I teach an introductory course on Zen and the cultivation of mindfulness at the University of California, and 30 or 40 people show up. I like teaching there because the kind of people who attend would never go to a Buddhist center—they are engineers, doctors, printers, artists, telephone men, the full spectrum of the population. What's drawing them is how to survive their lives; how to survive the pace, pressure, stress, complexity of modern life. People are desperate for guidance on how to have a life that is more sustainable and sane. Buddhism is a very practical path and the Buddha himself very pragmatic. It was one of the qualities that attracted me in the first place. The whole emphasis on how much our suffering is a consequence of our state of mind is so clear. When people are exposed to this lucid articulation about the nature of suffering and the nature of reality, it gives them direction on how to lead a way of life that is sustainable, wholesome and has to do with the cultivation of the heart. Our world is in terrible straits. As there is more suffering, there is more hunger for pathways that will alleviate it. The Buddha's path definitely provides that.

Buddhism is also becoming more non-sectarian. Increasing numbers of American teachers from different schools are interested in learning from each other and teaching together. More and more I'm invited as a Zen person to teach with someone from the Tibetan or the Theravadan tradition, offering what we have from our respective paths. You begin to see certain essential teachings that are present in all of the major vehicles. Undoubtedly there's enormous benefit in a certain amount of cross-fertilisation but at the same time I see a big danger in mixing and matching. Americans are very given to what I call the smorgasbord technique, and consequently don't develop a tap root. You know, I'd been practicing for nearly twenty years by the time I met Tara Tulku, so to take teachings and initiations with him didn't knock me off my home path. It was an illuminating and opening up of certain elements in Zen.

It is not just the different Buddhist schools who are learning from each other in this present climate of open dialogue. I've taught a lot in Christian churches, and many Catholic religious and Episcopal clergy have come in order to learn meditation practice without any thought of ever becoming a Buddhist. There are lots and lots of Christian traditions which are incorporating Buddhist meditation. Suzuki used to say that Buddhism coming to the West would be mostly to help people be better Christians—and I would add as an aside to be better Jews, because many people attracted to Buddhism in the States come from a Jewish background. What I see now is many people, especially my Jewish friends, returning to the spiritual tradition that they were born into and reconsidering it out of their exposure to the inspiration of Buddhist meditation. In the long run I think that might be the strongest contribution and influence of Buddhism in the West.

For all the surge of interest in Buddhism over the past few years, I seriously doubt that it will be anything but a minority tradition. Buddhism is non-theistic, with teachings of no beginning and no end. Those sorts of beliefs are certainly very challenging for anyone brought up in a culture dominated by theistic tradition, with the idea of a 'creator' God. There is also a kind of rigor in a tradition which asks each of us to be the chemist or the goldsmith of our own experience. That's very different from a faith-based tradition. Also, in the East the traditional carrier of Buddhism has been monasticism. The USA, however, has historically very little experience with monasticism (unlike Europe, Central and South America). The real question becomes then, 'How will Buddhism continue to be carried in essentially lay forms?' I'm not convinced that it *will* continue in a vital way unless there are some pockets of monastic life, because monastics create a long-term sustaining energy.

What I am convinced about, however, is that lay people can become fully realized. I have a lot of students who doubt that. I don't. I'm quite convinced it is possible, but it does mean making some hard choices about your life. You can't have it all. You can't lead a life that has a lot of busyness and distraction in it. You have to keep your life fairly simple if you're going to stay on this path of training the mind. There's only a limited amount of time and energy resources, and I'm convinced that regular, frequent retreats make a difference. For a long time I've been offering retreats for a weekend, occasionally for three days; two or three times a year I offer retreats from anything between five days and three weeks. If you have one day of quiet attention a week, and a weekend a month, and two or three longer retreats a year, out of that going deep you can sustain attention and presence along with a fairly full daily life. You can't do that, however, and work a 60-hour week with all the distracting things that are constantly right there in front of us. In this society we are enormously practiced in distraction. For a lot of people, just learning how to place the mind is a huge task.

For many students, what is critical is finding a teacher whom they trust enough to receive some guidance and feedback from. I've been lucky. I've had some extraordinary teachers. I've also been open to being taught. I haven't been afraid of having a teacher. For some women, authority issues are very big—it can be a challenge. It goes with the want of self-confidence. Personally, I think women will be hindered if they have not developed wholesome and appropriate self-confidence.

After 32 years of practice I'm more grateful than ever for the Buddha Dharma, and happily I do continue to change. I've been very fortunate. I have good company and continue to have good teachers. Life also furnishes us with permanent opportunities to learn. In October 1997 I was diagnosed with a cancer which required surgery, not chemotherapy or radiation. My first reaction was 'Oh, a test'. That came directly out of my experience as a meditator and mind training. Actually I was downright enthusiastic about the whole business, which was rather trying for my family. I thought, 'What a great chance to find out what my state of mind actually is'. I was pretty interested in the whole thing. I ended up talking the doctor and anaesthetist into letting me go into surgery without any sedation—they did a local paralyzing. I could feel sensation but not pain. Throughout the operation, which lasted four hours, I did a breath practice—being mindful of the sensation of a long inhalation and a long exhalation—and every 40 minutes I'd do about ten minutes meditation on the Medicine Buddha where I would visualize the healing blue light energy of the healing Buddha going throughout my body and then from myself to all the other people in the hospital. I started before I went in and by the time I got into surgery I felt I was in a kind of deep groove and I just didn't leave it.

During the entire time none of my vital signs elevated at all for four hours. There was no elevation of my heart rate, pulse, blood pressure, or respiration. It was an exhilarating experience, completely extraordinary. By the end of the surgery I was in tears of gratitude for everyone in the theatre and they with me. It was especially hard work for the anaesthetist; she had to watch all the time. She told me later she wasn't very keen on the idea and had only gone along with it because I'd given her permission to give me a sedative if at any time she felt it was necessary. She didn't believe I could intentionally sustain that level of relaxation and ease. I was pretty sure I could, but I didn't know and I really wanted to find out.

Interestingly the nurse who took care of me afterwards was a young Tibetan woman whose brother was a monk at the monastery where Tara Tulku had been abbot for a long time. I saw her name tag: 'Dechong-la, you're Tibetan,' I cried. 'That's amazing—most people think I'm from the Philippines,' she replied. She took care of me for three days in a way I'd never been taken care of. I felt lots and lots of people praying for me all over the world. I sensed an energy that was sustaining me that was not coming from within me. I have pretty strong conviction about the power of prayer. I'm usually doing the praying, but this time I felt it on the receiving end—to do so was a very, very powerful experience.

What that whole episode demonstrated to me was the vastness and the power of the mind. There's another piece to this. Most people say when I tell them the story, 'You can do that because you've been meditating all these years'. It's not true—anyone can do it. After my surgery, three of my students who have varying degrees of experience had to have medical procedures of one sort or another, and I described to each of them the practices that I did. They then had their medical procedures, doing exactly what I had done, and had exactly the same experience. I find that pretty interesting!

I'm 63 now and my two children are grown up. The closest I've got to grandchildren is the young Tara Tulku, the recognized reincarnation of my heart teacher, who is living with me here. It doesn't particularly interest me to look for similarities between him and the previous Tara Tulku, but from the first time I saw him, when he was not quite one year old, I felt a very strong connection to him, which is clearly quite mutual. We're very close. He's four-and-a-half and a remarkable kid. He's very, very bright. His imaginative play is just extraordinary. He's healthy, he gets to run around, to have a physical life. He's learning English, he gets to have some women in his life. He's a wonderful kid and I worry about him. The life he has in front of him will be complicated and challenging. But I think it would be in any event.

I have a husband, Bill. We've been together for eighteen years. He's wholeheartedly and enthusiastically a follower of the Buddhist way, and completely supportive. Bill refers to himself as 'the priest's wife' and is utterly comfortable in that role. If I do a wedding he comes along and carries the bells and bouquets and does whatever he can to be helpful. We sometimes teach together. He's given to being very scholarly, studying all the sutras, so our respective practices are extremely complementary.

I'm not as busy as I used to be—I'm learning how precious creative energy is. I've been working on a book on language, which is a way of teaching on a bigger stage. My primary focus recently has been on retreats and meditation practices, leading them and doing them personally. I don't want to teach if I'm not also being a student. I feel strongly about that. The retreats, which last the typical seven days, are quite rigorous and my body is not always co-operative. Someone said to me recently, 'You're a healer', and in some ways that is true. I work with people who are in great suffering of one sort or another. One or two people a year come to me who are dying, and I sit with them for extended periods of time.

I get asked to talk at a lot of venues because I'm a woman, articulate and am good at making traditional

Buddhism accessible. In a way I see myself as a bridge person, a translator. I'm much more traditional than most people imagine, but I'm interested in finding ways to make the core teachings accessible for this time in this culture. I want to work with what is possible rather than some ideal that isn't. I get my students to take in theatre, art, poetry and see how it relates to Buddhism. I'm interested in what arises out of our own Western culture that resonates with Buddhism. I don't think Buddhism will really take root in the West until there is enough resonance that comes out of our own culture base.

The Buddha's teachings continue to be an extraordinary wellspring for guidance, insight and training. If anything I'm more convinced of their accuracy and efficacy than ever, especially the Buddha's observations expressed in such profundity in the First Noble Truth—the fact of suffering. The older I get, the more I see how big that pointing is. I see how much suffering comes from not knowing one is suffering—being deluded or in denial about one's suffering and consequently being closed off from doing something about it. Recently someone quoted a poem: 'We were in paradise but we didn't know it, and hoping for something keeps me from the experience of the very thing I want and need, that's directly in front of me'. **"**

Key Buddhist terms

Bodhicitta   The altruistic mind which is focused on attaining full Enlightenment for the sake of all sentient beings.

Bodhisattva   A person who has determined to attain full Enlightenment in order to help others, one who is on the way to becoming a Buddha, a practitioner who has the Bodhicitta mind constantly. Only found in Mahayana Buddhism.

Buddha   A Supremely Enlightened One, an Awakened One. The historical founder of Buddhism was Gautama Siddhartha, the Buddha Shakyamuni, 581–501 BC, the first-born son of King Suddhodana who reigned over what is now Nepal. Aged 29, Gautama Siddhartha left his palace, his wife and child to seek the meaning of existence. After many years of study, meditation and self-denial he found his answer when he attained Enlightenment under the Bodhi tree, in Bodhgaya, India. He was 35 years old and for the next 45 years, until his death at 80, he expounded his teachings so that others might also find the way to Liberation. 'Buddha' also denotes anybody who has attained Awakening. According to Mahayana Buddhism (see below), Shakyamuni Buddha was the fourth in a series of Buddhas who will come to Earth to help sentient beings. The next human Buddha is predicted to be Maitreya.

Dharma   The path which leads to the cessation of suffering, and cessation itself. It also carries the meaning of the teachings (of the Buddha), the spiritual law of righteousness, the eternal law of the Universe, Truth.

deity   A figure, either male or female, which depicts an emanation, or an aspect of the Enlightened mind. For example, in Tibetan Buddhism, Chenrezig is the male deity representing universal compassion, Tara the female deity representing compassionate action.

Eightfold Path   The path leading to liberation: right speech (abstention from lying, slander, harsh or abusive language and idle chatter); right thought (having only thoughts that are unselfish, loving and non-violent); right action (conducting oneself in moral, peaceful and honorable ways); right livelihood (making one's living in a way that is not harmful to sentient beings); right mindfulness (being aware of one's actions of body, speech and mind); right concentration (developing concentration through meditation to the stage of single-pointed concentration); right view (understanding the Four Noble Truths and having penetrative insight into reality, or Emptiness); right effort (principally staying enthusiastic for the practice).

Emptiness/Shunyata   Profound and complex philosophy which, when fully understood, uproots the principal cause of suffering. Briefly, Emptiness states that nothing exists independently, everything is dependent on causes and conditions. Our problems start when we grasp at a thing—including a concept of an 'I'—as being solid and existing in itself (self-existent). The Dalai Lama put it thus:

> There has never been, at any time, inherent existence: there is no thing that is independent or exists through its own power. Rather, there is interdependent production, which has no inherent existence but brings all suffering and kindness too. Therefore all phenomena seem to exist in various appearances that interdependently originate, yet their nature remains that of being completely empty of inherent existence. Each known thing possesses two natures: a superficial way of appearing called relative or conventional truth (*samvritisatya*) and ultimate truth (*paramarthasatya*).

The most famous teaching on Emptiness is the *Heart Sutra* which includes the lines: 'Form is emptiness, emptiness is form; emptiness is not other than form, form is not other than emptiness; in the same way feeling, perception, concept and consciousness are empty'.

Enlightenment   The totally awakened, illuminated state, characterised by omniscience and absolute Bodhicitta. In the Mahayana tradition (see below), Enlightenment equals Buddhahood. The Buddha taught that Enlightenment is possible for all beings, and that all beings will eventually attain it.

Four Noble Truths   The first teaching of the Buddha, which he gave in the Deer Park at Sarnath, India after attaining Enlightenment, and which constitutes the fundamental doctrine of Buddhism. The Four Noble Truths clarify the cause of suffering or dissatisfaction and the way to emancipation. The truths are: that all conditioned existence entails suffering; that suffering is caused by ignorance which gives rise to desire, anger and illusion; that there is an end to suffering; that the way out of suffering is by following the Eightfold Path (see above).

Hinayana *see* **Theravada**

initiation To give permission to do the spiritual practice associated with a deity (see above.) Can only be given by someone who has received the initiation from a lineage master and who has completed a full retreat on the deity in question.

karma Intentional actions, usually translated as cause and effect. The doctrine of karma is complex and subtle but generally it states that our actions of body, speech and mind leave imprints on our mindstream which bring about our experiences in present or future lifetimes.

lama Teacher (literally 'high mother').

Mahayana The form of Buddhism practiced in the 'northern countries' of Tibet, Mongolia, China, Japan and Vietnam. Mahayana Buddhism asserts that all beings can attain full Enlightenment and strongly emphasizes compassion and the altruistic intention. The Mahayana practitioner is dedicated to the attainment of Enlightenment for the sole purpose of benefiting others.

mantra Sanskrit word meaning 'uniting and holding', i.e. uniting all dharmas and holding all meanings. A series of syllables consecrated by a Buddha and expressing the essence of the entire path to Enlightenment.

nirvana Cessation of suffering, individual liberation, freedom from cyclic existence or Samsara (see below).

reincarnation   The doctrine which maintains that after death one is reborn in another body. According to Buddhism, one takes a body and an existence which is commensurate with one's karma (see above). Thus one can be born in different realms of existence, including animal bodies as well as various hellish and heavenly states.

Rinpoche/Tulku   Literally 'Precious One', this is the title given to recognized/reincarnated Tibetan spiritual practitioners. Tibet instigated a system (involving lengthy search and testing techniques) to find the reincarnations of advanced meditators, in the understanding that such people had promised to return to Earth in order to bring all living beings to Enlightenment. The recognized reincarnation was then reinstated in his former position, usually at a very young age, to carry on the spiritual work he had been engaged in during his previous life. The most famous recognized reincarnated lama is the Dalai Lama. The present Dalai Lama is the fourteenth in a succession which began with Gendun Drup in 1391.

Samsara   Conditioned existence, or the endless round of birth and death due to not having eradicated delusions. Because we do not see reality clearly, we act in ways which perpetuate this state.

Sangha   Technically, a person who has realized Emptiness directly (see above). Commonly used to denote monks, nuns, or the spiritual community that offers support for one's own spiritual endeavors.

Shunyata *see* **Emptiness**

stupa   Traditional Buddhist tiered monument present in many Buddhist countries. Built to specific dimensions, it represents the Enlightened mind. Sometimes used as a reliquary.

sutra   Buddhist scripture or teaching.

tantra   An advanced practice based on Bodhicitta and Emptiness (see above) which seeks to transform negative energy into the path to Enlightenment. A feature of Vajrayana Buddhism, practiced widely in Tibet.

Theravada   Early school of Buddhism, also known as the Tradition of the Elders, practiced in the 'southern countries' of Sri Lanka, Thailand, Laos, Cambodia and Burma. Theravadan Buddhism adheres to a strict understanding of the teachings of the historical Buddha and has Nirvana (see above) as its goal.

Further reading

Martine Batchelor, *A Woman's Guide to Buddhism*, Thorsons, 2002.

Pema Chodron, *Start Where You Are*, Shambhala Dragon Edition, 1994.

HH Dalai Lama and Howard Cutler, *The Art of Happiness: A Handbook For Living*, Coronet Books, Hodder and Stoughton, 1998.

Jack Kornfield, *A Path With Heart*, Bantam Books, 1993.

Geri Larkin, *Stumbling Towards Enlightenment*, Ten Speed Press, 1997.

Thich Nhat Hanh, *Old Path, White Clouds*, Parallax Press, 1990.

Walpola Rahula, *What the Buddha Taught*, Grove/Atlantic, 1972.

Sharon Salzberg, *Loving-Kindness*, Shambala, 1997.

Sogyal Rinpoche, *The Tibetan Book of Living and Dying*, Harper San Francisco, 1994.

Robert Thurman, *Inner Revolution*, Riverland Books, 1998.

Choygam Trungpa, *Cutting Through Spiritual Materialism*, Shambala Dragon Edition, 1987.

Lama Yeshe and Lama Zopa Rinpoche, *Wisdom Energy*, Wisdom, 1985, 2000.

p150 - called - life is a ?
p210 - Becoming a respected teacher
p226 - the shadow
p105 - Jargon free
p73 - Mind Training - Art of Living
p76 - Solve your own problems.
p78 - Do anything you want. Only
your belief that you can't
will stop you.

p88 Loving kindness - a way of seeing
p89 Self-hatred
p193 God - Creator